CASTEGGIO 02-01-2015

SOTTILE SAVIOR

PRESENTA

PRESENTS

JUDAS

Youcanprint *Self-Publishing*

Titolo | Il libro da Giuda in lingua inglese
Autore | Salvatore Sottile
Immagine di copertina a cura dell'autore
ISBN | 978-88-91173-65-2

Youcanprint Self-Publishing
Via Roma, 73 - 73039 Tricase (LE) - Italy
www.youcanprint.it
info@youcanprint.it
Facebook: facebook.com/youcanprint.it
Twitter: twitter.com/youcanprintit

THE BIRTH OF THIS BOOK -P.1

This book was created with the acquisition of various ancient news from me elaborate, and from my imagination mostly depth. So the whole theme was developed with the help received from a general work: through in-depth historical information from the thoughts out of my mind, influenced by thousands of subtle reasoning and very logical and reflective. I must add that in addition to this, it was important mainly for the writing of the novel and understanding of the subject "Judas" the help that I received from a dream message from a dream during sleep. I do not deny that, even if minimal, specific and characteristic influence, of the subject, I have received well by the Gospel, especially in so far as the scriptures assert that Judas was very intelligent, and therefore the beloved apostle of Jesus . from this and a host of many other things I started thousands of reasoning, until these have led me to make a lot of assumptions and make me come many ideas. Some hypotheses and ideas, after careful analysis, in one aspect the thought fit for this work in the specific project and to identify the personality of Judah and then I considered carefully, others because they consider appropriate the unwrapping a priori. However, it was just when I was making useful this circumstance, capitatami during sleep that I realized that this work could take if the message had also associated historical information. Therefore, in order to justify their intelligence so acute in the opinion of the Evangelical writings about Judah, that's the message I received from that dream to how bizarre it was by chance really. I thought, great base to see the center of the personality of Judah! The understanding of the personality and the character of Judas has become important to do this work. The dream was also characteristic for understanding and split the personality of Judah, this made it possible to do this extraordinary work. So I started working on this dream experience, and all this work I did for a deeper understanding of Judah, led me, almost instinctively, to fantasize about the whole panorama view and a realism "all the time in my opinion" , and not just on the personality of Judah I saw the realism but also on society and much of that period. Honestly I made a profound work that eventually led me to complete the novel with putting together of many things: Historical information, my fantasy staff, especially the dream message. So my dear readers, were a set of things that prompted my creativity, have helped me to accomplish this strange and extraordinary. In the end I think more important than anything else to point out and telling myself that it was really the decisive contribution of the dream message to speak and understand deeply the personality of the character; thereby reflecting the historical idea transmitted to us from the ancient scriptures. Therefore he said I like him, he thought, like, about his person behaved and interacted with others, with the environment, and with the people he loved. However, it does not neglect the importance of his final act with the report JESUS ', which is determined by the corruption of Judah and therefore by his betrayal. A truth this indisputable because it came to us from the writings and stories of our ancestors, of which I do not deny the existence uses. Whereas, however, Judah the smartest man in the world, it is at this point that we must understand that in the intellectual dimension Jesus gave him the thread sgarbugliare, but Jesus had evolved as a human being reinforced from His creation and Spiritual Divine, for this reason Judas was embarrassed by Jesus, and perhaps this Judas included. However, it is notable, and also very clear that Judas believed Jesus to be the Son of God, but not to have seen him perform miracles, or how to talk or anything, but for the internal values deep in the soul who owned the Messiah and that he alone he discovers them. So Judas believed Jesus to be the Son of God because it includes human values, spiritual, His very being, here it is understandable that it is really then that Judas discovers the soul of Jesus, and recognizes the Son of God. JUDAS Well, even if if only for this fact, he really is the smartest man in the world and he knew this, so if Judas believes that Jesus is the Son of God, Jesus' really is! Because no man on this earth, "past, present and future," may face JUDAS in his intelligence, only JESUS 'could but because the Son of God.

FIRST DREAM -P.2

I dreamed that I was in a room, with the door open, he knew the house. The atmosphere inside was modest and peaceful. I did not know in what place I was and I could not understand it. Whole dream was situated in open countryside, as it was this house. I saw a young man; his body was squat and wide, wearing a brown robe. In the dream I associated to one of the

5

pillars, one of those who armavo and cast concrete with when I was a carpenter and bricklayer, so I saw him robust. After watching him a bit 'better, I realized to myself: this man with wide hips almost like the chest, her wrists are as wide almost like the muscles of his arms. - Amazingly, - I thought. I sensed this and I kept making considerations: This man, from the Mediterranean skin color is like a pillar. My mind at that moment he saw a pillar and associated it to him. I saw as if the pillar reinforced concrete and he were the same thing. Inside I was attracted to this curious figure, and I associated its strength and its mass now, in a new way: no longer a pillar but a large column is capable of sustaining the room where in, was there too ' I. I was looking forward to seeing him better to understand if you know him, but he purposely turned and gave me his side, and his outline is blurred, and I realized that I did not know. I felt that I had noticed but it seemed that paid no attention to my person, as if he saw me, or did pretend, indifferent to me, perhaps elusive, however indifferent and showed no attention to me. At his side, a little farther on, there was an elderly woman small and petite. Was enveloped by a long dress that the top was black in color and in the bottom seemed gray, his hair was long and straight, white media with long tufts blacks, I saw very well. Near the door leading outside, there was a robust old, small and squat. I looked at his face, I saw that it was a Chinese by his appearance and his eyes. Then I directed attention to the old, well now I watched, I noticed that it was not a Chinese. He addressed his gaze again unknown to man, now I could see only the side and also his face, although it is unclear and obscured by an opaque color, intravvedevo but did not understand with clarity the lineaments. He, as if afraid that I see him getting better, immediately turned, giving me your listing, it was clear that his attitude was as if he wanted me to discover who he is. In vain his bearing reserved and evasive because the same was quite remarkable to understand that it was not a Chinese: it seemed more of a Mediterranean person. After realizing that the man was not a Chinese, both at that moment I realized to be in

6

China. Then I turned to the old Chinese to understand something more. I watched him better now, and I contemplated his face and his person, I stood for a moment to admire his completely bald head with a gray ponytail that fell behind his back, they were just a tuft of hair but related assets, and they gave him an air of wisdom. I looked even better, it was closer to me the other time and contemplated. It seemed it was a Monaco, a teacher. She was wearing a brightly colored toned, between light and dark gray, with brown shades. It was an old man who felt very strong though small; He was stocky and well-placed; a round face with rosy cheeks, and 'was silent, as seriously as the other, but more sociable from the air and less evasive. I could see the old Master face and look him in the eye but not the other. I felt that he was fine and was full of his strength, and it seemed that it was too docile though his figure made him look like a very serious person, stern and determined to "unlike that other" that: I could see, just, only the outline of his person and just to realize that it was not a Chinese, but seemed rather to be a European, definitely Mediterranean. Then the old woman began to talk to me out loud, but if you would like that even those present could hear what he was saying to me, starting to talk about:

<< Only Judas Master taught singing and the wind words. To you it is not possible to learn this power. >> After a second of silence she continued:

<<Only Judas was allowed to learn this power, which is why he knows everything. >>
I in that moment, I directed all my attention to the stranger: I understood that it was really Judas, my emotions are reconciled to this truth. He now felt a heavy air and anguished, as if his whole being was wrapped in a sentence, and a painful and distressing feeling emanating from this sad person permeated the entire interior of shadows and darkness. I would wake and I removed the attention on him. I said to myself: this is his punishment for the death of His Friend Jesus.

Now I understood, and I understood his deep sorrow: << terrible anguish, >> I thought to myself, and in that moment I realized that what I had thought, it was really true. At that point destandomi from him lightly, and natural as not to attract attention to myself and to hide that I had taken a nice jolt, I directed my attention to the old man, because I felt more council and less hostility from this that the other . It was the desire to learn the song of the wind and the words of WIND. "I want to talk to the wind." I said to myself. Meanwhile, a slight wind could be heard outside the room; He is whistling blowing. The whistle sound was light, graceful, mixed with air blow of wind, he came to my ears like sweet music, harmonica, but in the meantime anxious, it seemed that the sound penetrated all the way to the heart. Inside me I understood, I said to myself: The wind knows he has to talk to him, is calling him. Quest'anziano teacher is a holy wise. He knows the words of the wind and the singing, talking to the wind. I have to learn this secret. I understood and now I was sure of what I had understood. Curiosity and the desire to understand and learn this secret, I felt stronger than anything that before had caught my attention. It was then that I decided that I had to take this chance. I felt a deep desire, strong and irresistible, so I had to learn at any cost this supreme secret that allowed the men, and even to me, you know everything like Judas. I realized that for me it was an opportunity not to miss for the world. The old woman was as if reading my thoughts all that I had seen. So he began to speak again, but now, louder, firmer than before. With opponent tone began to say, - but as if his whole speech was addressed only to me - but I understand that from the tone of his voice seemed that communicated directly above the old; in practice it was as if it came out a harsh, high-pitched tone of his voice, and seemed to invite him to listen better, not only the meaning of his words even from the tone of his voice.

<< Judah knows everything because Master taught the song of the wind, but you are not allowed to learn this power, you're only allowed to know that he knows! >>

I wondered: - What do you know? - And I answered myself; - All! - Then I would pay more attention only to this statement, and I understood that it was the song of the wind that gave the supreme knowledge to men as he had given it to Judas, and now I was convinced more than ever of this truth, and in that moment I understood , not with words, but through to the emotions that he was sure of himself when he was with Jesus, because he knew everything. I said to myself: << for this reason he was sure of himself, and when he was with friends, he knew everything, but nobody revealed his supreme wisdom, was ahead and no one could figure out why. He saw the world from top to bottom. >> In that moment I received the emotions that he behaved in a respectful and affectionate with his Master because he was happy to be with him, and in a different way he behaved with others, friends, and every situation had a different way to show his mood and personality. However now I was angry with the old woman who wanted to forbid me to learn of the power of the supreme knowledge. The you denied me the opportunity to know everything scolded me greatly. I felt powerless. That's when it seemed that I gave up, I reacted and instead m'intestardivo more I wanted to know, excited me the idea of talking with the wind. I understood that the spirit grunted know, and that he also wanted me to teach me to speak with the wind as he had taught to Judas.

I believed in my heart that it was unfair, two thousand years ago, that Judas knew everything and others not. In fact, I considered, that friends and acquaintances did not understand what was ahead for he had the supreme knowledge. Now the time had come to know. In that moment I felt the emotions of an ancient life, understood to be the one experienced by Judas, Jesus and his friends, and I felt that everyone felt embarrassed and amazed in front of Judah, because they could not read in his heart, but who I was at last he knew where it came from his supreme wisdom, and I understood well that he did not have with anyone Condivo this secret, so no one could read in his heart, and he was quiet. Knowledge of Judah came from the wind, where I could learn it too. I understood well that he through this his wisdom was able to be admired by Jesus and thus to obtain his friendship, but had not revealed where he had learned this supreme knowledge. Well I understood that Judas only Jesus had openly expressed how deep his wisdom, but not to others, so only Jesus could read in his heart, because only he had allowed to know him deeply, because they considered him someone, despite a higher being all. All these considerations were faster than a sigh, I was amazed.

At that moment the old as if I read the thoughts beckoned me with his finger, of: << No! >> I realized that whatever I thought comprendessi or the old one, automatically, he knew, I felt like a man who is put up against the wall. Just then I looked at the old man to understand if he was of the same opinion of her: from his face and his gaze I understood that he was obedient to the old old, but that basically was indifferent for him to teach me or not. I looked good again, and I became convinced that for him, if I had learned or not, he would not have made any difference and I felt that m'invitasse to dare, to be more daring, as if deep down I would not happen anything if I had disobeyed. He was neutral, and distant from the reasons and motivations. This sense of his opinion gave me the courage to dare, I understood that: with a different opinion, he would not hesitate to teach me, and I, I would have learned without any difficulty. Without my I expected, now, slowly, slowly it was preparing to go out, his attitude changed, became more negative, and the courage to dare I fainted. In the end I resigned I understood that I was not allowed to know and to learn this supernatural power and I had to give it up, and at that moment I accepted my resignation. This, however, she grieved. Then I thought about good the unique opportunity that presented itself to me, and I became even more curious: I wanted to go all the way and see what was happening outside, although I was not taught to speak and sing with the wind, I wanted at least to be a spectator, and watching him as he spoke, he would have me at that moment was enough. I was

10

thinking of doing this, and given the circumstances I had left nothing else to do. Then I had an argument with myself, I said to myself: first the old man seemed, although disappointed, he would teach me the same talking to the wind, and it would have done against the will of the old, who was really just her to contrariarlo, then it looked like, but after having heard better, change your mind, I hold good for her expression of before, as his last will and dare disobey. As soon as I made this decision in me, the wind seemed to be slightly increased, and became stronger his whistle. I realized that the wind was increasing his breath, but he did it to invite the holy man to go outdoors, to talk with him, and not to the decision that a moment before I had taken. When I understood this truth, that: The wind had agreed not to argue with me and not to relocate to the supreme wisdom, I more I became convinced of the existence of this power boost and I felt more in me a desire to learn this power; is the desire continued to aumentarmi, to the events as they were combined, up to when I became stronger, safer and more daring.

I now did not want to watch but I wanted to participate, and I knew it just me, the old like magic did not include more what I had inside of me decided, it was as if he had moved away from my mind, even though it was still present in the cockpit materially. At that moment, as if the wind would read me inside, and saw that I was determined, it seemed to have changed their minds, and manifesting agree with my decision, began to blow stronger and the sound of his whistle increased even as if he invited to leave the house even me, because the time had come. The wise old man came out and began to sing the words of the wind. I though I had been denied the acquisition of this power from the old, quickly went out behind the Master, hiding behind him and trying not to notice the remained behind and was imitating his deeds. Now that I was out with the old and the wind blew hard, I understood that the old no longer had any power, the games were made now, and that reassured me. I listened to the song of the wise old man who respected the rhythm of his voice and the wind whistling.

The wind increased the whistle and so is the old song, and I behind to repeat his words by increasing the tone like him. The song was like a moan uncommon, melodic, full of pain and melancholy, but at the same time conveyed a gentle feeling. It was the music of the real and material life that we live, but we do not hear that since our birth, and for each moment of our life up to the moment of our death, this melody is constantly heard, but we do not hear, and this port us knowledge. This is the melody of truth and of life itself, that the wind catches and holds within itself, and then the only reveals the elect men. The old man sang this lament like a slow melancholy sentence but was also light and how to fly. She sang and danced with her hands wide open, following the tone of the whistle. It seemed that the wind would listen, and in turn with its whistle to talk to him, and they were fused together in a supernatural communion. I realized then that it was not just a song of love and peace, but it was also a song of anguish and pain. I standogli behind began to repeat his exploits and sang and danced by following the melodic rhythm, and the words I repeated to him the same as if by magic. The I repeated identical to his, with an almost insignificant space that left me this my ability to learn, stucco. They were not real words, but an incomprehensible wailing and together with the wind whistling was created a melancholy tune that he knew at the same time of war and peace, and left inside my heart all his feelings of joy and sorrow together. I realized it was the music of real life, and inside this melody I felt one in particular that he knew of anguish and pain, as I had guessed from before. Just then I learned the melody, and it was one that sounded the wind two thousand years ago at the time of Jesus, I understood it was the same music, and I could smell and feel the same time. I repeated the words behind her, identical, with the same tone and cadence. Increasing the tone of my words and my mourning following the shades of the old Master who in turn raised the tone of his voice, to hand hand that the wind whistled louder, I realized that the song had reached a good point He advanced, and this consoled me as I felt to be merged with the old and the wind. All this happened in the mysterious dream. I at the same time I was amazed to be able so easily to talk with unknown words, and learn this great power so easily made me proud, yes I was right I was pleased with myself. I realized that through the old master I communicated with the wind, I had become part of him and he had become part of me. I felt at one stage of bliss, although the lament was delicate and painful at the same time, I was pleased with me. Here the wind I conveyed the pain of the past and the melody of that time who accompanied the men, suffering, lived at that time, that even they themselves who have lived in their moments of a troubled life could listen while being alive at the same time, since this is silent ear, audible only with the spirit, and I, I was elected, I could hear it, taste it with the soul and to finally know everything like Judas! I felt within me an energy that grew and became bigger and bigger, it is increasingly expanding more.

When I came into melodic tune with him and with the wind, I heard the old man, he noticed me, and he turned. He understood now the Master what I had dared to do, and looked at me as if she told me with her eyes: "You're smart state." I understood at that moment that he could no interrupting his singing, so I continued to sing his words by repeating them after him, now being left in front and looking him straight in the eyes. Now I understood that to keep up in front, my learning was becoming more and more perfect and deeper. I felt that my perfection increased because the wind was whistling in tune to my hand as if he wanted to communicate also approve of my participation, and his voice was a whistle that came from his breath, increased tone for having noticed that I was able to follow him. Meanwhile, the old man lent his attention all directed at me. Now he felt a mild light in his round face, as if he appreciated my ability of learning, and this seemed to manifest more pleasure to teach. From the expression on his face I understood that now appreciated more than before my person and he became like a part of me. I'd be amazed. Now you and the old man had become the same as if we were the same person. And while we would go well together, dancing with open arms and singing with the wind, the wind whistled louder and louder, and we also we raised the tone even more, but it more than us, and we more than him, in one go the endless tone. At that moment I understood that shortly thereafter I completed all my singing and I learned well. When I made this consideration with the mind, suddenly, in the most beautiful, Marta woke me.

He told me:

<< He has awakened me! What's wrong? What are you dreaming? Why do you complain in this way so melancholy? You made me scare? You louder moaning! >>

I did not answer, but I realized that my song from sleep was out in the world of cute, and who was sleeping, woke up, and so I had awakened from his sleep Marta. I was sorry for her and for me too. Marta had awakened me, as one of my most beautiful dreams.

WHY 'BELIEVE IN SOME MESSAGES? - P.3

To be honest, I say: I do not believe in all my dreams, rightly for their inherent variability, for their infinite meaning, for their bad association of representatives of other elements, all to be discovered, and many others things useless to list. Rightly to respect this dream world, sometimes for a few, it soon faith above all for the following reason: in my life I have suffered so much and have always been only in times of need. Discriminated against, marginalized, I lived in trouble and when they saw me, weak and helpless I have dates yet. My soul is full of scars and there are many prosthesis that the Eternal Father gave me. Therefore, I believe in some afterlife messages, because this way I have suffered many injustices by man, perhaps for my appearance that irritates the skin the next, or to my poverty, or other reasons that it is difficult to understand

and to explain. However there is a rule that fits for almost all the people like me: when you are weak, or barely recognized as such and seen in difficulty, if noticed only, it is slaughtered by "those" having fun and interest to do so.

Unfortunately for me even friends and relatives, as soon as they saw me needy, I have turned my back; So I have this world, and in this I think, in the land of the living are left out. So there are many things that lead me to trust a lot in the invisible messages, and I do not want to list.
Therefore, in general, what I learned from my humiliating existence, it is as if I had stolen from the men on one side, and as if God had sent me somewhere else. Verily I have only been often are. Nothing I was served, given or donated, everything I own, is one work of my sweat and my Faith. Beyond the life, no inheritance for me, the right, to be with others and to have something, I have gained through humiliation and submission.

So I who have taken part in the history of man, but he is not sure he has taken part in the story of God, I believe part of it now, and through this dream, and ye shall do no share with me if you read all this novel to the end.

For these reasons, I believe, in any way, in some of my dreams and in some of my visions, because I have nothing else; and when it happens not to believe it, I abstain and let myself be lulled by the doubt, but I trust in the opinion of man but only by faith in God. So these messages of the unseen world, some times, have proven authentic, and, masters of life! Especially useful with regard to the evolution and growth of my person, view, from the point of: character, personal, cultural and spiritual.

ANALYSIS OF DREAMS -P.4

From this dream of the whole processing of the personality of Judah, and the influence that it has manifested itself in a meaningful way throughout the novel, it is obvious. After this dream I wanted to support the possibility that Judas came from China, and, as in the dream had a holy man for master capable of talking to the wind, consider the possibility that he could have achieved in China spiritual and supernatural powers of a scope and depth unknown more men of that time, and perhaps even our own. I support this thesis in the novel, are reliable considering it because this hypothesis might just be true, because beyond what would justify his great intelligence, among other praised in the Holy Scriptures, and then somewhere this wisdom and intelligence had to save him, which the Messiah he recognized the values and is said to be the beloved apostle.

So on one hand this dream message gave me the opportunity to split the personality of Judah, the other side would have to make me understand: what the wind did it say? I do not know deeply, or know him but do not know to own it, but soon we'll find out together, dear readers, and seeing the path of this book, where it leads me, only then you will see more clearly what I understood from wind words. So what you've told me the wind in my heart, still do not know clearly, but I maintain that I received something subconsciously, even though I still is poorly understood in my consciousness, but maybe one day find out more about this dream so strange message and so complex. I initially I can formulate hypotheses, maybe that's just conjecture, however, expose my opinion now although risky, perhaps the wind seeking justice and wanted to bring to my ears the voice of Judah; those exclamations, made by his last words when he hath taken his life by committing suicide. Maybe the wind asks Justice to humanity, and uses me as a go between him and men. .... Perhaps Judas did not betray Jesus'. Sometimes when the man took his own life, nothing else he wants to prove that his innocence. Maybe. ... Maybe. ... Maybe. ... So many doubts. ... God knows the truth, for me now is incomprehensible, and only when God wills, will ensure that you can understand; unfortunately only then I shall understand.

However I fear the man as it is evil and that his illness he creates history at his pleasure and interest, and then some truth from the beginning are manipulated, and hardly any truth has been manipulated at the time of Our Lord, now we could be able to discover. But then with all theologians and scholars why me it had to happen to have a dream-like message of this magnitude? No answer in my heart, God the Father chooses the man for the heart and it shows that my blows the trust.

Returning to our discussion, however, that Judas is a traitor, or that it is not, for us it makes no difference, especially now that we know with what splendor, illuminates us the path towards the construction of this work and to the Lord.

Because we still have to follow an educational path of good, and Jude was not only bad, but also good, he has our respect. However we have to investigate deeply because a priori nothing we can say. I, like you, dear readers, I can not give confirmations without a thorough investigation and revealing of who and what was Judas. We try to investigate facts and forgotten CASES too quickly judged and closed. Of these events of which we are subject influenced by culture and teaching received during our school life, we must for a moment believe that he knew nothing, just so we can begin now to understand how they have turned out some things in those sad moments of two thousand years ago, and how he thought the man then environment has sentenced to death the Son of God. Therefore the above every concept we have come from schools that we have done, now ... this is beyond knowing. ... That still manage to do the same this novel because I felt in my heart, during sleep, the personality and the character of Judas Iscariot, then the novel can continue in an almost entirely independent of the information received by the man. I also say that perhaps this might not be enough to thoroughly investigate about things buried in centuries, but perhaps it is. If anything I would escape, surely when the Eternal Father will want you, dear

17

readers, and I understand it better, then he will retrace the dream, until you happen to understand what escapes us, and only then at that time, we revisit again this novel that has escaped can be taken up and brought to light. However by the time I say all of us be content with what we have understood and material possessions. With this as well as we can perform the way: you and I transcription of circumspection, and we give thanks to God for what he has granted us, and ask you to assist us in this long and difficult path. Amen.

CONSIDERATIONS ON JUDAH. - P.5

From here! That is up from this dream, I started to develop the personality and the character of Judas. Clearly it is through the "partial understanding can say" this dream that comes the desire to investigate and to say what I feel inside me. Pure is obvious to note "as the dream intends to make me understand" that Judas was a man who was acting in the spirit and mental power. I say that even though I do not believe in that power, yet now to give meaning to the historical description made about him, to everything else about him that, and above all to the same dream, I am compelled to believe can acquire this mental power at least if only it were only for its specific and unique case. I always though: "This mental power" I considered it only a statement made by impractical and individuals with few certainties, and from "those" who stated this belief, I do not trust; and I remember that I stated in various circumstances "their" being sellers of something unreal, and their statements certain, I felt almost disgusted when I listened to them, but now, I had to partially reconsider. Everything is unusual especially coming from me but it is the evolution forces me to consider the possibility that there really is mental power, because Judah acquisition of this power was reached. This mysterious force, said mental power, is able to understand things incomprehensible to the human eye, so it is said and believed.

I accept this creed incomprehensible, because, if I did not

accept this plausible truth, my novel would fall and it would not make any sense in its entirety because it speaks of an individual invested to supernatural causes of this power. I have to accept this truth, otherwise it would make no sense to believe that Judas had an eastern master without receiving a spiritual power; as it would have no sense to say that Judas was the smartest Apostle of all others, and therefore favored by the Messiah, if he has not shown his superior gifts Master the others.

However, returning to the possibility of considering that Judas had achieved during the journey of his life "mental power" we now, in the novel, we attribute this acquisition, and they justify intellectual gifts and behavioral almost supernatural. So all those qualities which allegedly possess to those who are hit by this power, we consider that he had to. So initially I say he is: Medium, thinker, poet. Capable of showing brilliance in the application at work, ability to understand things through, intuitive, possessor of the sixth sense, that he used the attack as a defense, would address with the action the surrounding world, and skilful in impressing it convince the next, almost seem hypnotist. ... Etc. Etc. Etc. ... ... so he had qualities of good and evil so deep and supernatural, and lived with these two universes, which belonged to him, so conciliatory, as able to dominate them. So he could have two opinions, contrary to the other, and dominate them at the same time, and over these opinions, could dominate the inner conflict as able to believe in nothing. He possessed a quick and almost instantaneous psychological transformation. He was too intellect forward to be grabbed easily.

I also have to consider that if he interacted with men of good like Jesus', this meant that he had a perfect control and great power over himself, so perfect enough to control his aggressive instincts and never to anything leak out that way of his devoted personalities not to believe in anything, to opportunism, the action, and if necessary also to do evil. Here Judas was an easy

19

man to boredom which requires new incentives to find satisfaction and pleasure in social relations, and friendship as he was led to believe that this could create the conditions to make it feel normal and not too different from the others. A man who was sports physical and mental workout to relax. A man focused on himself. Free spirit, ruler and evasive. Impenetrable he was in his heart, so is discovered. Inwardly it was as if he had a closed shell, secret, well guarded, that seals the truth of his personality. The truth that was his action. As he demanded ribollirgli feel the adrenaline in the blood, she needed a certain kind of movement and environments otherwise oxidized. So his character was different from that of Jesus and the other apostles, because what he was able to do them were not able to think. So he was discovered, but he also liked to attend that environment of Jesus. Surely because he found something in Jesus that attracted him. For this reason he could not live indifferent and could not deprive yourself to participate in the life of Jesus, even if they were opposites. This choice was pleasant and friendly, but also personal satisfaction. For he had to be where he turned the scene of the world, and this turned where there was Jesus. Judas could not miss this appointment, and this truth he felt within himself. Therefore, his supreme intelligence made him understand that Jesus was the star of the world stage, for this-I believe - that all his wisdom was opened in the hands of his Master, to conquer and stay close to him, I loved him for a force mysterious to us not comprehensible human, and his only weapon to win the friendship of Jesus was only his supreme knowledge. -

THE SCENE OF THE WORLD. - P.6

If we now consider that Judas also had enough ability to make money and feel good, so we can not rule out that it was a well-off, because we know where are the best money than anyone else, and someone like Judas the money and taking them up at home, if I wanted him, and doing nothing. So he also attended a certain environment of rich, so to attend and loving an environment like that of Jesus, it means that he realized that there would turn the world scene. So according to him the scene of the world was taking place among the poor in Jesus', not in the environment of the rich and to each other, but also where the Master lived and was a poor and marginalized as others. This means that Judas was really a special being, because all the rich were convinced then, as they are now, that the scene takes place in the world where they are and their power, their titles and all their honors, why the if history is written by tailored and please them, but Judah despite being partly one of them, you do not think so, even identifies the scene of the world not in the palaces of kings, but in the poor environment of Jesus and chooses and frequents, for which Judah is a supernatural being.

I THINK THAT NO ONE HAS EVER BEEN ABLE TO DISCOVER THE HEART OF JUDAH to understand the TRUTH. - P7

Which is why, he could do a kind of life regardless of the environment him to attend. So he to frequent or belonged to a different environment of the life he led in the dark and hidden, was not relevant, s'immedesimava in the new character who was supposed to represent, and each scene and environment had a special measure, however, warning! He was always the character of good and evil. A practical and adaptable man was Judas, in my opinion. Maybe too good. Surely skilled to understand the signs of the outside world, the messages of the individuals who avvantaggiavano for their understanding. He was able to understand the surrounding world, and skilled at reading other deeply. This makes avvantaggiava because if that was the case, it depended on the circumstances and opportunities of course, put him in the pure fighting aware of conditions which would be the final outcome. Maybe it was able to fight for justice in defense of the weak, this is characteristic of those who want to have respect and admiration of others, and especially if he takes pleasure if it is in view to acquire NSAIDs and admirers, a way of winning the next, it could be for Judah, so no doubt he was also inclined to show this part of his personality, everything depended on the circumstances logically. But he was wrong the conflict with Jesus, he did not even take to the competition with the Son of God, he was superior even to that. So conquer NSAIDs, I do not think he cared not if they did nothing, was in the middle of the fray to feel normal and only tried to have friends. Clearly, we must also support, that if we ascribe the power to Judas "Mental Spiritual" compulsorily nothing, he would serve if the first thing he had not used to always be well in sight, but only with those he said. Thus he was able to excel in any environment whereabouts or to frequent, but always in order to be appreciated by others, character that is in psychological game of who possesses superior qualities of others, and who is looking for fame or friends and admirers meeting into relations and cultural exchanges. So surely the opportunities that capitavano, he knew exploit them and take them on the fly just to be in the offing. I say this because this was the fashion of the super ego, and ME highest Imperial that affected the whole world of that time, and every one wanted to rise to the high evolutionary leaders to the point of reflecting Augustus, and at the same time becoming Divine! As it was believed that it was Octavian Augustus. This was the fashion at the time and the man wanted to reach this stage regardless of his social class they belong to.

OPINIONS ABOUT JUDAH. - p.8

One of my instinctive opinions is that he had to be, also, a good and just person. In him there was a very good part probably, or otherwise, could not be compatible with that of his person JESUS ': Just because he was a man of action, therefore, contrary to the character of Jesus', had to be a good or do it at the same time for temperamentally tie to the Messiah. Man of action means above all also be able to represent evil materially.

22

However if it was not even a good, could not deeply interact with the Son of God, this would like to point how complex his personality and how fickle and adapted his character. A good analyzer, and great observer. Difficult to separate the personality of a good man and bad at the same time, as shown, be that of Judas, but that efforts need me to do it. Instead Regarding act or live by the Spirit, it means, that Judas, owned a bivalent personality, but he was also able gestirsela, in order to be able also to find means and livelihood through his intelligence, his great cunning. We could say: << Judas was good and bad at the same time and in the same person there were these kinds of values. >> His was a unique strength but opposite, and dominated by his superego; probably managed "by him" as a code of their own life and the whole staff that helped him to create order within themselves in order to behave in the right way, according to the circumstances and the environment, and therefore in almost all occasions he behaved with wisdom and justice. Surely he had an extraordinary energy that allowed him to apply to anything that required analysis, study and understanding, and all what required competitiveness challenge, and measurement. He was on top of everything that could dominate, and if he lived by adapting their behavior to the circumstances and the environment around him. So he had good control set. Mental energy, if we tell her, or spiritual, definitely self regenerative and inexhaustible or otherwise, this mental power would lose sense, and he could not always keep to himself. After all that power was if you ran out? This is the mystery of the spiritual and mental power that I believe that he possessed: the self regeneration; Self education. ... Etc. ... Etc. ... Anything and everything, always AUTO, that was saying, compieva the evolutionary and definitive work of his life alone, believed only in himself, and therefore, was believed to be the smartest man in the world after his father, and God logically. His was an evolution that allowed him to live in alternating phase, so I think there was a period in his life where he lived spontaneously and without adapting his personality to the environment, without a mask. Probably, at some stage, he had lost all consideration towards others, but later fell, otherwise could not have a stable relationship with the Son of God. Go out and back proves himself a respectable government that does not understand that he was tied to nothing, totally free. A loose cannon, this was Judas, ready to explode, but you do not know how or when. So Judah had psychological independence, and some in the most absolute freedom to conceptions, and human influences, it was only within themselves culturally speaking. He, due to go it alone, that is none other than the supreme teaching received at an early age by the likes of his father and the holy man, so it was unable by his own psychology to recognize a superior man, so he recognized more than himself alone himself. Therefore, he can not become NSAIDs anyone, much less of Jesus, at least that in the Messiah, by itself, does not recognize the sending Divinity. However, Jesus, as a man of intellect, competes with Judah, and from beyond all his expectations. Competes because the Messiah is linked to the heavenly plan, you have spiritual gifts that come from heaven, and for this reason it is able to face and discuss with Judas drawing from this interaction personal satisfaction and affective, for himself, but also for the same Judas the same thing. That is what Judas includes, Divinity of Jesus: A man who can not compete, but there is with all his courage and faith that sustains it. Admirable for those who can not understand it. Judah came to be true to these evolutionary states of the next understanding? Yes! This was Judas knew all that was going on inside people morally and if he wanted to? I try to Yes! And our analysis could be more than truthful if our psychological journey is identified with the results that we all know, however, by means of the Holy Scriptures, we can say that this was Judah's intelligence in its pure state.

I personally hope to be able to make the idea, why explain it, it is not easy. You dear readers make this comparison: Compare the mind of man who possesses this quality. He becomes like an ever-access engine, and it is logical to ask of you: Where draws the energy to feed themselves? Why it does not end? The answer is obvious: Inside she draws strength and energy, and through "extraordinary intellectual evolution of a certain type" achieved, and learned in various ways during his earthly life. So for a power attained in the evolution and understood by the same mind that has come in elevation where the concentration opens the casket seals which we find the secrets of man you are kept the same, that he "Judas" But be careful! Hiding, for fear of realism? "Maybe"! However penetrate the impenetrable this is the evolution to the upper stage, and that man can not be achieved except by the spirit and devoid of your body that is what is dead, what puts us in a position to understand that Judas was something really scary , no less than it was Jesus, always in the intellectual dimension of course, because I try to explain how he was able to penetrate the secret of man, in other words open the chest. This is a capacity of Judah. This is Judas. Something implausible and incomprehensible at the same time, we could agree; but while explaining, his ability to know everything and understand all of creation: How asserts the old dream in which I did. << ... He knows everything. >> ... He says. ... Mental power because he knows things you can learn only by studying? I do not know. Call it what we want ... the result does not change: He knows the unknowable, discovers the non-discoverable, and contrary to all human expectation, he knows he is Jesus, and it is just so that at least we can identify it and display it to Judas. Judas was an autodidact at the end of the fair, because his Master could not, even if "him" he had wanted to, follow him over to teach him more, however, to consider that the old master has given him Judas the basic teaching , and he has turned on at the same time that psychological engine, which made him realize the truth, it is right. So Judah had as a party mechanism in his mind that he could never stop or go out unless he himself had wanted, from himself, or at least until he has discovered Jesus being the Son from God. So Judah on things that he saw and understood it was direct and intuitive, and self-taught of things he had not seen and did not understand, but which centrava and at the end, and discovered in them and its reality. Besides this evolutionary psychological stage, associating a physical strength that allowed him to take bold action, and associating the ability to use these two qualities simultaneously, one to the other service, he was a mixture of combinations to bring fear to whom it both, and not only he destined him to be successful in life. winning combination? We might also say yes! If the whole is combined to the experience! And 'apparently it was not lacking opportunities to make on that historic day. ... The thesis is appropriate. At the base of this evolution, we can say that it was in a position to develop within themselves, the personality of others and to understand: Weaknesses and strengths. Ability to be able to understand deeper truths, to unveil secrets and find solutions to "those" who have more intertwined problems of life. He was skilled, to study the world around him, inside him, taking the realism of the various situations. In practice we were ahead compared completely different. So Judas did not need a Master of life after having run away from his, as a boy, he served as Master alone. This understanding is clear if we keep the dream for good done by me, which I have described above, and what is said about him in the ancient scriptures. As attested to my dream, he had suffered a great spiritual master in his past, and plausibly as is natural habit, he could have overcome (in the course of evolutionary years). Why Judas for his personality and his intelligence, coming from another world, could be terribly envied and hated for its strength by some, at least as it was Jesus', although for different reasons. Its autonomy, its personality could lead to having convictions not equal to those of the environment, new, surrounding, and therefore, appear unconventional, unconventional and sometimes cocky.

From this analytical point we wonder! What connects Judah JESUS? I simply answer, the affection, the esteem respect, intelligence. JESUS 'was funny? True but not enough. JESUS 'attracted him? True but becoming NSAIDs of Jesus', for someone like Judas there has to be something real Son of God, of which Judas remains seriously affected and therefore remained tied in the Spirit for the rest of his life. Judas really want to love Jesus? Of course with all his heart. I do not see another reality, other than this. In my logical analysis:

Judah loves JESUS 'a clean and candied love and try a Love that is the same as the angels feel each other in Paradise. So between the two characters there is a feeling that humanity can not prove and can not understand jackets, is a love that comes only in Paradise. From their heavenly feeling engages friendship.

To me it is difficult to suppose that their friendship is born because both could be hated and envied by the world around for reasons to be decoded and displayed. there were no communions of interests! Why I not consider a sufficient motivation of the kind that can bind two people, at their level, to the point that one is willing to take their lives for each other even itself there was, at base, a betrayal pattern with repentance to cause suicide, would not be enough anyway to justify this act if it was executed without affective love, and if you miss, the feeling there would be no reason to feel guilty and to take his life. So Judas really want to love Jesus, this is indisputable! Since suicide is yes! Try: Surely repentance! << Of course, but at least it also proves to be a sense at least to bring the consciousness of the traitor, finally, is the consciousness that requires the car to condemn their own judgment to themselves! But to condemn self to death, it means that the sentiment that binds is DIVINE. >>

Finally a part of the presentation of his mind, we can say that Judas in intellectual form needed only a minimum of information from the surrounding world, after this information, could process the data and find the result of the truth of others and of the world within if. Truly amazing. And doing this process he could get to the truth of a matter or a material or psychological situation. In this way he could discover the reality of an individual or of an environment, even before some antagonists. Judas was a supernatural being. This realism, plausible of his nature, of his person, can explain many things said and told on him, come to us from the story itself. Another consideration of the character comes from his physical appearance. A square aspect, and though not very high, is well-placed presented. For this clearly Judas was a man of action; this I suppose to respect the natural law they call the man to fulfill the duty to respect the needs of the flesh, with strengths and weaknesses, and the needs of that massive body could be the action. .... And of that period it seemed that environment did nothing to prevent the man the fight and action, therefore, Judas two thousand years ago was the right environment for him, but Jesus, no! According to all these analyzes and information, imaginatively describe the events of the life of Judah to coincide with the era of the Messiah. Clearly, this is always a novel. For this we have two friends, (Judas and Jesus') one that claims by force and one that defends the sweet WORD relying on the heart and the feelings of others. So Jesus is turning the other cheek to all mankind, and for God to all people without judging anyone, and salvation is indistinct and embraces all humanity. What is unusual, however, defend themselves turning the other cheek at that period of history where heroism was commended, and each did his part to be a man regarded. And also for the religious of that time we have proof that anything made that turning the other cheek, especially if they were attacked. What usual defend himself with his sword at that time, especially for Judah who lived to feed on adrenaline.

The times were tailored to Judah because they were harsh times where the man wanted to compete and do evil with their own strength to the next, and this was normal to be praised and glorified, but JESUS 'is truly AMAZING in the intelligence and only Judas has the evolution and supernatural intelligence to understand it! And no one else! In conclusion, shared by Jesus' and Judas there are: the supernatural intelligence in communion with the laws of the invisible, and the feeling that comes from Paradise, this only! Absolutely no interest as well as love and intellectual sharing was in Judah. Jesus gave the time to become that man had better pick on the weakest, perhaps it was surrounded by: false friends, enemies, and people who had no problem betraying him because it is obvious that they considered zero, because it was not in compliance with social rules of the time. On the other hand we know that Judas is a man of action; therefore able to solve problems even killing if it was necessary, so it was: brave, intelligent, educated, prepared, thinker and trained to fight, and with aggressive control of instincts, a perfect war machine, and that human power is put on the side of Jesus', weaker and intelligent man in the world but that the weakness makes its power! There is nothing that would give grounds of the birth of the feeling of Judas and Jesus ', at least that, Judah with his terrible intelligence and mental power alone and does not find out about his business that JESUS' is the Son of God, but if they share a feeling that comes from Heaven, Judas becomes automatic to discover for himself the divine identity of Jesus. We all know that in the ground, when a man is seen weak, the marginalized, and now only after centuries is protected by social laws but relatives and those who call people closer emotionally, revolve back and not take their own lives for it.

JESUS 'AND JUDAH, TWO STEPS. -P.9

At this point we can share the life of Jesus 'in two phases (as logically we can also divide the life of Judah in two stages), however, we begin to divide the life of Jesus'. The first phase of the living Messiah, hiding your ego, and without opening up in front of others, not out of fear, but to protect themselves: so little it is open when wrong, or exuberance opens, others laugh at him and they do feel zero, and he knows it, so for the survival of the law is realized to open up too much, especially with those who have no certainty that you can really trust. But he knew that the man is a journalist, therefore Jesus is very careful, protects itself and certainly will have had experiences that have made us understand how to deal with MOZZICATARI. So even if we think JESUS 'was exuberant, his set is admirable control, succeeds despite the time and fulfill His mission. In the second stage, JESUS ', for a reason (unknown to us) encounters Judah. ... For because they have a communion of ideas and exchanging small talk. ... For it turns out that Judas Jesus' Son is from God. Question: Actually, dear readers, there may be a reason to interact with two opposing temperamentally people, if not only two high personalities at the highest levels of evolution? And if not the only reason that is intelligence, which have in common, or that of a Targeted Design of the Eternal Father, that, what else could keep them close? And it is here at this point that Judas takes shape sentiment against the Messiah. He has a Divine Design be their Friendship. It is here at this point that begins the new important stage in the life of Jesus' and that of Judah. A phase where: who in JESUS 'The teasing, or betrays Him, or Lo song, must be careful, because Judas is a man who kills for much less than this. Therefore Jesus did not need to have the protection of Judah, but combines something that makes it as much as humanly free, it was with the spirit. As JESUS '! Judah also has two important stages in his life: one is the evolution of evil and believe in nothing, or almost; the other is the evolution of the good that was born in him, but be careful though! Only if he is to recognize Jesus 'Son of God, or otherwise, since its evolution of super IO, he could not believe this truth even to themselves rivelargliela was the same Jesus'.

The basis of this decision of the Faith by Judas, the man has proof that Jesus' is really the Son of God. ... Because Judah can not go wrong. ... He knows everything like the dream said that I did, and that I have described. .. He 'afterlife to know everything, he, for the absolutism law, humanly believes only in

30

himself. ... And if it is, only himself to tell him: JESUS 'is the Son of God believes! Otherwise you will not believe! ... For that alone has unconditional faith; since it was his own voice of the heart to tell her, why she thinks! Why he loves Jesus', and loves him to the point of committing suicide if something horrible happened. At this point we are sorry for all the religions of the world, but unfortunately, Jude says that Jesus' Son is God, and there is no escape for anyone, Judah can not go wrong. ... You just have to believe in what he believes Judah, there is no escape for any human being, from north to south, from east to west. We have no choice we humans. Because? But because no one can deprive him from head to Judas that Jesus' Son is from God. ... Why no one has made up his mind, and no one could have had the power to do so. ... The self is put on her own head. ... And he it is un'assolutista that believes only in himself and in no other. .... And no one can win against Judah, he always wins even when he loses, so if it is not, so the same. He is a funny character, funny and smiling from this point of view of the conviction. On the other hand, logically he believes that God is superior to him, otherwise everything would lose evolutionary and conductive sense of the life of both. ... And it is precisely because of his pure faith in God that helps us to understand that He can do no wrong, Jesus is the Son of God, he says so and so, Judah knows everything, and he kills himself, because Jesus is the Son of God, no other reason would have pushed him to do so.

Therefore, only the Heart of Parents may sin as a child having made him acknowledge that God exists and is superior to every man, but not limited to, its supreme wisdom led him to God in a direct and real way, and he definitely understood that God was the one who embraced humanity with all its faults and married as it is bringing to the liberation, and giving him the salvation in heaven. Judas knew for this included the identity of Jesus. And it is the evolution that has given confirmation of this reality! So behind this Spirituality Religious, as Ethics, we, dear readers, we can say that he was part of a family that was regular and good education, although at certain times could bring out defects due to the varied nature of the crisis, as the rest can still observe in our days of incomprehension family defects due to the crisis of ideals or economics. Now is notable psychological work of Judah. On the one hand it must have to do with Jesus ', it is at this point must change his personality in order to do away JESUS' from his person. Because clearly JESUS 'might not have to do with a man of action made the kind of Judah, so it has to change its behavioral personality visually, at least when he is with Jesus', but it should also make you feel Jesus' great and higher, in order to give that importance that deserves to have the Son Almighty. and on the other hand can not completely destroy his being evolved for worse, for self-respect and his own evolution and finally the one that has led to recognize the Son of God. and Judah is a huge effort and a heavy psychological work he does in my opinion, to balance within itself the forces of good and evil, in order not to lose the satisfaction and happiness trying to be with the Son of God and in the environment of the Messiah! So Judah must in some way, not only manifest intelligence capable of binding and maintain an appreciable feeling, but must also represent the good.

So even assuming for himself the Messiah atmosphere was dull and unsatisfying, and rightly so because the characters are too poor and humble and free of psychological depth, hence unable to give incentives and rewards, he alone decides, as is the environment of Jesus, to be part of it, then it does friend's brother in spirit and takes lovingly part of his existence, for everything that belongs to Jesus he respects and feels alive, as if it were his own.

And when in the company of Jesus, absolutely must be good not only in words but also with deeds, and above all must show they understand it, this thing that is not difficult. And on the other hand Judas can not throw away years of evolution of the good and evil that have allowed him to live and to make a name, even if it were, that it is not, just for this, could not miss the opportunity to psychologically bind the person of Jesus, however, should remain adequate and therefore adapt to the environment and the different mentality from her. However, even the action environment he certainly does not neglect, therefore, albeit in a correct manner, in sports training in the environment of the struggle for life and for the victory, and represent pure evil if circumstances had requested, we and she was attending. So if hypothetically he had said, undergoing a hypothetical wronged by someone, you had to do a bad deed I could not hold back, it was his name and his honor, and even if this would have happened, in the period that attended the Son of God. Therefore Judah has to balance two opposing forces within themselves and must live with them and dominating them knowing how to manage. I do not think it was an easy job, and especially to live in peace with itself, he must have had an evolution, at the height of the hills boundless unknown, since we must not forget that the environment we attend gives us emotions and feelings which it is not easy to clean up with ease in our memory especially when they form us and accompany us in a profound way in important phases of our lives.

THE COURAGE TO WRITE THIS BOOK-P.10

The courage to write this book, I came from a dream.

Honestly I started writing but at some point I had pending. Because there was something inside me that I was not going. Then I finally decided to leave alone and forget about it. For me it was a relief, I felt better. Unexpectedly, that same night, the same day that I had decided to leave this book, I had a very strange dream.

SECOND DREAM. -P.11

I dreamed of a shadow man. I felt it was my enemy and would not show up, he peered the dark presence and heard only the words, they said: "God has given you his head you must give it to me, you is have you GIVE ME your head." I I looked and did not answered. I had a trickle of this shadow of unknown fear. his speech I associated him in the book of Jude, and I understood that the decision to suspend this work was sensible. When I understood this, in the same dream I was trying to I remember when God had given His head. Instead of reminding me that I could think of who had given me his hand to write, and at that moment I had the feeling, as if the entire arm of God came into my. Only this he remembered my mind. I said to myself: you're wrong God gave me only your hand to write. So know that he had given me only your hand, made me feel lighter, and the heaviness of my heart vanished . I was better now, and I felt more confident. This shadow dark, from which felt the evil and bad intentions, ignored her and said nothing, and I did not answered and not contrariavo his speeches, I kept a serious demeanor, and I kept his distance. He kept talking to me, but now, with a strong voice, strong and menacing: "Watch out I'm in charge, men obey only me, be careful that I'll make you pay."

The dream ended at this point, without my having said something. From the dream I understood that I had to return to write the book by Judas and finish it. I said to myself: "And 'God's will I have to write this book." I repeated this in my mind. The morning when I got up, almost immediately resumed work psychological journey. A path that I have traveled to the complete draft of the work.

SUMMARY OF THE PRESENTATIONS - P. 12

Because now with Judah pass from one stage of development to another, which is why we are required to give a brief summary, and say: The book Light, the Holy Book and the Hope book deal with the extent of our being, and the reasons of our lives and of our evolution. We are an energy of thinking light, bright with the human form of our body, that is from another universe. This energy; we are! It regenerates and feeds itself through Love, Whose, its apex is perfect, Universal Love. In the absence of quest'Universalità, the energy that we are, we will go out and die for eternity. For eternity, we can live, die for eternity, depends only on us, and exclusively by us. Only here is the final choice of our order, our destiny. Everything according to the road that we walk according to our will and our choices: the Good or bad determine our end, good or bad. These things we say in the book and in the Holy Light. The book Hope, explaining clearly the good and evil in its representation, material separates good from evil, "said and done" closes this developmental stage.

SUMMARY PRESENTATION NEW PHASE. - P.13

Judas opens a new phase, you pass has a different evolutionary stage. The book of Jude is divided into several parts. I mean mainly detect the part: historical, fictional, essay, imaginative and psychological. The various parties will ultimately go together and will reconcile each other. For this reason, the novel will flow harmoniously and hand in hand will take a logical aspect. So, this is a book complex as a whole and complex in its drafting, consisting of: mysticism, fantasy while reasoning respecting the historical era that is used to characterize, customize the character in his actions and his thoughts. What characterizes the book of Jude is a sense of unicità- singolarità- showing the character in dealing with the environment. There are some features of the character that basically reflect some sections of the usual personality of man for existence. Example:

Sometimes amazing things happen to us and we have to live with what happens to us. Sometimes we have to give a timely response if we are not to succumb to foolish and unexpected things from time, to time, happen to us in life. We are called in these extraordinary cases to behave in a certain way, in a way is

35

our uniqueness. Even if in the end it seems that the determination, the uniqueness sets us apart from others, however each of us has its determination and its uniqueness, just to make us all do not resemble each by its own unique response to a particular problem, however, to while similar. We are eager to be different, distinct and establish ourselves with a unique feature, original, authentic, in order to prevail or to point our image more than the others in our environment. With maybe they share ideas, interests and our time, so we share many interests and we seem similar to this, but we are different. Therefore, the character no less of other men, demonstrates his character authenticity, while sharing interests and habits with others. Up to this point would be normal, but we have to add that he had a bivalent personality for which he had a double life. Doubles were the habits in the environment, the greater its authenticity. It seems difficult to understand and yet it's not really that difficult.

An Environment was his of his being that reflected his person, harsh and cruel, perhaps with an own code of honor, but an environment that represented evil. The other an opposite environment where commanded and prevailed affections, the feelings and the representation of the asset, which applies to be Jesus'. At this point we can understand that Judah has not lost a fight or a challenge in his environment, Judah lost a fight and in the environment of Jesus' challenge and has lost feeling. ... For that alone he was defeated, by the feeling he had for Jesus' and from himself it was eventually convicted. This is a very delicate novel and you need to read it until the end, though, he wants to get on top. Before totally immerse myself in the subject, I declare, for the avoidance of doubt given the charge theme delicacy, which is not to be considered as I perform this work, historical relic; nor theological. This story of Judah is novel. This is a purely narrative created by me using all my psychological resources. I received help from my sensibility and my imagination. Here I express my psychological balance in order to understand the reasons and motivations that have pushed the character in question to have a certain kind of behavior that I have, he has labeled a traitor to the Son of God. He has a certain depth of intellectual evolution . And analyzing everything that belonged to that world, to understand the reasons, if any, any, that have led to betray the Son Of God. So we start from a logical analysis and rational considering the period of the time he had determined, customs. We analyze customs, culture, religion. Religions that represented different customs, and men who worshiped OF distinct while sharing the same environment and the same space. Finally we'll explain that in times of Jesus' s'iniziava to worship the spirit of Octavian Augustus, who eventually this custom, and induced people conditioned the next to want to acquire the super IO. At the time they worshiped many DEI but mostly they worshiped the spirit of the Emperors. For this man was fascinated by the "IO" super and consequently was always competing with others for the pursuit of perfection and their own super IO, he was measured in art, culture and physical strength. Thus he began the Imperial religion TIBERIO which imposed the worship of the Spirit of Augustus, the empire to maintain balance and to avoid a second civil war, perhaps! however notable that Judas, like all men, suffered this INFLUENCE Imperial. So it is for this reason that we make this historical journey, we are convinced that we serve to split the personality of Judah, because Judah was definitely influenced by this custom, though, he could've inherited from his father Simon, who though not was in use in his day, however, it is understandable that Augustus was venerated as a super man alive since he won against Mark Antony civil war. Thus Augustus was probably revered alive for his heroism, for his victory and for the ability he has shown in keeping the Roman Empire united. And then later on after his death, he was revered as a superior spirit, in this way it was maintained in the emperor's spirit as if it was among the living, and by his veneration sets, I repeat, by Tiberius Claudius Nero Augustus, I 'empire remained cohesive and a new civil war between DRUSO and Tiberius was averted. Notable that this new way of religion, prepared man to identify himself to be superior as Augustus, and at the same time to recognize a man as a superior being.

So I recommend to empathize with the environment taking into account, customs, mentality of the subject to the pagan religions and traditions, which influenced the culture of the Jewish religion and also the company. The mentality that was created was to aim for the devotion of the super ego, and to reach the highest peaks of evolution with the aim of becoming the super and perfect men; is this to blame the influence given by the adoration of the Spirit From Augustus. For this, it occurred a fusion of different, but mainly that you had galloped the culture of the super ego.

The influence of this cultural fusion with the conditioning that came from the Roman religious culture of the superego and adoration of the Spirit, predisposed man to understand the super ego of Jesus the Son of God; but only a few could have evolution to get to the cultural summit of the time, and to recognize Jesus' as the Son of God. One of the few to force must be Judas. I talked about in previous books about various topics but they are part have little difficult situations. What I mean is that: In this novel change a trickle, the intensity and depth of thought. You will notice that they are more free and more trained in writing now, than in previous writings. And 'this state comes from the desire to write and the pleasure of it. To know and imagine that you, dear readers, you notice these deep diversity in my writings, (just because you follow me), for me it is a comfortable and pleasant spronante and encouragement. I believe it is useful to your attention that especially helps me feel strong, because of the complexity of the topic I think it's very auspicious feel strong. Talk about a man trying with analysis and imagination, and a balance of his person with just what to say and he knows, it is not easy. We must rebuild a whole personality and a way of thinking, unknown to us, just having as basis what you read and what you called our imagination. A recollection process of small pieces scattered everywhere and who knows where. This process might seem an adventure, a bit reckless, beyond that each of us can judge it according to their point of view, does not deny that you venture a little foolhardy, the it is. I realize that the only starting point of the character and only his arrival that we know to be the final acts of his life, and they are: the betrayal and suicide. Tangible that's what we came here, and only this we. I'll have to break his personality, and take as an integral testimony of what he says, what is he has been written, and with this follow up to understand the evolution, the way of being and thinking. In the fictional work, manifest an abundant use of the imagination because it helps me a lot in completing a phase of life of the character in question. And while trying to express the story is true to a realism that we know through the old books, the fantasy it is indispensable for the completion of situations imagine, to make sense of events imagined in order to give a logical sense and continually to the events true given by history. Then it is to describe the life of the character, always imagined, we can find the truth known, and compare this with the logic of psychological realism of that time, and see if you can be of historical or unclear things failings. For this also the imagination I try to make her look almost real, or at least I try. To these arguments and the conclusions, albeit arise spontaneously, however, are conditioned by an underlying fantasy, you! Warning! Are to be considered interesting in the comparative aspect at the time, considering that historical period: logic, curiosity, human character nature, is devoted to good or evil, this is the manifestation of his natural identity, subject to ' opportunism, association, and victory to be achieved as a final award.

FEATURES ETERNAL. -P15

Besides, we must consider that humans are eternal characteristics, or at least personal qualities that you only change a little trickle after thousands of years, or maybe never.

And never! Man E 'managed to completely change forever and ever his inherited these characteristics since primordial times, and now part of its financial nature, because that is how it was born, and that's how it is (in part) for even now in our time, so not only in the past. Therefore he is: Opportunist, corruptible interest, unstable, executioner, self-destructive, envious, cynical. He is also enjoying, having certainty of the evil of others, regretted false, blasphemous, treacherous, ruthless, deceitful, and diabolical creature of habit. ... Etc ... Etc ....

These are the characteristics tend to hurt that man manifests to possess the ages of ages, and although represented the good, we could hardly say that from time to time can not commit sins under the influence of the characteristics of evil belonging to its genetic heritage. Therefore Man is EVIL. At the basis of this we conform ourselves to history, but beware! Let us go further and if we find something, that gives us the power of the doubt, let's boldly intend, if for no other reason to honor justice and respect for our cultural evolution. Certain man there are also features of the Well, which do not require, to be listed as all know them and only in front of them we usually see ourselves and courageously. Ultimately what I want to express that the man he was, at one time is now, it has evolved a lot, but in his temperamental nature has evolved the least. So the men of the past and of today have the same character, are the times have changed, the words are used in different ways, but the masks are made now as before.

After all, the man is an opportunist and he does not care who's in charge, but it counts only that "he" who commands materially guarantees, to him the good life, and to others a poor life in order that it can dominate. In fact, that would be rich if there were no poor? Nothing.

Therefore, beyond the wealth and material well-being, in one sense, to man the rest is of little importance, but it is precisely when he speaks well and the interest incurred to the rulers, normal thinking for all men! Those that are discarded by the thermal circuit, become idealistic and clearly struggling for a better world, that's part of the game. Therefore man is DIABILICO, then uses the tiny half and is on the side of all, and turns towards the interest. So man must feel great to the point of reaching a development that put him on a par with God, but this does not serve the other men if I do not recognize him as such, and must submit, and time he needs the poor, otherwise no one worships. Two thousand years ago is a poor man who is called Jesus and with his behavior tells us: << Money and teneteveli power, I am your Lord, who also believes in me will live if you die, you do not believe when they die he will be dead forever , the rules are universal love and the welfare distributed. Few believe, but good.

Returning to the theme above opportunism, in general, it was a behavior once enhanced features smart man, and this is now. Returning to the speech of Judah and of the novel, we say, this book consists, as we said above, also a part fictionalized, by a mystic and part psychological. There you will find the points of the phases and that for their uniformity, for their accurate description and for their depth, it would seem real, - ammirevole- but are not. It's still a job of my personality, of my morality, my thought that colors almost everything. With this novel set for myself a goal: that is to make you share my thoughts, give you a curious reading, pleasant, and seemingly real. I make conclusions compared to the realism of human nature to understand and feel the identity of Judah that I have seen in a dream and try to put in the time to see if it is in it connected, or if it is out of place.

This is why I try to understand how he could think and behave a man during his lifetime, and on certain occasions; and as a reference point it takes the kind of 'environment, based on the life that can lead, who can attend. In this way, I imagine the behavior that could have taken in front of others, any man she had: a certain personality and a certain character. I try to understand, given the time and based on the life that he could offer: the kind of people who might have met a man, in certain circles. Bearing in mind that to be in a certain environment and to attend certain characters, he had to have and experience certain personal characteristics that reflect the same environment, or otherwise drawing attention to himself negatively. Essentially in a certain way you have to think, in a sense needs to reason, to behave in a certain way, and in a certain way to be given answers to life's circumstances, if you want to survive, under certain circumstances and in certain environments. In the end these conclusions are drawn from me to identify the identity of the personalities of interacting with Judas and especially the identity that I want to compare with that of the dream to see if there are any similarities. Considering hypothetically that both that of my real dream and see if there is inside tolerated by historical events or is jarring and not tolerated. Finally according the events trying to figure out if the Judas of my dream is the true Judas, or not! And if the answers he gave, as written in the story, is proving with the personality that he has manifested in dreams, or if there is something wrong, or that escapes us scholars. Who is true Judas? One of my dream, or that of history? This I would like to understand together with you, dear readers, and it is for this reason that I do considerations and analyzes thousands and describing the most reliable. Under the respect and the influence of environment that frequently and people who attended the man, must give answers. Why in a certain way you must think and reason, otherwise man comes out of the circuit environment that attends, and his opportunism or interest decade. Using logic, I try to keep in mind the reality of human nature, reason with rationality, which takes into account the tendency of man to respond in certain ways and according to the circumstances and his personality. Understanding the trend character of being human, the face of events and the environment, for the way it responds.

Understand the personality of the individual based on the behavior that manifests towards others. Understand well, his way of thinking according as is expressed and how to solve their own problems. Whereas some answers are influenced by the experience itself, you need to understand their examination (answers) that kind of experience may have done in his past a man who gave these answers. Understanding the answer means identify the type achieved experiences. Bearing in mind not only the psychological dimension and character of the individual but the value and the thickness of the response, including the type of question that has received the individual from the environment or from the condition. measured response has a corresponding measured demand. Example: "If a man receives a slap, I return SWAT, and not a punch." In this way the conscience remains dormant. By performing this series of tests, we understand that the final answer of Judah that we know to be the betrayal of Jesus', was subject only has realistic shades of a certain kind: economic interest. So we get through this response connoisseurs environment under a point of view, we understand that kind of experience plausibly holds the individual, we measure his opportunism, and verify that gave this response. On the assumption that if we know the answer you gave a man, we can prove its authenticity through the study of his personality, and, well, we can understand much that is true or false that you say, referring to him. The personality is identified by examining: the environment in which he lived habitually, family, friends, the historical period, the contemporary culture of the period, the fashion of that time, customs. ... Etc ... Etc ...

Everything I describe, is inherent in that historical period. Through this study we understand the type of experiences that could make the man and describe his personality. When we understand the personality of man, we can know if the information that we received about the man is healthy, or if something is missing. All this we turn to JUDAH and see what turns up. However, with this base to investigate and try to imagine what might be his most intimate thoughts, so he can

44

assume at what evolutionary stage we can place his wisdom, his wisdom, if it is granted that we are able to locate one. also they express, through their material plausible representation of his thoughts, as can be seen from the next, as judged, and what feelings may attract him. Then pull the sums. Only in this way they have the ability to understand a certain feature of his personality. ... That may be, perhaps, tangible evidence of a motive for his betrayal. Including possible conceptions, drawing in its plausible experience, the personal qualities of his ego, will become comprehensible, and explained his actions, and we could probably find out more about him with this psychological and scientific research, in one dimension, of psychoanalysis. I give and I highlight as well, in the novel as the man could conceivably act, following his innermost thoughts and hidden of his ego to achieve its interest and survival goals. Also try to understand, what would be those thoughts that used to him, inside him, which put him in a position to reach those evolutionary goals of the self, that is true goals conceded only to the Elect, who are those who have an action mental significance, destined to not be destroyed or damaged by this supreme development, which could give so much happiness to be released a SENNA man! For this the personality of Judah is like thinking, and it is well as it does. And what he is physically and thinks, we did not detail how the historical report; We possess only a judgment that says: be a smart man and favorite Apostle of JESUS '. We can now investigate. I have my dream, the news that he is intelligent and favorite of Jesus', and the news of his ignoble betrayal. By means of these notions we can study and prove what you say. In this novel I try to open your heart and pull out of its deepest truth. .... That truth, plausible, it does not say, and that mask in the world and that only he and God knows. All this considering the human identity and elements that are: devotion to privacy, the protection of your balance, now we have to open them intelligently. Our strength is: reasoning, thinking and assume freewheel without any influence. I am more than convinced that the novel of Judah as a whole will be very curious and interesting for you to read it. I hope to have fun and give you some pleasant hours. To be considered, you can see, like the circular evolution follows its perpetual repetitive way in many respects. If you want to compare some facts of our times with some of the past, surely you would notice that the man seeks its own interest more than anything else, the betrayal in many cases, and a man's custom, corruption and speculation are the usual things in human nature, and much more if we compare. ... I am always the same and repetitive. ... Innate in man. ... ... Although there are stages of human improvement the road, you will notice, is still much to do to achieve purity, salvation and the Kingdom of God. This is why we consider human nature, and this is right believe, it is true both when it claims to have discovered something, in some cases, other have not found out something that was already there, but with each passing generation has been forgotten by us.

This something is the teachings of the Good that lead among God's arms. Happy reading.

PURPOSE. P16

What is being proposed to donate the book of Jude, to the readers? Why he killed himself, or rather, the reason that has brought forth within himself the death sentence carried out by himself. His was a car judgment "How P.111." We reveal the mystery that has led to suicide. - JUDAS has heard too much compassion for Jesus and so much he loved him and he was sorry that he can not resist the injustice of life, because a man like Jesus can not be killed! This JUDAS thought about Jesus! -

However we must also proceed slowly, along a whole psychoanalytic path, and above all of Judah, even to understand the feelings and consciousness. He as a whole is the proof of the depth of feeling of friendship. Great and strange word, but it reflects a feeling experienced and exists even in our times. The feeling of friendship, which cultivated can become deep and beautiful as a feeling of blood brothers, and even more. Something Divine. So that's what happens to Judas and Jesus', and I am describing. The reader must ask yourself an example. Two brothers are left in early childhood. After years they find themselves: the biggest, the strongest, for love tries to protect his younger brother, wants it always under the eyes want to control the world around him in order to protect it, and in this way, feel good and peaceful sure. The book of Jude tells us and points out that not knowing Jesus, eventually wants to protect like it was his younger brother. Sentimental prerogative that the Divine grants only to some men and not to all. At first he meets him, makes his knowledge, become friends, born affection and sentiment. Become like two real brothers, and yet they were not in reality, and were not even grown up together (if we give credit to the dream). We can ask ourselves: how can a feeling like that? The plausible answer might be: have cultivated a friendship without conflict and without rancor. We can ask ourselves: what mystery hides, the meeting of two great minds? We could answer, a degree of evolution achieved in intellectual dimension that puts them at a competitive level dialogue, understanding, and through what moral satisfaction and contentment. Two balanced magnets that attract. We can ask again: how does Judah try a similar sentiment, family of brotherhood against a man known only recently? What binds him in the spirit and soul to Jesus'? We can answer that: Judah have become inclined to have a similar affective communion with Jesus', must necessarily have had the experiences that accompanying him to have an emotional quality with the friends of this thick, although it was also a man of action, he believed in the feeling of friendship. We may ask further: what feeling test Judah? The answer might be, it depends on the thickness of the feeling that morally transmits the emotional and spiritual dimension, the Son of God, but surely divine, clean and difficult to understand for us regular people. We can ask many things, and all with a pinch of reasoning. We can try to give an exact and rational answer, but never be able to feel what he felt for Jesus' in his heart. In the end the purpose of this novel is the consideration that must be given to Judah in the face of the feeling of friendship that has immense value and not least, we are required to comply with Judah. Through this mysterious feeling of friendship that God has created for us men to make us live lovingly in peace between us, which ultimately as well, providing the conditions to know deeply and understand ourselves, we must have respect for Judah and his memory because he felt and he lived with this feeling.

Have faith in us, our feelings of our friends, is a way to prepare ourselves, educate ourselves and get used to living in the Kingdoms of Heaven. Judah also has Faith, believe in JESUS ', the feeling of friendship and the evidence proves it, so he too walked the path of preparation, education, which would allow him to live eternally in the Kingdoms of Heaven. Judah is smart, and it shows to the whole world. The fact that Judas, believes that Jesus 'being the Son of God, this means that: Truly Jesus' is the Son of God, there is no doubt that well. Humanity is obliged, when they know the personality of Judah, to believe that Jesus' being the Son of God. No man on earth is in a position to refute this. I have also a different religious belief, no matter who believes in God or not, he has no escape, because if Jesus tells Judas', is the Son of God, can only reply: "You're right." No man is exempt, to confident trust the declaration and the intelligence of Judah. No man can resist has an intelligence, without measure and in a magnetic, irresistible emanating   his   person.
The humanity of the whole earth, is bound to believe that Jesus' being the son of God, do you know why? Easy answer: Because Judas believed that Jesus' is the son of God. No man can go against this, as he will never, have achieved an evolution able to thwart and face, intelligence, charm and magnetism of Judah   .
Judah along its evolutionary path left of the material words, no

voice but materially visible, "are with JESUS 'until death." No matter how he died and why he went Judah; He died with his Master, was not with the people to have fun and to rage against the Son of God; disassociated itself from the bestial evil man, this is evidence of his belief in the identity account by JESUS ', otherwise he would die at the same time, and you would not be killed:

(For absolutely no reason at all he would kill himself).

With this book I give you, as well, the proof that Jesus' is the son of God. Through Judas, this is proof. Through a clean feeling, brotherly love, just wanted the Divine, between Judas and Jesus', this is proof. The book of Jude is a gift, that I make to the readers and to the world. How many things come to you as a gift from this book, which, although I do not know, and that you will grasp.

PREFACE-P.17

The book of Jude describes a dating situation corresponding to the feeling of friendship, which is the basis of brotherhood. The personality of the protagonist, I can think deeply and soaked thoughts that are partly rational. To be noted that I try to respect its nature, suggeritami from a cultural and informational situation. The irregular part of its duality is noted in his talk with the Master, a little 'bold and transgressive but deep in the meantime; partly silent, filled with emotions, with laughter and joy of simple expressions, drawn from the get-togethers with pleasure. Clearly, part of the duality of his personality, is regular, visible at the point where I do think with deep thoughts and conceptions. Since the birth of this book is deeply inspired by a dream, I remember that the effort I make in its drafting is considerable:

–   Why should I want to remind you that if something could not understand ritenetemi apologized because I justify it with you, dear readers. -

Judah is present as a traitor! So at the same time a victim of a scam from the same corruptive nature that Led to the Sanhedrin, our Lord; although are considerable different evil entity is received, and is different the quality of the substance that each has faced itself, however, the principal is the same nature. The suicide of Judas in this novel, becomes dress rehearsal of many factors and brings to light many contexts character of the character. Suicide treason trial, evidence of repentance; Suicide evidence of pain; judgment proof towards you, try suicide dissociation of malevolent society in association chain, suicide silent voice that Jesus' is the Son of God. .... Etc. Etc. ... ... All that we intend to prefer suicide is always with the aim to give full meaning to the character, and come to a saturation of his psychological situation. Referring, to spiritual purity, the priests of our time, in the emotional situation of the Messiah, I insert a dash of panache sweet and heartfelt joy. Combining a touch of gentle irony and sense of joyful, manifesting many priests of the Church of which I I've learned the admirable qualities, come from a heritage that comes to us already from ancient times through the faith that the Spirit of the Messiah there left as a legacy, that is: to smile even with joy, and ironic in order to maintain a harmonious atmosphere shared between people who respect each other and love each other. In this novel you can see phases with a pinch of joyful irony that brings a smile to the character in question. Judah, From the Messiah he draws the joyful and happy smile on his Grace, in order to be White Miracle by a deep pain that tortures him for the demise of his loved ones. That joyful smile emanating men in the grace of the Holy Spirit, this is one of the treasures that the Son of God left us a legacy, and that men most likely helped Judah to find the way of affection and sentiment that ' It led to bind to the Messiah. GOOD READING.

SAFE START WITH REALISM LAMPANTE-P.18

We have a vision of the Cross under a point of view. We see the Cross as the Passion of Jesus'. Feel towards the Cross something inexplicable in one respect, however, something deeply spiritual, but not as they saw it then. We must understand and understand it clearly as he saw the Cross, people to Jesus 'time, as he saw Judas and how Jesus'. This helps us to put ourselves in the environment, feel the air and breathe the oxygen that time full of life and strange at the same time. We require to understand the people, the people and all. Let's first of all in cold and direct way, that Jesus' did not go around preaching the cross in hand, so what we perceive of this symbol, is not equal to what was perceived to be. What was the cross then? Evil, the death sentence, the pain, the excruciating pain of the condemned and their families, representing the holocaust definitely. How he could see the people, the Cross, and how he could see the same Jesus'? Horror Symbol, executioner tool in the hands of the powerful they used to terrorize the poor. The cross as a symbol of fun and devotion to the cult of death for those who were there and those who never convicted could be sentenced. This was the cross, and this way he saw the people and the same JESUS '. So Jesus' founded Christianity, no symbol but with ideals.

OBESRVATION SOCIAL REAL -P.19

The reality is: the man is a social being and this feature visiting visit the cities to focus on living always close. The man is also a being executioner. For this for thousands of years man speaks well, he thinks good, but contrary is evil. There is a part of humanity subjected to powerful men who use them as objects. JESUS 'is to change the rules. Still we see with our eyes, that the rules JESUS 'were not accepted by man. And God has abandoned the man because they are not respectful of its laws

Benign, by contrast, is a sinner do not control her tormentor and slave nature. .... And is a liar, because: He speaks well, but only makes their interest. ... And then he proves to be false when he says he committed evil for work and for the reasons. ... Excuse nonexistent what it claims and intends to believe and let the neighbor, because evil has created by his own wickedness. If the Jesus' Brotherhood rules were not accepted, then we are in the hands of God's justice. This is the reality. The wickedness done to speculate on the next, for their own interest or to feed on sadism, leads man to destruction. We see wars and killings without any mercy towards the weak, without any reason. ... And that in the end I do not lead you to any improvements. ... The weak are always victims and helpless. This is the truth and the rest are words.

COMING OF THE MESSIAH-P.20

The Messiah is born at least ten years before the end of empire by Gaius Julius Caesar Augustus. First emperor of Rome. So he lives his life, seeing the two emperors governments: Octavian Augustus and Tiberius Julius Caesar Nero Augustus.

Tiberius at birth is called: Tiberius Claudius Nero, then just going on to become Emperor Augustus, was named Tiberius Julius Caesar, and finally Tiberius Julius Caesar Augustus. During his lifetime, the Messiah, sees two prosecutors in the Galilee; The other Valerio and Pilate's successor Valerio.

JESUS 'therefore, he does not live the conflict between Mark Antony and Octavian Augustus. The Civil War he does not live it, politicians end up noises, and 'He is born. Surely he has heard of it during its growth, but everything out of his living situation.

Tiberius was the son of the first bed of LIVIA. She had become the fourth wife of Octavian Augustus. DRUSILLA LIVIA was his mother, and was the wife of Augustus. Thus Octavian was his stepfather. The TIBERIO natural father was: Tiberius Claudius Nero husband of the first bed of Livia. Tiberius Claudius Nero, when it burst, the conflict between Augusto and Marco Antonio was on the side of Marco Antonio, then, was Antonino.

Note the oddity that the father and son had the same name, but this was not an unusual thing in ancient Rome.

The combination, of the conflict situation, including Marco Antonio and AUGUSTO, finds meaning in the evolution of psychological JUDAH. In fact this becomes reason in order that he will live the consequences following the path of his father, a path different from that of Jesus'; is the fate acts with the final aim of the meeting between Jesus' and Judas in adulthood; this is combined, appropriately, for a choice of part performed by Simon, the father of Judas: it was a ANTONIANO.

In conclusion, becoming Emperor Tiberius: the TIBERIO NERONE Son, he saw to it that many Antonian in exile could trust the new ROMA ruling political and decide to return to Patria. Who he turns Judea was changing, and becoming a vassal of Rome ROMAN province. favorable circumstance that sets the conditions to Antoniani to return within empire without fear of retaliation and revenge any. This is of great importance and will be decisive, factor in that: everything becomes a means, which needs, in order to materialize, the encounter between Jesus' and Judas, but only after obtaining both a certain evolution that puts them one facing each other to confront. A bond intellectually, we can also say between the two as an approach, and why not! Even this consideration there is.

The coming of Jesus' is a gift that God makes to man: The people, by His coming, they understand something True, Holy, Righteous who helps him become better and tastier. JESUS 'brings the Faith in God, something to believe in order to come through faith in God and His observances. How to say in a more direct way: give man the reason of the Supreme Truth which ultimately is the path of salvation. Well we can say that: through His Son, show the way of salvation to man, but through faith that He brings to us talking about his Father, who is God! This is what he brings to the world, the FAITH which is the Will of God (Leave all that to the world, having taken nothing!) Something to Believe, that truly reflects our history and the reality of our existence, and of our creation, in order to become good, and ripe to be worthy to enter the Garden of Eden! At that religious beliefs were varied, and not all men followed them with devout conviction. Most of them followed them, more for bias that for real Faith: we could say that to believe in something it was more a sort of costume that the true vocation. The Messiah comes at a point on the earth: - In a place. -

Where humanity is composed of people who are men of different cultures together. They use different costumes, as they have different beliefs, but the political circumstances, the Imperial customs, they create the situation of living in the same territory, to share life, having to also interact with their diversity. At that time the man, living with his neighbor, under the influence of the next culture, and at the same time, influencing others with their own culture. With this live you create a situation of understanding, discovery and even compromise, between people of different cultural and religious traditions. All this, under a profile of the charm and attraction dominated by curiosity and the pleasure to try the new, the man, is the exchange between the peoples of customs and traditions, by dividing and sharing customs. ... As if it was a way to understand each other, know each other, and evolve in different directions by learning notions of other cultures different from their own. New trends are felt alive the life and as if every novelty he rode the wave of success and modernity, breaking away and criticizing what is left of the years behind, dismissing those times gone by with the simple word, we modernize the whole world is changing this is the new life. In the end they are repetitive things for thousands of years and so have remained: the old way does not understand, the young man is modern it includes.

This was happening at the time of Jesus': a cultural revolution, religious, political and social. Usual things that happen and happen again over the centuries. In the end the poor remain poor and oppressed, and the rich change their names and words, but always remain rich, regardless of changing their way of thinking in the direction that the wind blows, always rule and if they take advantage of their power to achieve anyway command and control: for them what matters is not what religion to believe, is not what ideology represent, but has always being the leader of any ideology or of any religion. This is the reality for thousands of years for this world man is always the victim of injustice, this is called corruption. It was created at the time of this form, a live of peoples, cultures and different customs. ... Because they gave continuity to life. Therefore men spent the existence briskly, and with pleasing harmony. Therefore the campavano people without feeling any boredom, indeed waiting, almost anxiously, and called it the time for fluing faster because they were hoping to improve it and find happiness. So each, in those times of social and cultural changes, he was focused on his own being and his fate, it was as if waiting for something. Then the man lived, psychologically speaking, as campa now, and perhaps how he lived forever, calling the passage of time it waits for something to do or you have to perform.

At that time, he spent time taking with it the life and the atmosphere was lively performance from Rome. This air sparkling that came from the surrounding environment was born curiosity and desire to discover the customs of different nations, becoming for young people themselves, the most enjoyable and satisfying living. And 'the conduct of life itself seemed that offered more and better interesting future. The

man, understood the world of aliens of which came in contact that was different from their own. The older men differently conceived new cultures carried out by other countries in their own country, for this seemed more backward than younger people. Young people, a bit 'for the pleasure, a little' out of curiosity opened with momentum old citizens. His mind spontaneously opened. openness, attention, that one's mind and their psychological opened almost spontaneously for the rule of communion with men bearing new life from distant countries, of which there they admired strength and deeds, in this   case   "the   Romans   ".
In order to imagine and understand the world full of news that surrounds him, the man, with all these new situations, full of different communications, painful or not has to store information in order to evolve; and play a social role by opening the understanding to communicate with your villager though, he feels different and sees the new cultural and social situations so different from him. That's what creates conflict with their villagers and communion with foreigners. Jesus may have had in his retinue a willingness to interact with people from foreign lands. ... Like Judas. ... By contrast operates, or otherwise.

Man is, at that time, put in a share location and confrontation with his fellowman. .... Born antagonism. Given the circumstances favored the learning of the time, the learned man without being excused. .... The religious culture. .... Since it was also imposed, and was used by Rome to keep the empire under control. ... And all of the subject peoples. The ethnic situation fined invited him to exchange views and to 'learn. It would appear that he was ready and was open to learn new thinking that was the message of God. Humanity is in a stage of evolution and learning: caused by the expansion of the Roman Empire and the mixture of different cultures. The greatest contribution to humanity's evolutionary development came mainly from the dominant ones who were those "ROMAN and Jewish".

We can say, that: given the circumstances, humanity had become predisposed to acquire an ideal, or most ideal, is for them man was to fight, in order to achieve a higher civic sense stadium or different than that in he had lived in the recent past, or the one who lived in the contemporary time of that era; In order to make an improvement in their lives. Through the new opportunities that gave the modern environment and the man was trying to achieve a certain social status that would guarantee a better life, and to commune with the Romans it represented the possibility of good opportunities. There are men who believe in certain things and other men who believe in other things. For this we have a contact, where some remain for what they are other, transfer their ideals and beliefs in another direction. There are also those that combining the two cultures. Others who live with a culture and it tasted another for the sake of curiosity or anything. .... And there are those who look for people to realize their goals: dreamers, speculators, and corruption aimed at economic and social improvement first, and no matter how! For them has only his own interests and their own personal pleasure. ... Actors! Mystifying double agents. However apart from these individual qualities are forms of coexistence and reconciliation. The air we breathed was new and everyone wanted to do something for themselves. The mind spontaneously opened to decipher this air sparkling composed again, and to savor these myriads of new emotions and renewed feelings. Habit and inherited cultures, shared with other people, other cultures and other traditions, naturally the man opened to learn, to enter a new phase of evolution.

This was an era that received influences from different cultures. Different religions and beliefs. It would seem that the culture, the civil and religious Roman is the strongest, ready to prevail over the others and to dominate the world not only material but also spiritual, but this definitely officially, but unofficially, religious cultures were varied. So many were the gods. In addition to these pagan idolatry, there was the spirit's preference, the pursuit of perfection and superiority EGO, magic, spiritism. Rome, however, had declared the Imperial and mandatory spirit Imperiale "Augustus the cult culture" and later of all the emperors were worshiped. He, RE, was revered as a heavenly deity, or seeds of Divinity. .... One way to keep the Empire together! We must consider that the influence "Rome and Galilee" were bipolar, with the enthusiasm of new cultures that were compared to each other, fascinated by the Jews, and at the same time also the Romans, and some traditions and some Judean beliefs. ... Normal, which were influenced by the Roman tradition. For this we can say that apart from the standard, adherence to Rome as queen of the world by the will of the Gods that is definitely the text, there is also the Romans that they are carried away with pleasure and with interest, by the new religious cultures of the people who get in the hands of Rome. For this they create a coexistence and a mixture of customs and traditions. Then clearly each, even following their own opportunism. Beyond this, considering that Rome represented progress and better future, certainly in a sense could also consider and accept a certain reality and say that at that time the Roman culture was dominant and certainly obscured other cultures . The influence of Roman, was the strongest, offering more opportunities for those in search of a better future: let's say that it is clear Personal questions to it, easily the man he was fascinated and a certain attraction, which could shortly resist. God knows everything, is clear. The people Jew believes in Him. JESUS 'can only be born in this people to suffer religious influence, even if learned in informative manner all that the world could offer and all that surrounded him, he mostly belonged to an education that He predisposed him and prepared him as a child to the faith of the one God of his fathers. The Eternal Father, in order to donate the Road of Salvation man giving something tangible to believe in, He comes among men through His Son; one way: in order that culture devoted to Roman ideals not pleased by the Eternal Father, and in some way has stopped. Surely many other reasons the Eternal Father JESUS 'accomplished with his coming; this above, is definitely one of the many; to remember that many corrections had to be made civilly in all religions, because each had its dark side, so: many infinite reasons solved the Coming of the Messiah, yet not all of us can understand, but it was the right time and the 'era was ready for the coming of the Prophet, and so were! An era in which man must learn, because it is his time of learning and understanding by teaching what is right, what is evil, to separate these two things through and decide what the meaning of the Faith choose. What path to follow, if you want to go to God and save his soul. Therefore a man who believes in that time so many religions in the end does not believe in anything: live by lies and deception; only he pretends to believe, but it does not have faith in anything; and each man deceives and claims to have the best of God's protection; all a lie that leads nowhere. And the craziest thing in his nature, he knows he does not believe in anything but the same pretends to believe and conscientiously autosuggestiona. For this man knows that playing and it's all fake is all a game because in his heart he does not believe in anything, but wants to convince others that it is true its just believe. Nevertheless, it evolves - gave circostanze- and enhancing the culture and understanding begins to prepare its conscience before number choices, choices of Faith.

Faith affected by the recalled automatically consciousness evolution from man as head of the representation of good or evil, it is for this reason mainly required to give an account of the good or evil (done or seen done) to your heart, to the self, and understand what good and what is bad, and through the call of his conscience, choose the defendant road to appease the voice of conscience, in order to raise the feeling of pity. The man in himself, in this way, it gives the motivation and reason to justify this act, this took a psychological position, claiming that it was the right path to save his own soul and to enter into the good graces of God. ... still not clearly identified. Here comes Jesus' it helps this process is pointing with his finger the path of Light, man. Here this was the right time for humanity evolved and evolving the IO that was being perpetrated, to receive the message of God through His Son. Humanity is ready at that time, to receive and understand the Messiah. We might think, without any safety since there more we essays of the Eternal Father, and to assume in order to seek the understanding that: God's choice, to send His Son into the Jewish people, it might be understandable that the Jewish people believed God is tHE Venera ancient times, but it could be understood by the myriad of other reasons, as mentioned above. As well, one of these could be that the intertwining of religions could draw, given the evolutionary moment, the consciousness of man to improper analysis of the truth, and therefore, believe even more deeply (if we say with more cultural extremism and ideological) to false religions, passing them in a reasonable manner and deep attack them even more, than they were, the soul, the spirit, and conscience in man's own. In practice it was time to bring down the fake deities and rappresentatrici the false and evil, with the danger that it could return to devotion to god MOLOK. "This is also a reason" the understandable given that it was the right one. Corruption and devotion to evil were at the peak in those days, and God considered that the intervention of Jesus 'atonement was to avert the risk of greater attachment to evil that became deeper because it helped because of' evolutionary epoch of Civil relevance. I say this because considering religion presenter Roman teaching to become devotees absolute obedience. Be devoted to superior men, the years might have become normal and regular preaching and glorifying kings and tyrants. This would be for humanity a misconception because the dictatorship that leads man to accept themselves as less powerful teach him to look at, would never end. Thus the pagan religion and materialistic 'erroneous custom of ancient men, who worshiped the gods and men who claimed to be demigods because one of the parents was an Olympian god. Future generations would have a creed, where man worships only MAN, and the masses without understanding ethical and religious Christian who then is to understand that God made us all equal and therefore all those entitled to happiness, be happy to be sacrificed, as objects, and the powerful men who are at the top of the social wealth. So whereas Tiberius had imposed the religion of the spirit of Augustus, to be venerated as a God, they could remain in conscience bad habits and be mistaken for good and eternal things because man's intelligence was growing and itself during the intellectual growth he will associated custom and a wrong belief, the man would be intellectually grew up believing that evil was good and usual. And then Jesus' runs for cover according to the will of the Eternal Father.

<<The man grows intelligently and during its growth (in his rise to the understanding), God through Jesus, he puts in the way of the Well of Light, understanding of good values that lead him to save oneself and to God. to make this call all mankind has to listen to his conscience and to follow what He says. To do this sermon of the Good, Forgiveness and Mercy should be priority concerns for the man: Charity, and other values that lead to Universal Love, and all that in conscience feels right for his own good and the community he He must pursue. -

Therefore God enters into human history through His Son Jesus, but not as emperor, but as a common and poor man, but always the Son of God. Therefore, if the poor are represented by the Son of God, do not need to worship the rich as being superior to them, because they are their brothers in Christ and children of God as are all. Jesus fraternized at all there, in poverty and weakness. This understanding that the man got, was part of Christ's mission.

It can not rule out that if Jesus' appointment was missed, the passage to human sacrifice could be by evolutionary consequence of evil and religions that represented him. And everything would become normal to this day if you gave a breakthrough evolution of the man well. With the coming of the Messiah is the pity, compassion, new feelings even if it is not inconceivable that the man tried them, but it is clear that while it understands them so did the evil and was merciless, because he probably did not feel these feelings in a deep and right way. - Jesus brings these feelings and puts man in a different stadium. Now with our evolution we understand that a man can complete its life cycle without having to risk more disruption of their lives, prematurely, so unjust and violent for the same reasons as the threatened 2000 years ago. And it is right, it can complete its life cycle evolving and so can go by the Eternal Father well educated and ready to live with the angels, saints, and you Brothers. >>

POLICY JUDEA ROMANA – P.21

<<In ancient times he felt to speak of the Romans. Of them they said they were very good with small states that they submitted to them and they wanted alliances. This we read in the Holy Scriptures. In order also to be protected from their enemies, the Jews decide to put themselves under the protection of Rome. The Romans were a good match for those small countries in search of protection and and new relationships, cultural, social and economic. >>

They were loyal, who showed, fidelity and took charge of supporting the principles, the values and the Roman policy. They possessed an imperial culture and artistic avant-garde, even libertine and customs were very attractive for those who loved the fun and fashion of the new. Situation allures-ble to do to come to the citizens want to change their lives: the temptation to become Romans themselves, or at least be under their influence, and to behave like them. Judea was one of those nations that decided to put themselves under the protection of Rome, perhaps for fear of the Greeks or someone else nation, perhaps to progress, perhaps because in this way the bigwigs could get help from Rome to take in hand the own people, perhaps to broaden their markets to do business with them. For any other reasons, the conditions were all alluresable and affordable, and the conclusions, some were good for others a bit less, but the time was right for Rome that had become powerful, to expand his empire. However in Romans, the Roman Empire, the small states glimpsed the future and the security of tomorrow, so it was a fatal attraction without their excessive intravvedessero motivations.

The class knew Judea executive that if he behaved fairly and would pay the taxes imposed by Rome could rule their people and their nation by maintaining the same privileges always undisturbed from Rome, even Rome would enable them to remain in power their seats in their own country, this was a little more security for executives and Jewish leadership. So even if the rulers of Judea were under the orders of Rome, it mattered little because the Empire granted them privileges and wellness. Instill in Rome was only interested in the collection of taxes. Behind this priority interest of the Romans, who was loyal and reliable than had in Rome and signed in to the social and Imperial service privileges. Therefore Empire maintained puppets rulers in its provinces, such as Galilee, until they were able to comply with the orders of Rome. The Romans through the weakened taxes the foreign economy, and clearly became increasingly dominate less complicated, the threat of Rome certainly could not come from the states economically demolished, even more harm they received from Rome, and in Rome were tied (Yes the league bad as I have always said in my writings.) So since the era of the ancient alliance was signed between Judaea and Rome. A delegation was sent - in ancient times - the time of Judah Maccabee, and was entered into the alliance pact. Why Judea was one of those conquests of Rome not achieved by force but achieved through diplomacy.

Voluntarily were the Jews who offered their land in Rome. So the Jews became loyal subjects of Rome while remaining in the government of their country. strategic move of Judea diplomacy, which had attracted and wrapped by the cultures and customs of Rome. In the end, over the years, some of the men enlisted in the army of Rome, just to become Romans. This acquisition placed a man in a position of prestige. Roma gave security and stability. The Romans imposed their culture manifested and nothing else. Therefore, their culture was in the forefront both in use, both in customs and in the libertine tradition is understood as having all the carnal pleasures of life even if it meant unhappiness or suppression of others. It was well accepted by the Allied nations, which s'immergevano in it with fervor and delight. Many wanted to be like the Romans, and they also copied the gestures, personality and mentality. It was an era where man drew from others, and cultures mingled, but the stronger the more modern and daring was the one who was always better in use, because it gave more pleasure to the meat. The part of Rome was a way to feel with it, realized, and move on to a higher stage in human and personal way. The majority of people were happy to identify with Rome and with his people. So Judea was ruled by the Romans in an indirect way, through the Jewish priests. The priests, who were holding in their hands the people. In the event that a Jew was behaving badly, priests could accuse him and give it to the court of Rome. They could not be sentenced to death. Their religion, prevented, but they could accuse him and ask the Roman court death sentence. The court of Rome, imposing the sentences, exactly one required by the Jews priests, right in order that the services and good relations were always maintained and supported. Over the years, what seemed to the Jews, a good council alliance, became a profitable business for some and a pain for others. The people were boned from taxes, and could not speak, just because the religious leaders were with Rome. ROME more powerful and stronger; the allies were subject to Rome while maintaining rich if it meant restrictions for their people. For this, you could no longer get out of the covenant, the empire was the protector, now it was inside and had to move on. How can it, say, Rome supported only the most dedicated and the most capable to govern the Jews and to make money for it. We can assert that it was Rome to choose the Jews officials to better govern Judea according to the Roman point of view, it was always the same, to bring more wealth to Rome.

Why the law was well-respected, without remorse or conscience; There was dancing in the individual career, for which the Romans were no less interested officials of the states subject. The exchange of individual interests kept up the system. The people were destroyed, but the shows and surprises of the Roman customs, let him always amazed, amused, to the point of forgetting or just considering their inconvenient location. As if it were dragged into something stronger than it, which gave way, purpose in life, it was as if Rome and all that concerned with it, was the center of life SACRED. Why everyone was involved, and they felt being part of it.

RELIGIONS OF THE TIME ROMAN INFLUENZATRICE PEOPLES -P-22

Ancient Rome. Origin of its religions were primitive, and various branch. They were shrouded by fear resulting from invisible forces subject to faith in them. He was feared the magic, and all that could happen to a family, you wanted to attribute to the invisible forces of good or evil, which he wanted to see. Some things that were happening and where there was a clear lack of understanding were indicated as MANA, then the Romans changed in NUMEN. Name that applies indicating an event not easy to understand why willed by God. They worshiped, many deities that indicated the forces of nature and elements of existence, as if they were minor gods, led by other most important entities, which then were the same of the GREEKS. Each anything that was important and incomprehensible became the object of Divine worship. Clearly, the primitive religion of our whole planet looks like all are somewhat similar. For example: in the religions of India there is a fire symbol of honor and it should be borne in access for all, similar to ROMA is the same with the cult of Vesta. The gods: Juno, Minerva, Jupiter, Mars were glorified. ... Etc. ... Their glorification, was very relaxed from GREECE to GREEN. ... Etc ... Etc ... The increased representation: JUSTICE, WELFARE FORCE, all peoples worshiped these values from India to Europe, so in the same way also the people of Rome. Even some of the myths of the earth will look like. Odin in the North, with the hand and eyes you save a people. With the Romans, Mucius Scaevola, Horatius Codes, who with their eyes burns the opponent's king, and thus saves the people, and placing your right hand on the hot coals until losing it. Religion ROMAN had a branch also archaic, it was a little different, from the primitive religion. It broke away from the belief of natural events: water, fire, earth, sky, forest. Etc. ... Etc. ... They thought that around them there were dark forces, acting, they have the second, in a positive or negative way against them, and the same people, and these religions were named after NUMINA. From there slowly, slowly, religion was transformed into cult status. Therefore, no longer a religion of love or feelings, preached that of the state, but a reverence done in order to bind the man and the people of the Roman state representatives. Therefore they not performed the prayers but public or private ceremonies. Through religion, a citizen even if foreign, became ROMANO, she followed faithfully the directives. If denied, it could also be I killed persecuted. In this way we understand that the ROMAN were considered citizens of Rome he took a SACRED Patronage. They had the Temples for the areas around their house that in the end was a SACRED place, according to their custom. The cults were celebrated by the priests. There were priests of the gods who were considered to themselves like the gods: Mars, Juno, Venus, Jupiter, Vesta, Quirinus. ... Etc ... Etc ... And there were the minor priests, this is performed the ceremony. The chief priest was the Pontiff of GIOVE, and was considered the living God. He could not see the evil done in any man. Jupiter being representative of life, he could not see the death of any man. She wore clothes without laces and wore a leather hat of a sacrificed animal in JUPITER.

Other priests were three groups: Popes, Greetings, sacrificers. The pontiffs were sixteen men, of which the RE and the six VESTALLI, led by Massimo pontiff. Greetings were the interpreters of the messages, which sent the deities. The sacrificers were the guardians of SIBBILLINI books. The religions of the state did not represent Spiritualism, but the people bound for the same purpose which was to maintain intact the empire. However there were no official practices, many spread the empire that was the occult and magic. These practices were the search of the spirit, that state religions, did not give and not represented. In private, the heads of families had a certain moral responsibility, in order to preside over the ceremonies. Mostly rites were aimed at domestic Divinity: LARI E PENATI. However, every person, every head of the family, had his religious inspiration, and this garrisoned its ceremonies. As for the dead, was given to them the need for the afterlife, I was not a strictly religious ritual or spiritual, the idea of death had a profound religious expression. The dead man was invested by his honors, then he would turn into larva and was going to be part of HANDS, the gods of death was. The masses with the expansion of cities hardly took part in religious ceremonies or in political life. They were as if they were, marginalized, in a sense or oppressed. And their subversion. at the end of the republic was an adjustment and a religious reflection. Born new religious ideas. LUCK and VENUS. Respectively represented cases FREE, INCIDENTAL of life and its reality. In this way notable religious opposition to GIOVE that in his representation he does not recognize the case, nor fortune, and everything is seen in the form of order, and nothing is left to chance and arbitrariness. The free and fortuitous. They took effect in the masses, to the detriment of the custom civic, and its religious tradition came into crisis. So in this sense it is both VENUS LUCK began to take hold, with the consequence of becoming important in the political religious role. Especially VENUS, that was attributed to the legend of being the Mother of ENEA, thus the progenitor of JULIA, a descendant of a mythical Lulo, son of ENEA and grandson of VENUS. Roma now, away to where JUPITER, of which he no longer felt the need, although it remained Romanized. Now ROME needed a ROMANO by Emperor deified and deifying, the world was beginning to adjust to the new reality and religious ideological form of ROME. Despite that AUGUSTO wanted to restore the traditions, he could not do anything to the religious changes. On this road, finally he arrived TIBERIO, and made divination Imperial and the rule of AUGUSTO SPIRIT, so that it was the veneration of STATE. On this road, finally Rome itself became DEA to worship. ROME was now the DEA mistress of the Divine world. In this way, the Asian peoples and those conquered, were markedly influenced by the religious political culture Romana, and their traditions and cults fell into crisis. In private, of course, there were mystical beliefs, and collectively manifested the mysteries of life and of all existence. Public religion, however, was the worship of Rome as DEA and Patroness And worship the sovereign spirit caught in the path of adoration in VENUS. To understand how the religious transformation of the people, and way, way, undermines the sense CIVIC, and from hand to hand, religion becomes the object of imperial cult, and in the hands of totalitarian rule. Over the years, there exist close to the legends, so the goddess VENUS becomes Mother of ENEA, Later with some minor variations, ENEA becomes a child of God because VENUS. Following his descendants are the kings, and by right of descent of beings to worship as they glorified the gods. Then by the time the RE, claim to be legitimate descendants of Aeneas, or related to Enea and they too become divine beings. So finally the descendants of ENEA, allegedly in an almost direct, they are RE and IMPERATORI Romans.

Hence something that starts from the people in the end becomes a monopoly of the powerful. We have with some minor changes in the power reconciled with the cult and religion, nothing less than a Divine being AUGUSTO Ottaviano, of which Tiberius orders their spiritual veneration of the whole empire, so the cult of Octavian Augustus becomes the culture and custom of imperial religion. Finally something of the people becomes a monopoly of power and through this you hold in their hands the people. It seems an ironic joke but in the end this is realism.

PSYCHOLOGICAL SITUATION OF YOUNG GENERATIONS – p.23

At this point becomes comprehensible worship of the super ego and evolutionary research in order to become supermen, or superior beings. The doctrinal form that worshiped kings and emperors in legalized so as state law, influenced mankind to become higher. In return we can also say, that: In this way, indirectly, humanity is psychologically prepared to recognize Jesus' Son of God. It would seem strange, but the same ill prepared man to go beyond the evolutionary barriers and acquire what stage of understanding that it was not just acknowledge Emperor and his great Spirit as a God, but put in a position to prepare the man unconsciously recognize JESUS '. Of course, this time and place, for each human being, but each had its time and its place to learn this truth. In summary we can say with reflection, that: The younger generations suffered the influence of the super ego. Each flowed and waved to others his super stadium. One way to subdue to be revered, to be respected, feared and to justify the reasons for them to be placed in the company's steps and justify the rule. Delusions of grandeur, we might say, to be super man, the most: in art, in battle and in all. The search for the super was becoming an ideal environment to be achieved and to be pursued. Associations, and poor families, who helped each other, were the basis of subsistence, but also received the influence of this type. Those who could not socialize or to enter into a certain circle, was excluded from the opportunity to live and feed, and if by chance he could still there, was banished. Woe to become weak, the whole world if he took advantage. The suggestionarsi psychologically idea man God gave that strength in each conscious living being to be reflected in a man, like another superior to him, and at the base of this equality tap into the psychological strength to face, overcome the problems of survival and acquire a high degree of tolerance by the state difficult. The upper believe aroused the instinct to exclude those who thought they were inferior beings, even if they were men belonging to the same people. For this, it had to be better than others, and certainly not falter. You had to stay away to the excluded of society, or otherwise attracted to you if the same treatment or were lost shots estimation. The treatment given to the excluded, was not very appropriate for a dignified life and livelihood, and no one would want to approach them, just for the fact of not risk having it the same treatment. And not only for this reason the man avoided to flank the weak and the marginalized, but also to protect their own lives to an end similar to "them." The man at that time had this smart way to behave so as not to lose the estimation points in front of the community, relatives, friends. In compliance with this reality, we understand that a man who claims to be the Son of God, is considered insane and is not included, but in the same way to contradiction is justified, and somehow heard and studied.

Therefore, even if only for these reasons JESUS 'it would be approached, given the customs and understandable that only the elect of God were able to understand it and follow it. Clearly in a situation where each individual was to become a super man, and this was in constant competition, it is not easy to believe that there have been men willing to follow and believe in JESUS 'if that were not their supermen but no one clearly he knew.

Each held his own reputation, and who could have it good, he did not try ambiguous compromise. Farsi lugging defamatory rumors were unfavorable for those who wanted to become someone or keep the achieved position. However, we must suppose a consideration: for the lower stage of nationalities and walks of life of some men, if you had not been at the root of the birth of the culture the veneration of the imperial ME, they would not have used the encouragement to use the maximum of their inner forces to discover and follow the path of the Messiah. It 'was just a magical moment and evolutionary, that perhaps will never return the same, which has put in a man to recognize the Son of God. The king was revered as a divine being replaceable and almost comparable to the same Jupiter. For this religious Roman culture, predisposes humans to recognize Jesus' Son of God, even though this mechanism makes it spring unconsciously, in a conscious and those who claim to be so is considered out of his mind, just because no king and not the son of King. at this point we, humanity ready to worship a man as a God, a humanity in search of the super of himself, but for the contradiction we have the son of God who demolishes all this, the preaching 'equality among men of which he claims are all brothers and to worship God was the God of Heaven.

He speaks of BROTHERHOOD; we are all children of the same God to which all Brothers and talk about EQUALITY. Contrary to the political religion of ROMANA imposed by TIBERIO NERONE AUGUSTO, which was to venerate the RE, the International Principles, the IMPERATORI as if they themselves were of DEI. Why JESUS 'was opposed not only to the state religion of Rome, but to all the rites and ceremonies connected with it. Consider that ROME, through religion and the army obtained some force to prop up his empire, we may allude to Jesus' we were annoyed at ROMANS rulers. The history tells us that this occurrence there was.

For this most likely, if we consider that Jesus' was not palatable to Pilate condemn him to death, which means that the Son of God even though they were against the imperial religions, had such a low influence that was not even considered a threat by the rulers to ROME. His personality was judged and inferiority, is visible; matters so little that you condemn the people and let GOODS 'in his hands. It would seem that Pilate was reluctant to condemn him that made him flogged with the intention that this would be enough to SINATRIO, unaware that the SINATRIO had for some time decided the death sentence of Jesus' But, he wanted to officially decretarla was Pilate and execute it ROME. To this Pilate was required to will issue the sentence, which he did not consider it necessary to stain your hands a murder of an innocent and give the responsibility for this act to whether and to his empire, for that reason he gave it to judgment of the people. So with Jesus' there, they only people who despise him out of envy, that are related to the priests and to those who manage the decisions within the SINATRIO. After all Jesus' is not even a threat to them, just annoying for as preached and what he says and you want to free him in the Easter holidays, in a definitive way. Let us return to our topic. We consider that Jesus' has been socially excluded, therefore, not party to the collective productivity, and social activities. So when he showed his identity, and to feel acceptable, that many friends, acquaintances, and family members have taken distances agreed by JESUS '; both as a person and as having to do either with him, in any way you can imagine or think, not to compromise, and it is understandable, their economic stability, social, and reputation, that could attract to attend if they same treatment that was reserved for him.

Therefore, in the same way, even if in secret attended it. Therefore recognize JESUS 'as I said before over the top, was a fact time and occasionally, just to give reason that only a certain type of evolution could be understood in a man, that Jesus' was the son of God. For this to be assumed that whether to recognize Jesus 'would be determined by a certain degree of evolution, to feel that: a super man, and tied to the Divine plan it could have to do with Jesus', or only a few super men, linked to the Divine plan, could have have to do with Jesus', but always in the defendant's discretion, and the right time to get out of this communion, taking care not to attract consequences.

For this reason, and the basis for this reason, anyone who had anything to do with Jesus', it would be fair and would use a good confidentiality. gentle behavior as a protective measure car, again in order not to be, highlighted the fact that it had been a friend, always with the aim to retrace their steps as if he wanted to, and had considered it was necessary, so as not to to incur if consequences, and loss of social values, that basically were the basis of nutritional survival, and say: "I know him just of view, I was just curious to hear what he had to say." We can say that is cowardice, the yes is. We must understand that everyone wants to save, and want to avoid getting finger-pointing and, this meant being already saved half. Also because not follow the Roman religious directives it could be fatal.

At the basis of this speech, we can say that also your dearest friend or disciple Judas, had the same biases of others. So if Judas was the only friends or disciples, seeing the Master carry the Cross, this means two things, and they are: First done, Judas had decided to die, so he did not care to attract to whether 'attention, or he is seen by the enemies of his Master.

Second, Judas had a courage beyond measure, and knew of its value and the contempt that men, enemies had against Jesus', and did not fear them. These despised him, too. These felt a hatred and a free cynicism without reason and without motivation. ... Pure evil stage that manifests the desire to see destroyed and erased from the face of the earth individuals without reasons; the usual intelligent who despise all because you believe masters of sciences, art and wisdom. ... The world has always been infected by these individuals. .... They know everything and the others nothing. We may think and believe that if Judas had not been overcome with grief, seeing death his Master, now we will not know the turning point of the story and how it was the defendant. Therefore, since Jesus 'it brings the Pieta' feeling man. ... Consciousness recalls the pain and punishment, the evil suffered by innocent. JESUS 'brings just the Pietà, an important feeling in God's eyes.

COMMUNION -P.24

However, the communion between Jesus' and his disciples, we can not also assert, after this our understanding, that it was entirely secret, but it definitely was maintained with the utmost discretion. Of course, with the entry of JUDAS communion buy with a little 'harder, a little' more security and more respect and credibility. Before that, Judah will take part: There was more superficial. The Apostles were posted; each pretending curiosity. The Disciples were standing close but without much interest. Why on the one hand did believe Jesus' being good friends, the other side did believe people to be curious Gods of similar people in all nations. For this, the substantial basis of Jesus' friends was the man to make him feel, but in a way and sense, only individual.

Collectively the whole thing was denied, and the man who was in the individual comparison, became a madman against so many men. This is why Jesus ', did not represent the will of a community, the less he did not use his Will for a collectivity of men, let alone the people in the group could entrust their will to Jesus', since it lacked the sincerity and respect deep. Keeping this collectively, to express their nature, we can not be said though, that Jesus' is just. I think it should be noted that those who! Albeit discreetly, he approached and had to do with him but had to be now, during the course of their lives, a Super Man. As they say, but few coupons. This is why the strength of the Son of God, was not based on numbers, but on the IO value. At this point we understand that being close to Jesus' could not be determined by external factors, but was defined by internal situations and totally out individually. Or anyone who was close to Jesus', must have realized something during the course of his life, which led him to a choice within himself, from his influence and his own evolving understanding gained during their journey. Who was close to Jesus' supposed to be from before you meet him, become a Super Man, within himself, through the understanding and evolution THE IO, or otherwise was no and could not be in a position to understand, much less to follow the Son of God. and 'more than clear now understand that behind this, there are many roads that lead a man to the understanding and wisdom, each to its value, becoming essay is based on the road is It goes along but it is also is based on the ability to learn and reason. For this reason, even in an environment, of which hatred, death, etc. ... And other features were representation of values, appreciable and acceptable in order that an individual could be considered worthy, there were men who had achieved through their thinking, the deep well values even if they lived in a different era from socio stage their evolution, as if to say the sum of them I was different from what the way they taught. At the base of this concept, the ability to live within each of them, the conceptual opposite situation, and their same Council, determines, their super ego in communion with the forces of good, for which reference is the Eternal Father. Because of this reality, we understand, you! Who is true that Jesus' first prove to the world he had secured the minimum necessary for its future, through manual work, the level of economic stability, or otherwise could not prove to the world he knew well and had calculated it well certain consequences from this action, we can not believe that He neither was able to intuit the gravity and the retaliation of His Acts. Therefore it is considered that because He has revealed how the doors have been closed by the social community of the time, it is; the community in which he lived and in which he belonged by birth, His life situation had been reduced to just the barely subsistence. Since, at that time period, there was a certain tax oppression carried out by the Jews on behalf of the Government ROMANO, it was also difficult for the few friends helping JESUS 'economically speaking. For this to follow and pursue your own life, there must be compulsorily the Hand Of God, who through some man or some family could reach him or commission that is little to do in the workplace, in order to have that little to live, to have intervened for him. A procedure performed clearly and with the utmost discretion in order that the aid does not become free. Considering another aspect, that some poor were associated in order to share what little they had, and believe that in turn someone had something to give, within the family and in a friendly confidence. However, Jesus' suffering perfidy, marginalization, discrimination, the hoax of man, during His Secona STAGE life ie that of His revelation. This is why Jesus', was now cleared from a large part of the community, even before His death sentence. Only humans of a certain size and a certain degree of evolution, we can call it SUPER, possessed the ability to understand it, it is they were linked to CELESTE floor, so it was also JUDAH.

CONDITIONING, RELIGIONS AND CULTURES
diverese -P.25

religious cultures different to the comparison between them. A society, one in which he lived the MESSIAH conditioned by the customs of Rome, and at the same time conditioner ROMANA culture. Society divided by different choices that were made and dictated by different cultural influences, habits and customs. Influence which conditioned the choices of a man. Sometimes the choices were determined by the circumstances, and a man, had to reconcile the two cultures, not to go to war on one side. For this it was not strange to find someone who was of Roman religion and Jewish simultaneously. Or you could see the same person takes part has a Roman festival and also to a Judaica. The path of a road that determines the reason or the commitment to be adopted as a habit, though not radical in life, but simply to achieve an ideal, was forced. Or else you could encounter some obstacle to their own purposes and to their ideals. A better way to not get hurt none of the parties with opposing cultures and the people they represented. All this transformation and civil conditioning were very sharp and created many difficulties in order to understand which direction was best to follow it, for a man to pursue in order to secure their future and enjoy the rest of their lives. Of what they had or did the people in their lives, it was impossible to believe that it was what they really wanted, just for the fact that he had servants and servants, and not only what others had told him to do and what think, everything else is not considered as it was not considered the initiative of an individual. The poor, since the world, has always been poor and driven away. This since ancient times. And 'evident at that time, a company that pursues to Judea and objectives of the improvement that it always leads over the arms and Roman culture, the whole world shakes to whether and shapes it according to their own ideas and personality, it meant becoming a province of Rome and at the end it was so. The company though not Roman, became with pleasure and satisfaction under the thumb of Rome and its customs and cultures it is a part, and I want to take participation with pleasure; though: we could consider the individual's social facade that hides the pleasure for culture and the Roman customs, proving just hypocrisy towards their fellow citizens. These new fashions confuse integrity society. So the new way of religious indifference dictated by convenience makes the man unholy birth. And the poor man does not make him understand to be the servants who run behind the promises. And, they remain servants, and are always found in the situation of wasting their lives for the pleasure and well-being of others, who are in power, what else do not have the heart to the contempt for the poor citizen helpless, condemning him for his petty-ria and poverty, similarly as if it was the same one and only guilty state of decay and poverty in which it is located. Certainly becoming strange false and twisted, but also for the fact that in the end the poor, so they felt less convinced that their car to be guilty of the same social status. Everyone crazy and twisted at that time, but in reality the social status offenders and depravity of the poor middle class, were only the powerful rulers in association with the Jews that they were the temporal foster the power of Judea, appointed, most of the sometimes from the same Rome; but above them always a Roman prefect as Firefighter established power and order. And in the meantime a fearful society and oppressed by decades belonging to the same people, guardians and vassals of Rome, who were loading their own people with the weight of the taxes to be donated to Rome in order that the circuit is not interrupted and whether they could always have the privileges of the Romans, that they guaranteed its perpetual enjoyment, if the perpetration of the services was always fair and affairs of a certain type were kept in a certain share.

That this company was brought always to betray his neighbor in order to live and to enter into a circuit that was allowed a few, it is more plausible although frightening. This determined also that an individual could be master of the destruction of its neighbor or his brother. Just those who know you, is that studies and makes money in exchange for your destruction. It incited a game in those days by the customs and the objectives of ROME who were always the ones to raise taxes and recognize deserving the most loyal to them and to Rome. Taxes are always a huge medium used to enslave the citizens, and not being able to pay for them will become victims and then indirect cause of their destruction. The lights that signaled the possessions in order that the justice of Rome could plunder, and the people suffer badly of its villagers. This was the air you could breathe in a state subject, and in an overhead line, or in a social position in which he was born and lived the MESSIAH. All this had had for devotion, spontaneous for some men, for compulsory easement for other, in respect of ROME. However anyone when it came to eating, though fearing the order consists, sought benefits or satisfaction; to see another, even if they belonged to the same environment, suppressed by Rome and its laws, he drew benefits. Betrayal, connected interest, is a modal feature that follows the man and tempts him during the course of his life, under various circumstances. Everything seemed normal, since the people, was indoctrinated as if he were himself an integral part of Rome. ROME involving the people of vassal regions, in such a skillful way that gave him responsibility and hand to hand felt ROMANS all, and eventually became Roman regions. Therefore it himself, involved in the moral dimension, could not understand and realize that it was brought up to the service and to waste one's life for the well-being consists of those who usufruiva the beautiful and rich life. The men, caught and having to examine them individually, by the people was attracted Someone was pleased by the culture, customs and Roman cults, but likewise had to be careful to honor their customs in respect of their culture and tradition, because some of them, covering a higher grade in society, were in business with the Romans, and this could be dangerous for those who abstained to manifest respect for the traditions.

THE WOMAN TOOK FROM ANCIENT ROME-P.26

The ideal woman in ANCIENT ROME who sought the subject peoples. In the times in question, the women wanted to become like the Roman. For this they took off the noose. A clearly for each environment: social family, the woman takes on characteristics, and learns ways, influence and education. What goes around in the air in the times in question, and that women of the peoples subject to Rome, they wanted to become like the Roman women. It seemed as if they would acquire more rights, in a sense they wanted to improve their standard of living. Clearly if circumstances permitted, there were few who did get out of hand the opportunity to become

ROMANA town. ROMAN The woman was the better future.

n this time the woman had acquired freedom and was also more educated. Clearly we must always consider that all depends on the family and the social one who attends and where you live. However, the air, the fashion, that we breathed was definitely more freedom, more empowerment, more taking prominent position: both within the family, and both in the social. For that although the woman had family roles: look after the house for the children, could take part in the social life of her husband. He could also have a certain freedom and a degree of autonomy: leave home, attend public places and do things that she liked to make. The woman could be in a position to be part of a good family party, it depends if she was lucky enough to be chosen to form part of the relevant companies.

Therefore to possess riches, honors, have used and servants; have a certain influence in public institutions, but depended on its beauty or the family lineage branch.

The Romans had the cult of beauty! The woman could assert their opinion and beliefs. Why, he had obtained over time, a fair draw, which put her in the same plane towards the man, who placed it in a position, to act according to his own pleasure, your own judgment, and to live a better and better quality of life as . Certainly, we must consider, that many men, engaged in the army, because it ROME increasingly demanded soldiers and officials, for the expansion of its domain; The women were in a situation where you become more autonomous, educated and emancipated was natural, because many men never returned to their families; or because it was the death in battle, or because they found a new love among the conquered peoples. This made the population more and more women than men. The situation clearly gave many opportunities to evolve to the woman, and some male roles were recognized and entrusted to it. The Roman man was influenced by the female figure of his own nation, and this his way of being free, expansive, exuberant minded; they passed on to women of the occupied peoples; In this way the women of the conquered peoples, they saw in the Roman soldier, a figure that could offer a better life than the one that could make their own village. However women within the empire, were liberated and occupied a prominent position in society. Their power in the end had put them in a position to divorce her husband and live freer and richer, with the right wanting to maintain their wealth even if he was getting married. Why many marriages, were combined properly for interest, just because the woman could take with them their wealth. Certainly, we must consider that at the time, the woman even though he had attained emancipation power, a quality of life happy, if you became a dishonest wife, the man could divorce her. Why not for all women and for all social and family environments, the situation was identical. There were women item you buy, like any one thing and enjoyed a better than a master wants. The imperial state was varied and mixed, but opportunities, to be taken flight to a better life, with the Romans were always ready to arrive and the women were always on alert, and ready to risk everything to be able to enter the situation. However, the woman became Roman from hand to hand, the models for other women scattered in the territories occupied by Rome, and the soldier Romans conveyed, through their behavior, the other women, the characteristics of the empire WOMAN. Roman man, in this way, the other women saw a better future and the modern emancipation, just because they imagined the different kind of man. In this way the race at best, second judgment performed by women, and families who had young daughters and virgins to fix, put the Romans in the condition of having a wide range of female choice and be able to enjoy every sort of sexual pleasure in order their own, they did not know how to do sex or what experiment to find pleasure and satisfaction. Everything was always at the expense of the people who were involved or were involved. Why not everything worked according to the idea, in most cases, the most daring were left alone, the soldier had his family, and they were launched to the street legal in commercial sex. To say that the city markets were offering opportunities for earning money at all. The poor people of the neighboring nation, emigrated in Romans territories, so, there were provinces and flourishing cities that offered money and a lot of possibilities to those who were looking for a change, especially brave and strong men and beautiful and emancipated women . The latter could be: Artist, educated, female musician and dancer. artistic and poetic skill, matrons women in ancient times, the woman in the Roman Empire had become modern, with intelligence and ability to reflections that are the envy, full of wit and charm. For this the era in question, the women were compared.

In some circles, social and family-minded, those who were married also suffered the severity of their husbands, they sentence that became bulls, censors and d exercised full authority over them. If the woman committed some shameful act or ignominious, he was severely punished. I have to stick to a certain behavior, demeanor morality and sobriety. If he committed adultery with another man, it is punishable by death. The woman could be put to death, if he had committed adultery, without the husband will suffer judgment. If it had been her husband, everything was normal. The severity of her husband was very marked. Usually the wife was also repudiated for minor acts, such as: the bad language and prove in public or in society too glib. Married women had severe drawings to follow, especially had to be obedient to her husband and to refrain permission, to do or go, that his wife was the permit. The husband had to know and be aware of the public sorties of the woman, that she he went to markets, games, public pools, or otherwise. Many wives, were infamate by rejection, but it was a way to frighten them, and remove the defect or the temptation of the same in their minds. In conclusion, women ROMAN in the period in question were considered to be almost equal to men. They did not carry out menial jobs but spun and wove with their daughters or domestic. They not always remained locked in the house, but they were free; in this way they could also pass the time outside and they could visit friends and relatives. They could receive visitors. They could also come out with their husbands, and accompany them in parties, receptions, theaters and more, even if they had to maintain composure, morality and stick to a moral and decent behavior, avoiding euphoria and spirited beverages. The women participated actively in the public life of their husbands and their recommendations were taken well into consideration, both recommendations were of little consequence, whether they were business advice and trade. Roman women were highly educated, in fact, the purest Latin language was spoken by the Roman matrons. In general, the tasks of the Roman woman summed up in: the care of the home, children and women's jobs. These quality hand in hand that passed in the Imperial Rome were little marked, but I think that has been basic quality, which could hardly be lost or replaced for a long time. Certainly there are shades of questionable morality of some famous women that still should not be generalized with a polar behavior, even though the modal transformation, cultural, was very attractive and tempting. Women of the people had a more honest behavior of what we might believe. After all she was the queen of her house, and some vices, of which a certain social class can be wrapped, the women of the people for various reasons remained clean queens, honest and loving his family and his home. From their hands he emerged from all good, in foodstuffs, in cleaning, in order and in spinning. There were women who were dressed by the Vestal Virgins. guardian of the sacred fire. They were virgins, and if it were sex or adultery, were buried alive in the field of the wicked places in the hills. To them they were given food, a lantern, and in the grave remained abandoned until death did not come to free them from suffering. The pits were covered so that no one would understand that beneath there was a buried alive. Their seducer was flogged until his death. Even women who were part of the normal households could be considered VESTALI, all based on their honesty and their devotion.

ENVIRONMENT. P28

We have spoken of the Roman women, but the Jewish, as well as being similar to the Roman women, in the family factor, had a different situation, ie: they had to interact with newcomers who were Romani. Not all of them had family. Why prostitution was legalized. Although for some women married off his halter means to be killed or repudiated. However, the situation recalled stranger, clearly, the money, or trade in girls, gave opportunity of easy money. Corruption taking root among the wealthy people of the occupied territory and among the ROMANS.

The environment was influenced by traditions and customs of the Romans, and the traditional identity of the people were dazzled by a new wave of innovation, which was bringing with it a host of new things, curious and exciting, but who put in identification crisis community. The influence of the Romans of that time society was considerable. In the subject peoples they were put customs that are not sure they were also consumed in ROME. In a nation of which you should take advantage of the resources and adoperarne people for personal pleasure, we can imagine that morality was disintegrated in the conquered peoples, but of course no doubt the Roman women, or at least some of them were not sure with his hands and HAND let you amuse with sex only husbands, so as to believe that Roma suffer in some way the fate that made others suffer. The Romans represented the vanguard of civilization and the contemporary era fashion. And all could believe that the customs and traditions, new, though excessive, were also held within the empire. Why in the new colonized, it dares to be excessive emancipation and recklessness for not less to the colonists. All this confused the people, and did not understand the political strategies and their sinister pacts. For this, the people were subject has a situation, but I understood the real dynamics and the reason of the situation even though they lived in a direct form, and at the same time. At that time it was clear that there is a mechanism, military, religious, economic and political forefront. This system was devoted to the exploitation of all types of human resource, also the beauty and carnal pleasure. They soon became the subject peoples, places of pleasure, human bargaining chips, and even business opportunities of all kinds. In this way, the East, in its totality was pervaded by the crisis of identity, the growing evil affair, corruption, poverty, crime and prostitution. At the same time he bound them to Rome when the Roman Religion and cults. Roma held the balance domination through religion, habits, customs, poverty and wealth for those who were able to prevail. The poor were fighting each other, they had lost the plot. The rich were always right, even if you do not know the problems of the discussion, rich and in communion with men who ran the political religious power, were always right. To survive, he was willing to do anything to make money it was willing to engage in something more than the others though, if he dared. The betrayal was the basis of the beginning of survival, and the man became accustomed to this mechanism, up to connect the betrayal in personal developmental dimension, and in this sense evolved in the scam technique, and bad deal. Learn about the evolution of the personality, the people and its characteristics, it is not something very easy since the revolutionary era in the cultural side, the depressive economic situation, opportunistic and ruthless in the side of survival, deceitful in the economic situation, the improvement of quality OF LIFE ITSELF. The Jewish rulers had reduced the people to abject poverty while becoming better and better and competitive with classes ROMAN executives. The Roman culture had invaded and changed way of thinking about life, but according to the opportunism Imperial. The exploitation was the end of the Empire, the leaders of the subject peoples, were associated with the objectives of ROME in exchange for welfare and assured protection. Finally the Della Judean leaders were nothing but renters of their nation. The customs and traditions and the Roman cults were in contradiction with the traditions and customs of the Jews. The Romans had gods, the cult of the RE and the Emperors, but in the occupied peoples we added the cult of sex and the liberation of prostitution, the cult of war, force, subjugation of peoples. It's twelve years he was older. This is why the environment and society were indoctrinated from Rome, so that the same was venerated as a DEA. Commanders Jews in their turn were assured from Rome, to be able to maintain power on their own people, in a kind of tenant covenant, but in the end the resources, had to be exploited by ROMA. Religion put at the service of politics, enslaved peoples, and through it ROME, kept the Empire together, and it ensured the loyalty.

The Romans had a political, strategic, in order to make use of the well-being of the peoples and to serve also the same people, for jobs and for sexual pleasures, for the wars and everything concerning the risk of life. Everything was used in the service, and all that was opposed to recognizing the religious political authority of Rome, it became an object not to use but to destroy. He had to ally with Rome and become like ROMANS, in this way the man could be sure to keep the continuation of their existence. No one could rebel against this because this was mostly accepted by JEWS executives. And so The economic policy forced the people to ask for they themselves to the Romans, to be taken at their service and be willing to do anything to eat and to settle down. Why the Romans had no need to force, servants, slaves or girls for their situations, but they were vying to enter to take part of these tasks and to be taken in the Roman service. This was a competition performed for a multitude of reasons, including:

work, fame, wealth, security of life in luxury environments where it was protected and had not been touched easily. People were competing to adjust his life. Accommodation and survival. The religion was mixed together: ROMANA, Judaica. Follow the Romans costumes and interact with them they allowed to become citizens ROMANS if it was True, and if Roma accepted. The people could keep their religion but they also had to venerate and observe cults Of Imperial Rome.

THE CITTA'- P. 29

Despite all this realism, in larger cities ironies of fate there was an atmosphere interesting and lively. And each worked to do something, to earn some money and to get by. The merchants were doing good business, and there was a bustle of strangers. At the time, age twelve, legalized prostitution, and looking for a great coming and going of strangers all over the city. They came for business or other, and someone did not disdain to an encounter of love. All the evil was not considered harmful, because it was coupled with the sexual pleasure, and the ability to settle down forever if it was believed to unforeseeable circumstances.

Men in sight and powerful buying girls and they did what they wanted, and they were also happy to be similar to the Roman people, to find more and more sexual pleasure and give more sex to others happiness. The race of the female sex became an invisible competition among teenage women was to try more and more pleasure in sex and see if you could always try and More. The evil that began with pain and sorrow in the end was gladly accepted, and the habit led people to want more and more and to want to compete against each other to be the best and become richer. So apart from that you could imagine, many merchants do not know that there were men entered that signaled wealth to the debt, and told all these executives. Somehow legally the poor victim was plundered and the spoils divided among collectors, managers and ROMANS. To this end all the power always came back to the source. He lived in the illusion, but no one understood. This realism was accepted in the singular form only when each one had to compare with the death or bad luck. The friendship and the bond with the Romans were of great importance, assured life and guaranteed survival. It was an era conditioned to have tough and uncivilized behavior towards the weak. It harmed at no cost to even taste their strength, says workout as well. The man lived to fulfill its ambitions, glory, honor, heroism and eroticism, comparing and identifying oneself in the heroic personality of which the ancient Romans were representatives. Behind this hurt became normal, usual, customary and costume. The feeling of pity was almost nonexistent and to survive a few people had really only obey and worship the pagan cults. JESUS 'brings the feeling of Mercy to all men in the world.

In order and in justice we consider that: The Romans did everything that the Jewish leaders and the priests asked him to do against some who felt guilty of crimes. Beyond the crimes which they considered to bring a man to trial, even considered, their personal conflicts, their issues and if you could strip away every good thing if it were only that, no hesitation to proceed. Rome, Always under indication of the Jews commanders, some even condemned them to death. This extreme rigor was also for personal questions. A fun behind the condemned were commonly usually the same. Wrapped some curious, sometimes boys, who followed the prisoner out of curiosity and excitement of the event. A way to celebrate, another who was talking was curious excited. A form of entertainment. This was an imported culture. The priests could not be condemned to death, their faith forbade it, but they knew how to convince the Romans to condemn someone to death. The prisoners were reported by people who were not Romans, but they were the same people of Jesus. The central part of the company was happy and content with this way of life because they had their pleasures. The low morality was so that man stonasse in the dimension of understanding and goodness. For this evil in all its representations, he did not think the Jews and their involution in understanding the good and in splitting the right dall'empio was considerable. The limit could be imposed by the rules and customs of the Romans, but also by what some of them ricavavano. This fold is reached the peak of evil and injustice. There was the cult to massacre and torture the defenseless and those who believed it was a bit silly, served the show and if he dies, it is not a great loss. So it was thought. The people wanted to believe this, the Romans were practical to do this was related to their worship. The priests and other men of influence, not dirtied their hands, they made her lordare to the Romans. They brought the condemned in judgment, even for arranging issues of disobedience snub or jealousy. This way of being became a cult, and it was fun for them to find the village idiot and torture him to the end without reason and without mercy, especially if around him there was no one, and if the family members were away from him. The people saw the show, but he enjoyed we can not really say, however, were the times and there was no television. And things were told to pass the time. So long as man remains he influenced. When some listeners lost the pleasure of the story because repetitive and you do feel tired, speakers altered the facts of the story until the fact was not listening socket. Like now, in a sense. Going back to the past, the Jews were essentially themselves convicts among their neighbors and offered them to the Romans to be sentenced in the public square is in this way was made the party. A fun I think that was the one part of the social, the so-called untouchables, or the part of people connected to men of power. Usually they condemned to death those who had stolen something or other, but in the absence of these took the most isolated and the least protected. Some light to get in to the ruler of empire, brought their fellow citizens, presumed guilty or not, however they were also judged for minor offenses or illusory. They flocked prominent men in the court and to ask for them, sometimes the death sentence. Not always there was the prison. The diversion was following and inferring of a condemned man. In this way the priests were holding in their hands the people and made them feel their importance as much as that of the Romans. They were put in good light against the rulers by massacring and killing people of their own people. Everything just for the sake of fun and demonstration of loyalty to the rulers, and to feel as an equal and to understand their subjects who were always them that they should fear more than anything because it was they who control the life or death and not only the Romans. RUFFIANARSI and show devoted to the Romans meant respect, food, and consideration. The society of thought only to the values praised by the Romans. Sex, death, devotion to Rome. It had to carefully observe the power of the priests, or otherwise they paid the consequences.

Therefore, on this basis who was obnoxious or aroused envy and was not considered in the society of the time, it was taken by the Jews reports, delivered to Roman justice and was suppressed, and the fact he felt like an excitement festive. This was a mindset, or rather a Tradition of the moment. The Roman culture for their ruthlessness intrigued all other cultures. And the Roman customs were considered and expressed with pleasure, they were fashionable. The Romans had the cult of death as entertainment, beauty, how am taking advantage and protection, and sexual worship as the oblivion of pleasure. No one was sorry to follow the Romans cults indeed all had pleasure to appreciate and to follow the example of life. All we had to be careful not to expose themselves. For this among the people is always lurking spies who reported everything to the priests. The priests then once knew everything and everyone. And according to this understanding decided who touch and those who leave quiet. So for a man's salvation, in a vital dimension inherent to their existence, and the continuation of his life, it was to enter the friendly situation with the Romans and with them bind and connect; or business, or servitude. ... Etc. ... For many, the way forward was to enroll in the army ROMANO. This represented security and some protection for his family. The fear of bad interference was preventing before curing, so the kin, communions were desperate. The choices: from enrollment, to the gifts, offerings, sales, marriages of young girls just come of age, the link to some good party, offering lovers, etc. ... They were targeted choices just to get friendship and gratitude by the Romans. To consider given situations, friendship with the Romans, they could always be somewhat favorable way. ROME was the guarantee for a new future, for the protection of his enemies, and for the continuation of life. It was only necessary to enter the Due to a representative of Rome or a good Roman citizen.

DEFECTS- P. 30

Vices them must have those who can afford them, or by grade or for power, others received the punishment of the envious or what comes from the ill-behavior. For this bravado made to want to identify with others, if you are not careful and if you do not keep your eyes open plausibly they pay the discount. A warning that was true then, it is important now in some cases. In ancient time, some men in the face of some vice condemned by moral education, they were apparently reluctant, but corrupt in secret. He lived at the time of Jesus' in a new world, advanced for its time, dominated by ambition, self-interest, from falsehood, and each lived for their own pleasure. Falsehoods to achieve that ambition aspired to as a final award. Falsehoods for the momentary pleasure, that suffered immediate that seemed at the time, as now, it was necessary and was one source of happiness. The believed then, as now, to strive to succumb vice that gives immediate pleasure and relaxation, it seemed impossible to find the strength to be able to refrain and to overcome the temptation. This derives from the ancient times, a bad judgment and in some cases fatal. It was not death sentence for the value or intensive depths of vice considered indecent and sinful, but what he recalled the thickness of the sentence was the value of the person who committed.

So if a poor man felt miserable and idiot could satisfy a vice, he was suppressed for the sin committed in appearance, but in truth was suppressed because it was a poor and counted for nothing in the world and certain satisfactions should not even think of them right because it was considered an inferior being. If the vice or sin made him a person of a certain thickness, and connected in a certain social class, she did not notice anyone, and who they made consciousness, did not mind for convenience. This made fake people and always looking to cheat others under the action of their frustration and their perfidy. Of course we can not think that people are not amused before the Romans, but the changes and the new culture they remove the halter even moralists boldest. However societies divided and we can not make lump everything and not all individuals who are the elements of society are equal. At the same time, because of the customs and oppression, then we can see a society that is afraid of Rome, even though it grasps the customs, and admires the culture. Some men view and control that were directed to the contact with the Romans commanders, sometimes to please and judge best emitted sentences, collectively, without any kind of remorse, just because you had to make sure that the company feared and he was afraid. The fear and the fear of being obeyed, and adhere to a certain way of thinking that forced a man to stand in his place or otherwise became example of justice through its whipping. For this people a little 'smart hardly reveal or advised to the next how to do to be better than it was; because there was the fear of being overtaken. Fall behind it meant to be eaten by the LUPA, and LUPA was Rome and the Jews chiefs. So good advice desist to arrive. Everyone looked at her head and lands, but at the same curiosity about others in order, to be seen as well as possible by the commanders heads holders of bureaucratic and political power. The keepers of the rules to enforce, were that part belonging to the people, but they were bureaucratic officials, that the evil people could not speak, much less appeal to them. They guaranteed the squeezing of the people, to give the coffers of Rome. For this they had the keys of the control and administrations. They also said they were in communion with God, and thus possessed the absolute obedience of the people, both did their own interests, those of Rome, or otherwise. ... Etc ... Etc ... Etc ... They had protection, were untouchable. They commanded the people, and used it to their liking, and they had the ability to put one against the other. Certainly they were in communion with God in their view, it would seem that every night God went from them to discuss themselves for their people. With this realism imagine a man who claims to be the son of God and talk to God and socially, and only a poor man with no power, and even has a considerable reputation, as it is seen and it is loved by a part of men year in hand the keys of the society and decide their fate at their pleasure. Surely he saw with hate and anger. Returning to our analysis, we could understand that. Some men to survive, almost forced way be required alliances and friendships with the Romans, and likewise serve the keepers who were the Jewish leadership, conferring with the central power ROMANO represented by a prefect, with all the devotion possible. These alliances that guaranteed them the future automatically led them to repress their own people, their own brother. Because alliances were connected to the devotion to Rome, this is manifested in the ability to demonstrate loyalty, demonstrable searching out enemies or people being disrespectful of the Roman rules and pass them to justice. Rightly for not having dates drawbacks the customs that were at that time, it was better not to focus the eyes on him by anyone.

For this just to have some advantages and alliances that assured him a good life, they not made many scruples, even in the face of suffering, and if they had to make a spy-born most likely for them, could represent a good opportunity to get even if the trampoline was someone's head. In fact, it is possible that some people of the people, hatred, or revenge, or to be considered by the Romans, or to be seen well by the Jewish leadership, they could sell and betrayed people connected in their affective circle, family or social. On this basis, even innocent, if there were circumstances, they could become guilty without knowing what crime, victims of the executioners, just for interest. Always a way to make a career and be put in a position of respect, it became spies and accusers of a weak or one that was defended. This treacherous behavior could bring money and sympathy from people and commanding views. The money was the way to buy the life of a human being for their own emotional purposes, working or sexual. ... The more servants had the more he was recognized the nobility and the supremacy. The desire to stand out in order to have the power and reputation that he could afford to buy a sweet and tender creature for its own joys, was very deep rooted. The coveted prize could also be characteristic for the continuation of one's life or healing of their sexual frustrations. Unfortunately must inform you that in those days humans were suffering from sexual frustration, in the sense that: so much sex and did so much they could never accomplish that was not enough, and sex were frustrated they did not know how to do and what to invent. They did not know then, as now, that the woman is ground, the more work it is more and more need to be worked. So perhaps it was cheaper, pretend not to know this truth, sweetest seemed pleased. Rightly worship and tradition of ROMANO sex, they did glimpse pleasant things, that many dreamed, and end each, in some way, trying to win her hand. People who accept suffering, just because he was aware that if it was good he could have made the power that changed his life forever and if not forever at least satisfy their vices. Vices that made him happy- course each, according to their point of view, to see the things in life, but at the bottom of the bear, despises honey to eat it all. The crocodile cries when you eat the puppy, and so on. ... No. No! In the heart I am: I would like to do it too! So they think inside people, who are fighting for justice condemning the abuse. Not all certainly are few wolves masquerading as sheep, and sooner or later come into the open. Prostitution was legal, custom connected to what the man revered and wanted. Clearly it was a way to create more concubines possible and of all ages. Rome was a source of cunning and intelligence, laws and religions in favor of Rome. The soldiers or anyone had to move for reasons of state, in a country vassal, he had to play, and what better thing is to become legal and sacred what is fun? The occupants of a nation must adapt. The conquerors, although clearly the expense goes, han some of the people, and then over time produces the boomerang effects, meanwhile plunder. Cunning administrative ROMANA, made her feel conquered peoples involved in projects Romans And part of Rome, in order to enslave them. Eventually we might consider that the customs of the evil of Rome, just as we in our times we classify them, were also addressed to themselves, but unfortunately at the end of the ages, the conquered peoples were hoping to enjoy something, but fun were the most LUSTRE social classes, and less luster remained open-mouthed and with a finger in his mouth. This unfortunately is part of the realism of a social structure dominated and subject political deception of the rulers, who in their psychological dimension, seeing the people as inferior, or as a subspecies of humanity, you take the luxury to settle for anything what needs to materialize in order to take in hand the collective will and to control the mind and thoughts. This clearly we see if we study the times, of which I speak living JESUS '.

However, if there was a right and rebellious man to the established order, or unconventional, and not he submitted or rebelled against the rules, the risk of being overwhelmed physically. Death was a cult ROME, and above all was the way he had sent a man to death, and plausible accusations it put to him, that were questionable felt that it was a cult give death to the next.

The cult of the dead became a sort of show and fun to do. For this there was a much morality, nor between ROMANS let alone among the conquered peoples, and in the end though of a different culture will let engage with pleasure from ROME customs. The Romans were privileged children, and protected by gods of a certain power, proven existence, and unquestioned reverence. From their point of view other peoples were wild to use, capture, engage in their culture and in their empire, in order to connect themselves and civilize the empire as ROMANS. This was the street and it was allowed, you had to be smart, with all sorts of means, to travel it. The poor of the people and the oppressed, for the most deluded, they crossed a lifetime of servitude, slavery, and vain hopes. Knowing this material reality had to be in a few, the rest of the men had to think differently to that which materially finally did by compulsion. This was the mindset of Rome: Power, cults, pleasure, and run to the wisdom and art in their own way, and keep everything under control through taxes, which in the end was the instrument of authority, and to maintain a submissive people and give him little time as possible to think and reflect. What men submitted themselves, with their will in this way of life now rooted in life, they were considered and left to live. Those who opposed the sentence was, that all in large part, contrary to how it should be civilly, felt right, even if it was not the right, but amused themselves until, they themselves were not condemned or someone dear to them.

PERVERSIONS DELL'EPOCA- P.31

The fashions of the time. Gave fun and please the powerful, sorrow to the people and in some cases means of survival, to the poor. As mentioned above the prostitution was legal. Clearly, it was the culture that created prostitutes. The need for some people gave him the opportunity. In other words, if a woman wants to be with a man for a reason, or a gain. ... Etc. .... Etc ... And 'a man wants to be with a woman for his reasons, or even because at will fulfill the self-interest of women, no one can prevent, is something other, and is part of their private communion. This was a fashion imported from many cultures, not just those Roman, but finally by ROMA were venerated more than the others, for the reason: What brought the girls to bed and children. And in a legalized way. To consider that this was done with the peoples subject to Rome, but in the heart of the empire, this could also be done in a more private form, which is secret and which is represented in the normal way. They were family, at the time, adult men with young girls. This could also be understandable. compose the family limits the evil and depravity. This is a situation of the time, but in that story had become a custom hunting and religious cults imported from ROMANS. Prostitution, in that era was born, for a violent form of sex and impose the pleasure. They 'clear that he was a vice for the pleasure of ROMANS soldiers, that having sex as legalized worship purpose situations to their advantage, always aimed for fun and personal pleasure, and subject peoples and considered inferior, were clearly used to pleasure and ROMANS fun. The whole thing was a bad thing, but it became routine, normal and accepted. Prostitution was also a consequence of the cult to the pleasures of sex. Worship and female culture, to be the best object used and used by a man, in order that these so feel amused by thanking and come back to her.

And 'the female acted in this way, just because this education had taught and this education, was involved in natural form, and completely normal. As usual it was any other thing though subject to forced acceptance, in order habit, is becoming normal practice. For a woman at the time transform their being an object of man's pleasure, he became a religion, and as such ingrained within him. The thought and the personality of the well were modeled so that the well was logged and accepted as normal and rule of life, even the evil and wrong things, that there is a modal form. Clearly in this cultural religious direction, a woman became a beautiful object, and the more he felt interesting, intelligent and appreciated. As a woman based her intelligence in conjunction with sex, the kind of pleasure that was, even by the amount of sex they could do, and their physical appearance. According to these accounts a woman, posed and approcciavano next air of supreme intelligence and higher wisdom, to the contrary, if these values were not by nature. Still she is raped and fucked with fury and violence, until it hurt and yelling with bad predestined as a child to become a wonderful bitch. This Roman soldiers knew that, and Rome has been quick to legalize everything. Of course, then they chatted a little all, both ROMANS both the representatives of the people, the so-called guardians of the Roman Vassallo. Royalists deceived their own people, not only in taxes, in the properties, but also on the other. ... Etc ... Etc ... Etc ... And 'everything was normal. Imagine you that little girls, already have their spigano the sex mothers, and that going to cheat with adults ROMANS, were good. In the psychology of an infant this system grows with it, and with it grows to maturity. So inconceivable to believe that this person, do not hand down the mentality, customs and traditions, to the next generations. Clearly, given the cult of sex and beauty, we would think, that sexual perversions were free, and acceptable. We must consider that everything has to the social status variant. For this there was that part of the people who were honest to various factors. Or why they could not competer in the form of attraction and beauty, then no danger of getting a reputation and then not be able to keep, and then stood in line on the side of the Puritans and honest. Clearly there were also those for the principles and traditions were honest or at least seemed that way, but in the end under, below, she does not and did not care anything to anybody. The people looking for sinners, but in the end all sinned in secret, but he liked to point fingers, although the day before had done themselves what they condemned. This shows that the cults of pleasure were privileges to some and severely punishes others, it all depended on the social scale in which an individual was connected. Clearly, if he diverted it was a poor, unprotected by her beauty, it followed a failure and a bad reputation that was a consequence of the situation that had sought. He was judged badly and end in some way the situation was created for the purpose of oppressing them, morally and physically. They infuse were all dirty, especially the moralists, more than others, even though they felt protected because no one could suspect them, or because they were radically disappear, traces and witnesses. The deviations were all normal and acceptable, if these were made by the powerful and wealthy. And from those who were protected by their beauty. A nasty whore, was killed, a pretty, was glorified. This was the world. A whore who was neither good nor bad, passable said, had to be careful, and rely on his luck and try to understand those who went with, or otherwise in bad hands ended badly. This was the reality that was the cult of beauty. What you do is fine if you are beautiful, if you do that you're bad, you attract him to the condemnation of the moralists, who maybe are the same who have enjoyed. This was a very restrained realism that the sins of the people. Before getting in the way you had to know, and know well their chances. Clearly, the world revolved around the hour to power and wealth. The most beautiful girls were taken from the most prominent and most powerful characters.

The sale of virgin girls then no was no view as an act of oppression to the weaker sex, how to say yes on custom. Indeed these were competing and can to be chosen as the first to be sold to the rich and to the Romans. Legal prostitution, was a rewarding result for the Roman soldiers, in order that they could have fun, and given the top rank by right of birth or of belonging, this created their happiness to be and to do what they were performing during their life, that is: All that in a moral situation can be prohibitive to them was consistent and due. Clearly, the people were involved from customs and traditions, so those who were on the ball could access its part, rewarding and satisfying. Why everyone wanted to become ROMANS soldiers were fine as much as the Emperor. Extremely popular situation in the cultural complex; of customs and traditions, some things also condemned so severely. It was always a form of disguise, or ways of being seen moralists, but basically in a situation of each individual opportunism, outside of customs and traditions culture, did not disdain to make use of carnal pleasures that life could offer. Moralism, was only expressed in form, but no doubt that was in force then were more a way of being rogues, seen and because outside of morality, individually, each wanted and demanded their share of pleasure, of glory, of well-being and without getting many scruples. Clearly those who saw money pass in front and having the possibility to deduct it from, were moralists, seen and because part of that money was used to buy virgin, wrapped enjoy them and sometimes sell them. These were people connected with or related parties of the public financial administration that moved on behalf of ROME. For the weaker sex, or rather for the female sex, sometimes it happened that expose themselves in order to be bought and end up in an honorable house Romana, caused her not to be chosen. This eventually led them to make the prostitutes. Clearly, a prostitute, having the opportunity, to go with many men, it has the option to choose the horse of his size. Clear girandogli of money in the end can hold the man who wants to fill it even at the cost of money. Everything was subject to customs and family choices but so what would seem not normal and unethical, in need of family survival, even this way became a normal way to live. We do not exclude that some families were eating through this ancient work. As we do not exclude that even then there was an organization in order to raise the money, or part thereof, to prostitutes, as it is not, rule out that some prostitutes willingly gave money to some hunk in order that would cover and give them that pleasure of which from childhood they are seeking. Clearly the prostitute, since ancient times does this right job because she likes. And this is a craft that in most cases begins at an early age in order to become an integral art in the life of a person. If not, they would lose all meaning. A trade that comes from sex pleasure, and in the end comes the passion of the trade and is used with pleasure. Case not, that no whore in the world, is born to do this job, she used to do to fate or another, but in childhood. Then in adulthood, nobody made, accepts alone, it becomes a very personal choice. Always a pleasant choice. A woman is a whore because you DO nice for her. If she did not like to be a whore not executed it. In adulthood means. Clearly, some men support this female choice, just because they have a life and a way to lead the bitch is required have it close. Some men do not support this choice, and are smarter, they act secretly. The latter, create female job roles or commitment, bogus, or unimportant, and thus they too have always been close but honest bitch, fuck them and others do not. In turn even he knows how many customers, honest as well as he has his sweet lover. And the world was spinning then, as I turn now. The sharing of love in complete form, that man applies to himself and to his fellow men, but always clever. As there was in those days, a woman who cheated men and boys than women rubbed, in the same way humanity has passed customs and traditions but, with reviews of verses even though realism has always the same remarried.

Grass we can not make a bundle. To believe that it is, people who did evil, both people and they did not, they had one thing in common. Both recognized, what was good and what was evil. Strange but in the deepest nature of man, whatever it commits knows what is the right WHAT and knows what is the wrong thing. In most cases during the period in question, I think that people, obedient to their own conscience, and the call of the well, there were also many. human beings linked to evil. Strange thing when a person is linked to evil, at the time of separation, suffering at least twice by the separation from something that bound him to the good. People who are bound by evil, and that in the end if they did it to each other, were really too many. However everyone knew what was good and what was bad because in their judgment and in their soul, they recognized the distinction that in the end is one thing in common that possess the nations, and then this is what constitutes and change the world It puts them in a position to fight for justice and the right to happiness. Perversions turned all the focus of greater perversion and most coveted. It was that of sex and represented by the person of their dreams hidden, able to become the object of desire and achievement of happiness. Sex, seen through the eyes of man pleasure in itself, if it is, he has to do it. He sees the woman as a main her to meet his pleasure and their perversions. Then later, in a second half he saw the woman as a symbol of family, to love, in the clean and less selfishly. To achieve the woman object, other perversions, even the most evil against some families of the people, were implemented. The world that then turned around to religions and their cults. And every thing that man did in life was always aimed at achieving the religious pleasure and to consume the most delicious cult that was always that of sex. All that is sought, needed in order to arrive at having pleasure. The most coveted was to have the power to conquer and to buy the object of sexual desires represented by a beautiful virgin or a wonderful woman. Every road that ran through the end he was the one that was intended; the sex magic, his cult and his possession. This was the main perversion, which attracted other. Power and women. That which was outside of this surface was considered, even if necessary. When it came to power, and women, all scruples, and every principle decayed. Clearly, as then and even now, be a shame if, while, forgiven by God, brings up a penance in extent from sin, you have to make. And this is something no human being dispensed, especially if there is the continuity of sin. For this it is clear that from this point of sexual violence did not exist for the Romans who occupied a region. Indeed it was imposed on all form of religion and celebration for it. The most coveted dishes were barely legal young virgins. From here we understand why you became older than twelve years. Why he wanted to become citizens of Rome and soldiers of Rome. This culture in the colonized peoples drew the lynching and perversion chain of a company's group THE bad. In this form the lynch was opportunism I have a vendetta, even though it was denounced as a purifier event and punishing the bad. The coming isolated from patients or friends, and being excluded from a group meant being weak. A weak person in danger of becoming the victim of a perversion and evil that suffered by a social group. And for whatever reason or excuse he was lynched and plundered by all his properties, including children he had, and even the woman. It depends on what a woman had, the best thing was that he had a bad. This was risky custom, do not forget that the example was also from Augustus, who took away the LIVIA woman to Tiberius Claudius Nero. Who is the Father of Tiberius Claudius Nero. Same name as I said earlier on, the Son became Emperor Augustus had added ilo name. T he wife daughters took her away as historians say, that he fell in love as soon as they saw her. I can not put no doubt, but rightly un'incinta married and had to fall in love? It may be coincidence but her husband was a ANTONIANO. Everything fits in the theft of the bride and disagrees in love. This was the air that is breathed in society to JESUS 'time.

AGGRAVATED -P.32

With this realism we consider the aggravating circumstance that are the habits and customs of the Romans, or better to say; the customs and traditions that Rome shows in places devoted to them, they are educated to make use to the subject peoples, in order to derive fun and joy of living. Which they are: Devotion and worship to sex as art and life principle. Devotion and consecration of beauty. This incited the man to fight for themselves women of better race. Devotion to the struggle and war for men in order to broaden the empire, devotion to the Imperial religion that served to keep the people to him with fidelity. Devotion and consecration to death. Devotion to the arts and culture. Devotion to honor the gods of Rome, as if this was a principle which he demonstrated his loyalty to the empire. Religion gift a center that is idealistic, in order to maintain a guarantor to the Roman hierarchy and to keep the empire under control, and through the United religious customs. A clear view of the time, and in its real depth, makes us realize that humanity required a control and a change in thinking, why is the son of God. Underlying these principles ROMANS, it is clear that: In a subject people are those who have these qualities that lure the ROMANS, and that the Romans, when they notice someone there, certainly involving, has a change of existence. After all cults are religious customs and involve people who have qualities attractive to the custom, for ROMA it is also a religious duty. Of course we know that if a person has to eat and want to live, if it possesses these qualities mentioned, must interact with ROMAN, to show off and get noticed. Of course it was necessary to respect their rules, the commitments that s'intraprendevano and pacts that stipulated. This was definitely not an obstacle. The certainty and security of the future is the radical basis of life and for its continuation in the improvement and well-being. The devotion to the cult of death, in the form of diversion festive entertainment and leisure, was also a ritual although macabre and pain for some. Kill or do kill was a way of exaltation and give pleasure to life, and in the meantime a warning, addressed to those who wished to oppose the system. It was a show that did not require the people now see for the pleasure but out of habit. The people proved to be underdeveloped, but it just was only brought up in order that what inflicted the ROMANS, were not only seen as a sort of punishment but also as a fun reason to viewers, and warning at the same time. Everything became normal in general form, even if we consider that in the affective domain family members of the condemned were suffering, but they were few in comparison to the suffering of many who were amused, but in turn, everyone could fall into the pain network. The people of the people maybe taken by one, by one, they were beings with sound moral principles and compassionate towards the slaves, but when they were en masse, had fun just because the bad happened did not belong to their general but individual affective domain.

Clearly there was a social partner who had moral feelings,

loyalty, and compassion for the unfortunates who needed to die to entertain others. That was the part of the people, which became a moralist, by age and 'experience, but likewise not claimed, officially. The generalized form environment certainly did not favor a growth in the good, in fact created a block to the evolution of the plural society in the direction of benign and altruistic. If this plural form we compare the evolution of the individual and this unique, associamoci poverty and fear, we understand how difficult it was to evolve in this way, and it was difficult to follow the good or who for goodness devoted their existence in preaching it and present it publicly, as did the Son of God. Everything under consideration would seem normal, for those who could not make it at that time but normal, because they were not: most of the people could not. It had made arrangements for the powerful and they lived with devotion, even if the cost was the waste of his very life.

There is to be considered in this historical presentation that some people were very conditioned environment and the fashion of the time, it was conditioned by culture and cutting-edge modal that Rome was usual to bring in subject peoples. The culture was not just imposed as an obligation, but more people were involved to the point of becoming an integral part of the same Roman culture. The leaders of the Vassallo who administered the people with their laws, most were like guardians of their own country, while seeing their people suffer he did not care, to them was interested in being part of the Roma class, feeding on luxuries, vices, and Roman culture, even if this meant death and hunger for their people, get rich and make power for themselves and for their loved ones. Clearly these people, they had the protection of the legal system that they themselves administered, had the keys of life on earth. There were others who had qualities that interested to ROMANS, AND somehow tramiti steps of pleasures which used to receive the keepers of Vassallo, could enter into a social dimension that assured him of joining the powerful and wealthy families and so they passed from one social class to the poor in a prominent position. Some thought they had these qualities, and in the end, most probably are due to change his mind, but in the end he did text realism was the belief, that it was, by means of, or other physical skills, you could make a career. In this way the future was assured. The adapt to new customs and conform to the different ways of understanding life could ensure survival. Not all people are equal and not all and were drawn completely from the fashion of the time, and new cultures or other, even if only with your fingers you could count nonconformists, they were there.

HISTORICAL STAGE AND REFLECTION-P.33

The historic stage, since the realism of the time; highlights the supremacy of evil against good, invites to understand the reason for the coming of the Son of God. Clearly we are men, and we can not be able to understand the wisdom of the Eternal Father, but we can understand the reality of the time that is contrary in what was once praised by those who by descent were Faithful to God's laws. Therefore, God sends the Son for a reason we do not permissive to explain and understand in its entirety, but we understand that Jesus' gives man the Good and Faith as Half or way to go in order to save his soul, searching and representing Well, the man follows the path of salvation. Rightly it is said that Jesus' died to save our lives. However, on this I agree; but I also believe that there are other reasons that explain the coming of the Son of God. One of those reasons is:

That Humanity pretends to believe at the time, but what is materially represents: unbelief. In fact, he believes only in gods that only serve to help the man to behave in a way that is similar to those who do not believe in anything. So when Jesus came, the man pretended to believe in gods and pretended to believe in God, but in truth he did not believe in anything. The man pretended to believe and nothing else. Otherwise Jesus would not come, and any prophet could have put on earth a message from God. The man before the coming of Jesus pretends to believe, but do not believe in anything. He lives in lies and opportunism. The man does not believe in anything before the coming of Christ, but pretends to believe, and it does so for reasons to study and understand. However the truth is this one! But the fiction continues to wait until the coming of God, and there was talk of an imminent end of the world, and this coming of God seemed liberating, and it was said that God would only have saved some and not others. He pretended throughout also on what you preached was not believed, only the interest and nothing else mattered.

Clearly, we men, we can not decide how he is God, as we can not understand how God has taken, to see the Son sentenced to death by a part of the people, in order that they too are his children but that is they are stained hands of His Son. Clearly, the die in one way or another in the same way Jesus' fulfilled the divine task, but this does not justify the hatred, which is a crime connected to evil, shown by man against his Son. << But the man hates feeling like the man, and this even without reason. He lives his bestial stage. >> We can not think otherwise how are we to believe that God does not demand the condemnation of His Son to save the man. Many things are in the dark of our understanding.

"God willing one day we become more learned and knowledgeable of the situation that grips our intellectual nature, He will make sure that we understand, for the time being we must accept and share with us what He has allowed us to understand, and render merit and thanks for this good to us, bestowed upon people of good will. "

Returning to the old speech: Of course we can not assume that the convict JESUS 'under the Easter festivities is a challenge, driven by some of the brothers against the heavenly Father. We can say that they did not know what they were doing, as our Lord taught us. We can say that Jesus' was born in the people, he is a man of PEOPLE, and it is for the people This means that in an era situation, where humanity requires its coming, he manifested the will of the Heavenly Father, who always sees injustices that the people suffer, and intervenes by sending Jesus '' in order to educate the world with his Word and an end to the injustices against the people. And the world through everything, and sacrifice inclusive, leave the Faith. E 'reasonable, because at that time the man was losing the good road beyond repair; because it is considerable that humanity had lost the compass and had become an integral part of the evil, the coming of Jesus' through FAITH, redials the balance. We do not know if Jesus' had not been sentenced to death if we would no longer need to seek salvation by following the path that He has shown us, but we'd already saved.

These things do not know. And everything that we could assume would be only a guess, we must adhere, religious teachings, Christian saints who have written and prayed with FAITH in the heart and the interception of the Spirit of God. We do not know that if JESUS 'had it not been sentenced to death, we could not remember him, and our salvation would be compromised. This is why we entrust our intellectual virtues in the hands of the Eternal Father, and with faith we rely on him and his Saints. There are things that our intelligence, however skilled, can not understand deeply. However, the same reason and to try to understand what Heaven allows us to understand. We know that we must pay FAITH to those who have lived with He and the Gospel and all described in real form and questionable in its authenticity, that their other Scripture can not be that the Divine inspiration, connected to CELESTE plan as equally it is the musical melody I described in the book HOPE, connected to the flat Celeste. If the man said to Jesus' came to the world to offer himself in sacrifice for our salvation, we must pay us this FAITH, right I was wrong in that analysis is logical, we must pay FAITH. You ask why? I can answer simply, for a man for the simple fact of not feeling in the wrong and to give a value to his criminal actions performed against the Son of God.

Moreover, if the man takes believe it must be right to give himself. And it convinces autosuggestionandosi, that God thinks, otherwise it would lose the stimulus and COERANZA of salvation, which gives the FAITH and his way of finding reason and motivation to acts committed by some ancients erroneously. Man needs to be right in order that your evil is taken under an exam and is given a sense of Right with the aim to GOOD; in this way to get understanding and forgiveness from Heaven Divine; or courage for herself and from himself that allows him to continue his life. This is to have reason to believe. Us, even if we were to think otherwise, however, pay FAITH man, we too are people and we have to believe in man. Certainly God can forgive us or not, this is connected to our repentance and how we make our way to the ground and especially to His Will. We know that being men, we have an obligation to forgive our fellow man, God clearly does His will, and that we do not know, but for the Faith, we go back to It. And this speech is necessary for me to have done so in order to detect, beyond that from any point of view, doing evil, even the Son of God, is a crime committed by a part of men who are always Creatures God, but we can not judge, we must forgive, and entrust us with FAITH in God. we must now understand that social class which belonged to the Son of God, was that of the poor class. These poor people were considered inferior beings. These poor people were hurt and betrayed each other, to achieve a breath of oxygen economic or social, which was the reward for their treason. These poor people were ashamed of the other poor, wherever they merit from the higher social classes. These poor thought in most of their time how to survive and how to live, if only to eat. These poor people were not in a position to lose a few hours and devote their thoughts to another poor, who had held any rally. For this to be treated as inferior men, the feeling for because of the customs or other, people look with disdain by aristocrats, it happened that the class of the poor suffered, and as was to try the bread, in the same way as the JESUS family ', we must take into account, a realism, that Jesus' was just! And the poor with all the problems they had, possessed a brain and almost no thought. Therefore, you JESUS 'was just But God was with him. And if he managed to get to the point of leaving the FAITH as an inheritance, is a practical demonstration that Jesus' is the Son of God. There are no solutions, it was too messed up both socially, economically, only if he was the Son of God, he could do and let what he accomplished. For this is mathematical JESUS 'is the Son of God. These are the reasons that lead us to do a certain reasoning. We for this reason we can not exclude that Judas did not have considered, and who fails to understand these things that Jesus' has certainly lived during his life kid. Namely, Judas studying the childhood of Jesus' understood definitely that exceeded situations only if it was protected by a divine hand could overcome. Or he might have thought that: JESUS 'exceeded during His childhood, certain situations it is impossible to overcome them, and to have them drive past this man who is? Finally understands that it is the Son of God. We are obliged to offer hypotheses, it is part of our research. Returning to our discussion. For this one man speaks only when you create a base and a minimum of security, or otherwise does not speak. This is why Jesus' speaking in adulthood, when his intelligence is able to build up a base and that minimum of self-sufficiency, to live, in order to devote himself to what He had come to do in our world and at the same time guard against any enemies.

I say this because as I mentioned above at the time, was in a phase that the weak were trampled on, and not to work, not having a base, could lead enemies or people to become right enemy because I saw weak. Clearly I note that to be successful, to be poor, to tap into a future security minimum, in that society, and in that kind of environment, necessarily being connected to the PLAN Celeste, and that God was with Him, and helped him through some men, to work and to make work, in order to achieve a minimum of core stability and security for their future. Surely, He, Official so could not and would not be presented to the world as the Son of God until he failed to have a base of subsistence for the future, in order to dedicate himself with the mind, thoughts and body, to DESIGN BY GOD.

THEREFORE 'JESUS' KNEW OF BEING THE SON OF GOD; BUT ONLY KNEW HIM! - P34

Clearly, he knew that we are an energy of LIGHT thinking, that regenerates or generates itself with LOVE and goodness, in the absence of this energy, that is us, we disappear. JESUS 'knew that man has need to join en masse and to concentrate their will, in one individual, any ideas he has, man requires this. How clearly Jesus' knew that he never had the power to be a will to action in which the mass it would follow commands and orders. Just because he was a poor and belonged to the society of the Poor, who lead a regular life and fear of being judged by God. Therefore, we can not believe that he had qualities that could be of interest to ROMANS, in order to enter the their circle and that they be protected and revered made rich. This is why Jesus' NON'ERA NE 'BEAUTIFUL NE' UGLY, was a simple man of the poor people, just a simple man whom God made it his Sword, expressing own will in this way and to the beloved Son Up, he wanted to give the Way of Salvation man. Can the sense of the Divine Right, through JESUS 'be understood? Yes sure. The Divine teaching has shown the way of the Just man, by means of the Messiah. Well because it represents the man in his human value, has no follow a discernment between them, but simply considering the man for how it was created, which is rich, beautiful or ugly, intelligent, of a nation, or another. ... Etc ... Etc ... In Front of the Jesus' eyes were all men,

111

sons of God, and all the same. This way of dealing with creatures shows that he was incapable of offending, and honesty towards all humanity, which shows an evolution Spiritual Divine. His sense of the Right to man is applied by God through the Son because the Son is honest towards the man and obedient to our Heavenly Father. By means of this initiative and Divine manifestation makes concrete the hope of change, of Justice and of the triumph of Good. Now clearly waiting for the man manifest his honesty and his obedience to the teachings of JESUS '. JESUS 'His part has done, it's up to us to make our own. Underlying the success of Jesus' in doing His part with regard to creation, to save us, the Father. ... Etc ... Etc ... We can now believe and believe that Jesus' was connected to the Divine plan, and by Divine aid he had created a car sufficiency, economic social which allowed him to survive and so devote to His Divine mission, and to fully its part for Creation. Similarly we can not exclude that from the moment he began to Prove to the world, a lot of work and livelihood of the bridges have been cut, this is intended to be more than plausible. God was still with him, this was giving him the strategy and the strength to find the social economical solutions within themselves, and the means that God could use him to find certain solutions to problems, were: The intelligence to use to educate one's self and through this process achieve or have the inspiration. This is why even though Jesus' had not obtained certain experiences, was able to give answers like men who had lived experiences related to his answers.

This is why Jesus' experience or not, had a great spiritual evolution, which reached him by invisible forces, which are Governate by God. It was this that enabled him to impress and to find solutions to the unexpected. Unexpected that the man, for one reason or none, put as an obstacle from time to time in your path.

We treat the theme of morality in order to understand the dialectic of the Son of God. Jesus' clear, just to do the moralist, because surrounded by few and those few are supermen. Little or nothing has to teach them. How could he make the moralist with a character like JUDAS that always the why and the solution and the excuse of human behavior in your pocket? And it is always ready to give way to an answer and a reason to each behavioral condition of man. Not easy to be a moralist, you can reason, discuss and find convergent points, with his Disciples. What does Jesus' is being presented according to an Benigno perspective. A slide being in its natural totality, and an indication of how one should live and d act against oneself and in others in order to have God's grace and to be happy for eternity. JESUS 'declares the world to be Son of God, this mainly ago, it was inconceivable that the moralist, or did the teacher. He tells of the Heavenly Kingdom, and shows how to get to attain eternal life going in the Kingdom of Heaven. He only says how you should lead a man in order to save his soul and in order to live happily with others. He does not judge anyone. This does not rule out some conflicting opinions that may have expressed, to those who believed in a lie. Moralism without the practical demonstration, we men know that it's just false. JESUS 'could not be faked, so hard to believe it was a moralist, perhaps a counselor, yes! He is no exaggeration to assert that the moralist has been. Definitely one that declared the truth, and sometimes bother! With this we can not rule that would discuss and express his opinions, but between saying their beliefs and make the moralist is a bit 'of difference. Therefore no man could say, here is did the moral and now with that evil person is speaking. No one could say that this thing does not like and now to change your mind. Etc. ... The need to interact with people who unfortunately are also the mental conception and different custom led her to refrain from judging others.

JESUS 'does not come close to making the moral, but to discuss, if it was felt, considerable in his person, otherwise, leave it alone; hardly, I think, he did offend or allowed himself to be hit with words alone, rightly because it was penetrating in the discourse and wishing also pungent. The approach was sympathetic with a mixture of joy, happiness and affection. The moral clearly an intelligent man of his reach, it can only gently so as not to offend the sensibilities of others. And I think he had a lot of tact and in this respect, otherwise it still does not speak of His Work. For this he was not certainly a moralist fanatical and convinced, but it was one that conveyed joy and happiness to others. Just so the neighbor was not bumped into his sensibility, was tied to Him, and accept to interact with Him. That is JESUS 'was a joyful man, smiling, peaceful temperament, conciliatory, and transmitted peace and harmony. He extinguished with his temper the hot tempers and familiarization people with him because they felt as if he was their family and a lifelong friend. This makes us realize that even if not always to frequent certain persons, they still remembered him. It makes us understand that the people to love and to be happy to be with him, it means that He did not hit their sensitivity. And not to offend the sensibilities of others, first of all, we must not be moralists. Everything is mathematical.

JESUS 'knew that the smile and smile, chasing evil within man. As we now know this too. We know that hospital smell, and smile, they flee the devil that lurks in man. Jesus had this power, to escape the evil that lurked within the man. To do that you have to accept escape. ... Etc ... Etc ... And turn it into Well. Although we can rightly think and believe that it is natural, that: the moment between two characters you establish communication, respect, affection and confidence, the right and duty to make moral are indisputable, and therefore almost obliged, just to respect of feeling and for the good that you want to the next. For this clearly JESUS 'he did not lack these

114

qualities, but was at the time and had to part as quoted. For this his way of being anti-conformist, individualistic, expressive and sociable neighbor, he is even more loved by those who are at their side. He was able to approach anyone. The people aroused sympathy and benevolence, for His exuberance, his expansiveness and His Miracles. The people, regardless of social class or trade that little loved. And whatever the character of the people ... I wanted Well, even if it was out of fashion his speeches contrary to the prevailing customs. For this, the Messiah, could interact and have contact with different environments. Where he could discuss with scholars, famous men in the social, it was the occasion or circumstance interacted with anyone without any kind of prejudice. The people, the poor, working families ... everyone was nice and pleasant because of its envious Miraculous ability and his way of presenting to the next. This capacity, engaging, came from the fact that it was not a moralist, otherwise would have to change clothes for each time had to pass from one environment to another, which he believed, not too important. For this he was with the learned, he became product, whether it was with the workers, he also became one that works, whether it was with the homeless, became this as well, if it happened in an environment of achievers or evil, He became neutral, and if he could, he expressed his opinion, but hardly these kinds of knowing men could involve him in a bad deal. This humble manifestation of adaptation makes us realize that Jesus' had, for His Mission, to save all men, regardless of their inclination. This always singular, right form because to bestow and to give something to the evolved could learn the message, or else who was not the evolved, bestowed the understanding, the Son of God, he could only make his life difficult. This means that we can find smart, among the poor, among the rich, between the honest among the dishonest etc. ... This means that we can find killers and devoted to evil, in any environment, and we can find good and devoted to the good in any environment. This also means, that we can find fools, among the poor, among the rich, between the honest among dishonest. ... Etc ... Etc ... You mean the world is variegated, and Jesus' knew this, why he could not judge. He knew that good and evil were interwoven. He had, by Divine Grace including the heart of men, and skin included what had in mind and what was in their hearts. His way of being, holds a positive force that embarrasses, those who confront him, attracting and involving in the center of His people, those who esteem him and wish his friendship. Similarly was born in some hatred and treachery that, in the end, as history shows us, lead to a perversion hurt social chain, dominated by those who are the representatives of the people and their will though few in number, it becomes the collective will. JESUS 'has a sort of magnetism that attracts only the most advanced and most intelligent people in the Spirit. Something miraculous and extraordinary possessed JESUS ', which was to attract to himself all the people but few are able to magnetize and to remain connected to Him, and only the most evolved psychologically speaking. Other people, though fascinated by His being, His evolution, he could not make the magnet with He, just because they lacked the degree of evolution of which was really necessary, for restarne linked forever.

They are confused and the Good that they lavished became the midst of confusion, I think it is not ready to understand for lack of the kind of evolution that has not been achieved, the individual was born a sort of embarrassment and apprehension, almost like if the same message too deep to become a means of apprehension. He still gives everyone something. The people who approach Him, and why derive from them, but we can not assume that these were able to understand it and to know it deeply. People went to derive the well, and the rest could also forget it. JESUS 'did not judge this, He went His way as God The indicated. What Jesus' bestows in intellectual dimension, it is something that only a few can learn and accept, all in conjunction individual evolution of each of them, understanding super men, or rather evolution Deeply spiritual and independent of evolutionary influences the man traditionalist culture that era: that rightly created by the powerful and those who have had a relatively low contact with realism and with the sufferings of the popular reality and of life itself. The apostles were men who have not been influenced by the thinking of the conservative culture, although they studied, their brain had remained pure it is not infected, from that culture made by lords of the court, which in the opinion of some: they had always eaten and drunk behind the people, had cried for a scribe who carried home their kitty. Characters are maintained, spoiled, convinced that they are the best, observers of the people contemptuously. The Apostles knew, knew this realism, they had resisted to not be brainwashed by these lessons to glorify the living rooms of people who had always represented evil. The Apostles had canceled in their mind of man phony culture, and of his heroism at the expense of the weak and losers. They did not believe in man spoiled and powerful, devoted to sanctify maxims and nonsense rhymes, turned to the good of their own and against the neighbor. They knew the car sanctification of the powerful intelligence. They knew that through the power, the man handing out this cultural product that was nothing but a diet to become evil men like their teachers. They knew of the muses and the stories that were written down by those women I had plenty of them, and that they create another culture was a kind of contest between them, in order to see who was the best at writing bullshit. Clearly were they to decide honors, glories and to give titles of nobility and reverence, only to a few favored, finally, the chosen were always children and family members of men of power or of those people who were always in the powerful social classes. The apostles knew that despite being an ark of science, what they said they had nothing, and bullshit that someone said that was tied in the manger of the powerful, it was pure gold. I personally believe that in different historical circumstances the man proves to have faith that intelligence is a purchasable gift with power and wealth. Unfortunately not, intelligence is a natural gift that all human beings possess.

Clearly in the Ibero referees man decides how to grow it and how to evolve it. From this factor stems the prejudice, and believe that a poor, not having had opportunity to attend educational and cultural environments, has not been able to cultivate their intelligence, so it is considered unintelligent, unfortunately this is a man's fault. Returning to our discussion above, in this way the apostles by Jesus', began to create another culture. A new culture teaches us to do good that speaks and teaches the realism of one good and loving God with His creatures. Elected to this understanding, but a few Super Men, capable of owning quell'anticonformismo, who challenged the whole situation and evil animal, human power over the people.

One of them was Super Men JUDAH.

NOTES TO DISCREPANCY-P.36

Now we understand, that the Messiah, has a way of balanced interact with others. Adapting his personality in order to create a communion and sympathy with others. At the end of your adjustment, it leads him to keep himself clean in the soul but little moralist, reconciling himself in this contradiction in order to communicate His being the same Divine, who was standing in front, making it not so much the reasoning recalling but the moral conscience. Therefore, this determines one part anti impression factor that Jesus suffers from the other, of the other factor is the impression that he transmits to others. That is, Jesus can meet any man, of any culture, any social status that does not make any impression. You can speak to a king or a man of the poor, without showing no difference between them in His I and His way of acting or thinking. While adapting to the difference of those that the Front capitavano personality and mentality. Basically, Jesus' face if he sees only a MAN, and nothing more than this, whoever he may be, or whatever it is, he sees only a man, which to give His message. This makes us realize that Jesus' can not be biased, be all, just because he saw the same floor and felt no embarrassment to talk or make friends with anybody, what counted that made her feel welcome, important, pleasant to be with him, and that the attention will transmit a sense of liking to His person and His way of seeing and thinking. At this point Jesus' opened and astonished, who was ready and mature in order to understand him and follow him, not physically because everyone has to fight for his life, but certainly psychologically and morally. Therefore JESUS 'was not emotional, but it was He impress others. This way of being involved, that some men who are rich or is poor or any status they belonged to force majeure had to be evolved to learn and understand the Son of God; By means of this phenomenal evolution they were with Jesus'. Clearly being addressed, from JESUS ', in singular form, among them believers, they could not even know each other. For this we have men who are Apostles, and believe in JESUS 'and among them you know, they have also men who believe in Jesus', had to do with Jesus', like the Apostles, but among them are unknown. However we should note that these are superior beings, or otherwise could not learn that evolution that the Messiah conveyed, and could not stand for Him, much less interact with Him. This realism leads us to understand some historical discrepancies, because most likely, some Apostles, while attending JESUS 'between them was not known. You have to consider at this point, that the strides made by the Apostles and all those who followed him was the same, though the culture and doctrine were not the same. For this we find men of different nationalities, of different cultures but who have understood the same things in life, and they arrived at the same evolutionary apex while studying and coming from different cultures and societies. Clearly behind this concept, there can be no organization among the Apostles, and those who believe in the Messiah, even if the same evolutionary stage, there connects to the flat Celeste. Surely they organize themselves in order to follow and represent to the world the teachings of the Messiah, it took place after the death of the

Same. We can not be surprised if we understand that the Son of God, does not require an organization, but the application to communicate with people who can understand it, with super people. We can not be surprised if Jesus' makes friends with a homeless man, or a king, with a prostitute or with a home in His Heart are only human, what is important and that they are ready and evolved enough to understand it and believe in him. we can not be surprised if he is excited in front of people, much as they were so excited. The power was not in the organization, but in the choice of suitable men in intellect to the WELL laws.

SINGOLARISMO AND PLURALISM-P.37

At this point we find two behaviors, different under the communicative profile of the Messiah. One in front of an individual. One in front of most individuals. Clearly Jesus' going to communion, as circumstances posed to stay for a long time in front of more than a friend or more people. However, while I understand that the consistency of a collective judgment, which identifies a man like Judas traitor and so condemns it, leads us to consider the possibility of a certain group in the communion and, at the base of this concept, we do! We see a collective opinion expressed by a group, but the texture of a collective judgment is not enough to try the action and cohesion of organized group. The proof of pluralism lived in a singular way we see that it is a single project as hindering their enemies, that is Judah. Only obstacle to corrupt, for those plots against the Son of God, and with the aim to achieve the goal of be condemned to death, is Judas. This forces us to think that even though there is a group, did not act uniformly, or otherwise the enemy would have to involve a whole group, rather than a single for their end. This is why the non-existence of cohesion between Judas and the enemies of Christ, serves as a mechanism that facilitates criminal intentions of the enemy, because uncontrolled and therefore unknown. Clearly, if there had been a cohesive group acting on behalf of a single will, and this singularity could stay quiet and he remained quiet relying pluralism, those who wanted to condemn Jesus' would have more difficulty performing their project, because corrupt, there was not only a man but more characters. Instead the obstacle was represented only by a man, and this was Judas. The pluralism was not distinctive in order to create the space to JUDAS fosse- -if so they can act according to their instincts and their own interests, diverting friendship affection and esteem for it he felt towards the group and , detaching it for the love and affection he felt toward his Master. To consider, which according to this reasoning, the group of the family of the Son of God could not take part. Otherwise, the embarrassment of Judah in front of the brothers from Jesus', could play a certain role and what could have prevented the erroneous act of Judas. To this as nature allows there to be a competition among men of the same family. On this final point, it is understandable and clear:

That being with Jesus', the follow Him and believe in Him, it is not a familiar factor, but it is an individual choice, determined by achieved intellectual evolution. Certainly the brothers of Jesus' suffered his own persecution by the community. Why they were persecuted regardless that they had to follow the evolution and to understand their brother or had not. Of course then later another brother, though not all have followed in his footsteps. For this evolution to the painful end or unwillingly had to achieve it and understand the coming of his brother. I say unwillingly because they began their social persecution, and other choices they could not have. Social persecution, rather than a choice of personal evolution achieved in the psychological way in a spontaneous way, led to a partisan choice and mandatory defense. Still remains the sacrifice, to suffer evil without having understood, only to the bond of family kinship. It would seem strange, but the family of the Son of God, in the opinion of the community and of the same behavior, it would seem, that the only food he was, hated and thwarted. So it is clear who were men of action, maybe not as smart as Judah, but action, and it would seem that The Thunder brother of Jesus' was a man of action related to a family of Syrian murderers, so the Romans and the priests have found bread for his teeth. If you read the history books, I understand that Rome was forced several times to enter the army in Judea, and the reasons are. They say that these riots were the fault of taxes. But I say that there was a civil war and hatred based on revenge. Let us not forget that Mary Magdalene, who was a prostitute action, has had his retinue of evil Greek business people, we can not believe that the death of his spiritual brother, although it had become CATECUMMA, has given blows to the Pilato family .

And this is likely, just because the Romans were GIANNI (men out of habit always go with the courtesans) for religion, and where is it written that something to them has been prepared? Do not forget that Mary Magdalene had the power to dominate men and to be obeyed by the worst kind of assassins. Considering also that Judas could have friends of killers environments, we can not believe, that all have remained with their hands HAND, even though deep down we do not know much, and it is for this reason that we only speculate, considerations and assumptions. He was a man of action, you have to see how they took her friends when they heard that a man like Judas who killed payment under the traitors, he has passed this species. We do not know as the year taken in its environment but wrote with a knife, because if they had written with the pen, do not know what we would read them and how they think about the betrayal of Judas do against his friend. As we do not know how he Filippo taken that it was he who watched the JESUS 'body after death. Do not forget that Filippo had within the same family of assassins, who knew also knew that Judas and Judas, this was a place where the living man is survives only if it respects his word and the rule of no betrayal, they are worth for all those who are part of it and not. Why Judah has not the mentality of the traitor. Unfortunately we can know with certainty that the Apostles, Jesus' inclusive, could not imagine that Judas COULD be good and COULD be bad, depended on the circumstances. He could save a man, killing him as well. Secrets that only he knew, personal privacy. Yet we are supposed to believe that he had a code of honor, and he believed in God and in His Son, or otherwise he would not have made sense for both the fellowship. And what he had with Jesus' and the apostles were good, and the good part of his character manifested, when he was with them and with his Master. Certain that when friends have asked him of the evil, surely, what was he doing with Jesus ', he will have truly proven to be a super man, because surely have answered: JESUS' is not like me, and like you, nor . He is the son of God, I am with him. Demonstrating courage is a lion's strength. On this basis the underworld who esteemed him, could not contrarialo in his friendship choice. Now on this basis we know that the underworld, is with his people, rightly or wrongly, that JESUS 'although was evil intent on the street, there was always someone who took his side, although he did not know why and he did not know the identity. This is mathematics. Clearly revenge called hate, the expense were the relatives of Jesus'. These are, however, conjectures, and that has to be considered, I write what I hypothesize, but clearly we must pay Faith and tangible evidence. However JESUS 'has forgiven all, and all had to wash their hands of the situation. Pilate washes his hands. The priests revolt evil against Judah, and they wash their hands. Judas kills himself, and this too can be a way to wash their hands, perhaps. The Apostles hide and wash their hands, the people say that he died to save them and washes his hands, the family would have at least some say, and to him who is there said of getting into trouble and to attend the little people recommendable? This is also a way to wash their hands for which he won the rule of forgiveness that God in His infinite goodness and mercy, gives us sinners. So I think you have to follow the sacred writings, and follow the example of God and finally that of FORGIVENESS. And we should also learn to forgive wrongs, after all it is our moral obligation as well as being an act of FAITH. It becomes noticeable that despite all that has committed a wrong morally visible against the Son Almighty, He was able to complete his mission and to make sure that your teaching is followed even in our times. This is the Will of the Eternal Father, a will that no human being can deeply understand how it is, but that ultimately they are all worthy individuals. For this there is the saying: "I make my business to me." This is also a way of apportarsi to the next, and not just a spoken or a way of thinking, which in many cases separates us from the bad interference.

Wise phrases, or ancient sayings, we invite most likely to engage in dubious behavior to the Creator's eyes, surely sometimes a pinch of participation in more towards life and other people's problems, we would reward at least, in a human sense and eyes the Creator, however, good men are not always found in the circumstances they can afford to do heroism. Returning to our discussion above, clearly, we can not consider Judas, one of the Apostles rappresentatrice will of the group, but we can consider, that Judas, was highly respected by the group, and perhaps more than we can imagine, just for the reason that he was able, though by interest, fail, respect and compliance of the group. That was to be loyal and faithful to their Master.

Similarly, we exclude a priori that Jesus' could act as a single will to collective action, also because his spirit free, sociable, cheerful, and full of emotional brotherhood, could not put it psychologically to the size of organizing a group headed by his Will.

The principle of the Son of God was individual autonomy and each had to think and act conscientiously, and with his conviction, under the influence of Love and laws that refer to the good, of which the Apostles' behavior had to demonstrate for personal conviction, and not to others' suggestion. In accordance with this principle, natural that he follow the Son of

God, they were to be men, really special, disorganized justly for their super ego self, but very evolved. At the base of this realism, ease of falling into foul, which comes to JUDAH, and totally free and arbitrary, with no second thoughts and remorse under the reasoning of the profile and individual reflection performed by Judas, before the betrayal was as he consumed. Unfortunately we have to give credit to what has come to us about him. Clearly, after the confetti, they feel the pain, so judgment of Judas becomes different from that, performed its analysis before he was the infamous act. The realism of the action carried out and its intensity and different from the one imagined him inside.

CONTEMPORARY SOCIAL JESUS-P.38

I can understand that in a city like Jerusalem, there was a bustle of strangers. A bustle of travelers. This determines thriving commercial activity and well controlled. Also determines the need for some foreign families had to settle or to move there for work or business, or to make money through prostitution, etc. ... Jerusalem had become a metropolis, crowded and full of life. So it is difficult to believe that Jesus' lived in the heart of the city, patch corruption and transgression. I imagine you more of a device, adapted to its evolution and its mission. With this, of course I do not say that He would not go into town, but definitely not so assiduous and definitely not in a stable manner or stopping for long periods. This is what we are obliged to think, as some characters, while hurting, had a bit of rethinking. Clearly the place of rethinking may be only a tad away from the nest of evil. This tells me that he interacting with people of different cultures and many trades working, these commonalities between them had an instinctive balance and behavior between them almost like it could be for example: to understand the good and try to heal the bad, when they were involved and which were fed, from time, to time, they consumed when they went in the heart of the city. This is why those who have to do with the Son of God and almost inclined to understand the behavior of good and evil, and to resent and repent of the evil that has been feeding or feeds occasionally. This regardless of their way of life and their way of thinking and manifest to others, that is true, the more prone to pleasures that it is in meeting the temptations, or to seize any opportunities for corruption, and so on remain attracted and attempted.

However everything was in the process of change, they were about to reach the time was that the JUDEA from Vassallo ROME ROMAN became a province, so some resentments, used in acting and living worse, distracted the conscience, and what was wrong if you gave pleasure or satisfy interests it became right. Behind this who resented having their conscience behavior objectionable material, seen under the sensitive side of the human mind, he could have repentance and remorse of conscience. And this kind of people had surely an education respectful and civil. This is shown, where corruption and transgressive social emancipation, has failed to take root deeply and radically in some person. For this, Jesus', and many of those who follow him do not live in the heart of the city, where lurks, corruption and bad deal. Clear that they possessed thoughts of resentment if they had participated in the evil, were predisposed to do good is to achieve the teachings of the Master himself. And who had already achieved an evolution with this address and this fold of the well, were in a position to recognize the quality of the good represented by Jesus' and be with Him. For, at this time given the variety of social customs, was all in flux. And given the desire and the desire to achieve material happiness, which guaranteed the lustful satisfactions and pleasures related to wealth and power, the surprises social policies followed one another from time to time. Alliances between men wrapped competed and at times, were en route, all without scruple of conscience and remorse. This situation of change, and alternation, had a great importance for the evolution of some destinies intertwined with each other and come to face to fortuitous circumstances as a result of personal choices forced by situations that others created for citizens and persons likely to suffer changes adjustments because of the selfish choices of others. This is why many people of the land, intertwined by fate relations, with whom it had to do with the Son of God, or who have had to do with the Son of God, and with him directly or indirectly through others, they were not dispensed to know JESUS '.

This is why many men who came to town with an intention, remained fascinated by Jesus' or by those who spoke to him, they learned the good and the thought of goodness, and if this understanding, became opposed to the project that had led them in city, they thought it was a sign of destiny. And follow the ideology contrary to them, was not only a choice of reflection but it was a sign Of God, of which you had to take it into account. Here are some men who follow the Messiah, even if they are in mentality and different countries. For this it was born on the feeling of friendship, affection, and that's what keeps the stability and the continuation of friendship.

Assuming that God is Love. Starting with the premise What Love is Joy and Happiness of Living. The Greatest qualities that could have and possess the Son of God, was the ability to convey Joy to the next, and the desire to live with those simple emotions which man begins to feed as a young man and life but unfortunately hand it becomes adult, clears slowly, slowly, to make it disappear for the track forever.

With this quality and with the force with which the manifest and makes sense to others, the Son of God, is the miracle of all, and especially with those who are grieving, and as if by magic, the pain, the pain vanishes in their hearts and in its place come the smile, happiness, peace and joy of life, and all the emotions connected to the Good and Love. Why he can not go unnoticed, and those in contact, remains, in Well, forever marked. And the amazing power of God is manifested in this way: The more time you're away from Jesus' and the greater the desire to see him and be with him. The less you try to think of it, and the mind develops thoughts of Him.

So even His enemies, who have had to deal with him, they were marked to the point to turn against themselves and STAY on His side. JESUS 'leaves its mark for which He, though in miniature, and if even a small part, is the character of the personal will of God. Of course we human beings we have reached has an evolution that makes us understand, that is clear, temperamentally the Son resembles the Father. The men in the contemporary SOCIAL JESUS ', they do not know this, perhaps, but still live it. For this, the said Imperial susseguito in the near future after His death, "Christ Galileo, Thou hast won," represents true under some judicious look. It means that man has understood, but is unable to express what he understood why he always sees, fight the competition and the power that blurs the vision of realism. I guess you know what he understood the man. What he understands is: If I man, I'm brutal, sinful, demonic, kill my brothers, responsible for the death of the Son of God, when they are in front of the Eternal Father, change completely. Change because I have to give a straightforward answer to God. Because the answer I have to give to the Heavenly Father puts me in front of my consciousness, and this is not affixed, they are automatically against the part of me that is bad. So they're on God's side. So I collapse in me all those beliefs in which I had lent faith to selfishness. It is this belief that led me to give pain and suffering to others. However now I have a weak man of flesh and sinful before God, I'm against that part of me that is worse and lives in sin, reason for which I only ask forgiveness. This man has understood that God Vince inside man and inside of himself. Jesus' being the Son of God, it is the same thing that happens to man. The basis of this we understand that the more man tries to kill the Messiah in his heart, so the Messiah increasingly shape reborn inside her soul. And 'mathematician.

128

For those who directly have created evil and gave him pain, you even more before you have to deal with God have had to deal with themselves. We now understand that this realism, JESUS 'could not be popular in official form, but in truth he was little-known officially speaking. However, at the same time was known in the singular and individual form, in its principle bring: Peace, Joy and Love. ... Etc ... Etc ... And as a gift to the next, this is how materially representing Well, we understand that: FAITH other way that does not materialize in Action to give what you can offer to those in need, even if in most often they do not receive anything in return. This principle puts us in a position to understand that we humans can become saints only if materially represent the Faith with our goodness. Donate what you can to those in need. Representing materially our goodness, and preaching the good, love and peace, we become saints regardless that God, through us, did or did not do miracles.

START-P.39

SIMONE
Simon was a young man of spirit even as an old man. Born when Judea was a vassal of Rome. It had become a Roman citizen for services provided to about it. He felt more a Roman than a Jew. He belonged to that people, even if of a different race. Judea had taken part in Rome in a way identificarsene and almost all households identified themselves to the customs and traditions of Rome.

Simone underwent This attraction and became a Faithful of Rome, for ideal, ambition and why we believed. As a result, these ideals, this irresistible charm that Rome exercised over himself, became a citizen of Rome, and from Rome made services. He was like a Trust Agent, a secret man. Soon he enjoyed admiration from Rome for his loyalty and his services. Although he had become Roman citizens, however, he reconciled within itself the two cultures. Roman, who has worked to live as a man and as such evolve, adapt to the times, to assert; one Jewish, which was that of his ancestors, which he kept with him the tradition and kept it lovingly in his heart. He was attracted, he loved and respected the value of religion handed down from his fathers. He knew how to adapt, and included how to reconcile the two cultures. Its capacity was to keep him, even two opposing ideas and take action against both reconciling with himself and with the world. He was a man of action, and very courageous. His relatives when they realized his choices, they felt almost betrayed, he, they say, contrasted the Judaic values and passing on the side of Rome and that you disapproved of the methods are ill suited to their religion, of which he learned in the new deployment Simone From Rome. Simone as a young man proved to be insightful learning, manifested a great vivacity and courage in the action; a good talent to live and survive given the violent era and his little-mode Orthodox representatives to interact with others and to enforce laws and rules of ROME. His relatives were regular people, ordinary, like the majority of the population, instead he was biased, and the ball did not touch her interesting emotions in personality, so ill not suffered any mental disturbance. cold, calculating man, is understood to persecute their own ideals, and the fight is not made him uneasy. His collaboration with Rome was first secret, then from hand to hand, it had become obvious and known in the environments that had to make alliances, or to clash with Roma. The character was smart, intelligent, very sly and cunning. A self-confident man. A person who knew their limits and possibilities. His ideas were clear clear as they were his goals. He knew what he wanted and how to work hard to get it. Handsome and willing in its commitments, estimated by those who shared his deployment. Judas was a character with a strong character, a man all of a piece. He was a man of his word and loyal to its commitments. fierce person with the enemies. He was a person able to cope with difficulties. He was a loyal and sociable man with friends, but tough with enemies. It was a determined and resolute person, and with fierce enemies. of medium height dark, handsome, computer, speech analyzer and the environment in which he was and the people with whom he was dealing. He was a man with an impulsive and direct. A person courageous and faithful. He was a loyal and good man with friends. Judas was consistent person with the world, and respectful of the weak, and kept their commitments and the word "date." A faithful person to their ideals. A man of action who could operate the brain and as a result, achieve their goals, in any way and by any means. He worked for Rome, and some characters of Rome trusted him. They were a group of trustees who worked for Rome and obeyed some powerful Romans, where he was deployed. We can say that, it was a secret service, working in political office, together with the teams, prepared, and ready for action. He believed in its powers, and only they relied, confided in his craftiness, and his sword that he handled with great skill. Only this trust and this alone she felt, really safe. The type of job that was leading him to trust only himself, in the end every situation could have followed unexpected, was part of its commitment to face some unexpected. So he developed a certain instinct, which in extreme cases, in addition to save his life, the rising of the mess. However their social situation, and its ties allowed him a life of a certain socio-economic level. The kind of life I was leading, and put him in a position to use your brain and know to run. Always ready for any eventuality. He dreamed of making career in the army, perhaps one day, and become a powerful ROME.

It was now a young man, handsome and sure of himself with his triangular face and his broad forehead. When the outbreak of civil war. The Roman army was divided in two. Simone had achieved a great personality. Its Gospel was: - no man can be superior to me, and I do not think other than God, is superior to me -. With this conception faced the world with courage and with sword in hand and a deep faith in himself. All that concerned its characteristic merit was the devotion to Rome and to his ideals, loyalty, honor, and be of those who were with him and who pursued his ideals.

He had its evolutionary side convention has only one God, and believed in God, like his ancestors and how they had learned. Everything had accepted from Rome unless the religious part, that had remained intact and faithful to that of his ancestors. The live the Roman mentality puts us in a position to assume, that he believed in everything, and at the same time nothing. Two ideas, contrary to the other, but that he could reconcile and pursue, either one or both the other concomitants in the circumstances that they came from in front of them. He believed in everything and do not BELIEVE in anything, and do not underestimate anyone. This was a feature of his being. At that time, a situation was created which the choices were vital. He had to stand on one side or another? The right choice if you guessed it ensures safety for the continuation of life. The choice not guessed could prove fatal. If that part, where he decided to stay lost, then you have to get away if you do not want to succumb to the reprisals of the victors. This happened in that distant era, a civil war, shocked the Roman Empire. Simone had sided with Marco Antonio, who fought against Octavian Augustus. He had attempted to guess, had chosen for conviction of being right. Even considering that Simon somehow was already part of the deployment. It is found there, but there was already. With his relatives, in that same period, the total fracture occurred. Understandable, good people could not be reconciled with a man, even though relative, thought leapfrog, and at any moment could be frightening even with the only way of speaking and behaving. Simone, at that moment, everything seemed nice and easy at the beginning of the dispute. already felt the victory in his hands and those of Mark. With this conviction, his actions, became excessive, until it became very cruel to enemies. This put them in a position to be known in the public and of some importance environments. Eventually Augustus won, and Simone to avoid the tribunal of the victors had to flee to the east to China. Others as he followed the fate to rebuild their lives away from Rome. Clearly, given the role of Simon to be top secret, you can not think, they were trying really him, but plausible that those who were with Mark by someone could be recognized. - Better evitare- thought many do. Prudence, and knowledge of some enemies of him and the position he occupied at the time of Mark Antony, prudence dictated by the cunning and intelligence, he preferred, like others, to move away from the place where he had experienced and had performed actions , on behalf of and in favors to supporters of MARCO. The Romans were already over there in the Far East. He knew this, and in that place he wanted to start rebuilding their lives. Wars did not want to learn, instill his ANTONIANO party, had collapsed and he wanted to rebuild his regular life, like his father and his family. As it was customary at the time, married with women much younger than themselves. So Simone he married a much younger woman, of Jewish origin, made his family and began to work devoting himself to it body and soul.

The new place no one knew him, and those few connoisseurs of him were like him. However these proposals, with some were removed, ultimately remained a void of memories and some distant knowledge. Simone was a new life, a renewed closing existence completely with his past. Sure had a lot of experience and this was a good base to resume and to reorganize a new existence, absorbing and applying renewed ideals. At the bottom was a way of conceiving the future in an inward and personal revolution. Equally, the same way that it agreed, prove to be Jews, when it was convenient to show that it was of Roman descent, did not hesitate to do so, given and why the Romans around the world were considered, people of a certain quality, and special in a sense, it depends on the environment or the people with whom he had to do for interest in opening more thoroughly.

For this he lived with those honors that you agree to a Roman.

The company's doors were always open for him. So although far from his home, his life took a successful defendant for a man of his rank, and in the new country had had implanted as if it was his country, or even better than his. The success and well-being, not long in coming, everything seemed to have had him. His former social class was taken very into account. For lineage and personal merits, given his intelligence and his shrewdness, he had become a man respected and honored by all citizens of the new world, and while not exercising public office became influential. He traded and did his best, especially as a good businessman who was Roman. Led a comfortable life, a life in the work in compliance, well-being, and in the enjoyment of the esteem and respect of all his countrymen, and his friendships were increased in number in day to day, until you get a reputation . He married a good woman and good religious Jewish origin. And she bore him a son, and named him Judah. A name suggested to him by his wife, a strong believer in the religion of his people, and he wanted to renew family traditions and the people they belonged to his ancestors, and her. We may think that being a citizen Roman, he could please his wife and at the same time imposing on him a second name of Roman mold. After all it would be normal and understandable, but this second name, did not know anything, but our hypothesis might be true. Simone had many qualities, among which had the advantage of being able to identify early intellect characteristics of Judah, and teach him all he knew him, and giving him the opportunity to learn even instructions, from screws teachers, as wise, as scholars and intellectuals. Besides this Simone had many excellent qualities, including self-change, with the ability to adapt to environments so admirable, able to adapt to the circumstances of the same life and the same fate. Simon was also a great teacher of life and a great instructor and Judah saw the student suitable and capable of learning all his knowledge and his being. Simon was a super man for his part, yes! A skilled thinker, and thus was able to identify him Judah, after studying it deeply without reservation. He had long worked for the transformation of his personality. The rebuild a new life, is to love this like previous civilian dimension in achieving the idea that everything can be united and love within themselves, it is not an every day. We must consider that, excluding the possible loss of these deep feelings that bind us to the past, you have to, return to love new faces and go unfamiliar streets, this change calls for a considerable effort for those who have a lot to leave in their homeland. Simone in the future it could also have a slight regret for having left his country, it can be surmounted psychologically, no doubt, but still morally relevant. Simone definitely with its timely and decisive choices showed one of his principles. Who they were these ideals: << Wherever I go, it's the people and the place that you must attach to me, more than I can attach to them. >>

Simon also shows that sometimes a man to survive must have the strength to implement a radical change in his life, and put into question everything, which earlier had been pointless. However, over the years, only slight regret the past, remained in his heart, and the feelings of close family members counted, only those had the value to be remembered and sought in his heart. Whenever he was conducted by the circumstances, to rebuild a new life and start all over again, its ability to adapt and comply with the new was admirable. On every occasion of rebirth, he was the solution, convenient, attractive and good substitute for what he had lost. Willingly he accepted the transformation, and has this psychological concept, he was the satisfaction which leads to value life, love for the ideals that derive from it, affection and interest in new knowledge. A compensatory dimension that is to accept a new way of thinking about living life, and find interest and satisfaction from it. This personality work, and its transformation checked and accepted, for the laws of compensation completed it in his character and ability dimension to transform situations, even apparently disadvantageous, in phases, advantageous, because it all became basically a game, and only the most skilled player could stand out of trouble and win disputes. Through the victories accomplishments that each report provides the winners in each comparison and in any social environment, they gave more and increases opportunities for easy money and to affirm one's own ego. For this to be understood that Simon was a skilled player of life. The outlook on the company, its work, the role that each man had in society, no longer appeared serious as before, under the eyes of Simon, but it appeared only a game, and what mattered was part of it, and realize as much as possible, while maintaining the principles and values in order not to be put out of the game, from the same environment that for a series of accepted him circumstances.

In the end his only obstacle to rebuild their lives from scratch, it was only the minimum and indispensable engagement. Therefore nothing easier to start from scratch. For him it was necessary above all things to conceive and work on his own personality, finding in it the various solutions, in order to reap the benefits and to adapt it, in any type of social environment confidentially. He lived entirely controlling the world around them and following their instincts. The experience in this case was important. Decipher the world around him, even with the instinct and read your own intuition, she placed him in a better situation to the next, by means of this he was easy to adapt to a new life; if he wanted to adjust, with renewed ideals to pursue and fight for it. And all that could ensue from the change, he was loved and lived in full. In the same way had the experience, and honored provenance origins and well taken into account, to get in a good light in the situation, social, whenever, as circumstances deemed necessary. For that Simon knew impress, not only with their own personality or your talk, but also with facts, just because he was a man of action and on this psychological basis had evolved. We must consider that in that period of history, fashion, mentality, was to become a super man. We could say that man evolved trying to become the super. It was the culture of man god or demi-god, to learn that the Romans kept her and made her become stronger with their religion. It was probably an ancient culture that has always nested in the heart of men. Rightly it had been retaken by the Romans. The revival of this culture could demonstrate, in the eyes of God, not evolution of men. And back in a circular evolutionary situation it became a perpetual cycle, and what to evolution was attained finally returned again and resumed the old ways, were brought back to light with more impetus. This cycle was interrupted in some way by the Messiah.

JUDAS-P.40

Judah during his life he had suffered from his father's influence ROMANA culture, in which man was bound to become a super man, a demigod.

Similarly also he had the influence of the culture of the mother, that being a religious virtuous woman fearing from God was giving him the rules of good and the respect of religious ideals.

Judas was growing with two conceptions of life. He had actually assimilated two different cultures between them, and one that is compare with the other. Therefore he had to adapt to live with it.

He grew in that social class, where the poor were viewed from top to bottom. He was from the top. It is that the virtue of respect for the good and the weak, connected to religion, as he had learned in a genuine way from the mother also attended the people who were at the bottom. He learned the understanding of man, in any social stage it lived. He made no discrimination and had no preconceptions. He grew with the honors that you agreed to his father. He grew among the people who pulled ahead with difficulty and honors he had few. Sometimes it seemed that he would find more enjoyment and satisfaction among the simple and poor people, and between the high class people and all ABBINTATE and complicated. The two cultures, imposed by parents, they led him to live different life situations, and to make a multitude of

137

experiences.

He was addicted to the study of philosophy. In writing. He practiced mystical meditation. He possessed a special talent in the arts. He was also skilled in fighting, the use of arms and sport. A comfortable life was his, spent in the nobility of the place. If he worked for will and his own pleasure, it had no need to work. Because he liked, accustomed, to do different experiences was dedicated to all that the right was curious to experience, until they got tired and no. She felt more pleasure in doing what was not customary to take, for one of its class. So Judah had everything, he lived like a rich man, in his father's house, and even knew how they lived those less fortunate than him. He was gentle and lovable all respected him. The father was proud of her son, her face and clever eyes, which showed obedience and great virtue in the arts and in the studio. An honor that Judas was respected in the same way that was respected too. Were Romans and honor in ROME was not quite clear in respect of color that belonged to this nation.

His father was his first teacher of a certain kind of life: The one dedicated to becoming a wise demigod around and able to do everything. His mother was his first teacher, although he taught other. Judah was supposed to be a respectful religious religion of his fathers, this was something not debatable, and Simone willingly accepted this performance. Judah, also he attended the doctrines and had many masters of life and teaching. From his father he learned the first secrets of life. Judah learned among other things, and many also processing of their personality, and through this process understand how to solve problems, and how to deal with their enemies. Finding solutions within themselves, analyzing oneself at all times of daily reflection. Analysis of himself, in order to find, identify the nature of their problems, correct, errors and improve their personality. Knowledge of itself. Simon soon realized that Judas was shrewd and learned like a sponge. He wanted for his son, draw a starting point of evolution, in the sense; transfer to his

138

son all he could from his person, in order that from Judah went away a legacy that started from where he had come.

He did a job, interesting but not easy technically. Everything matched, since the temperament of Judah was brought to learn all that his father taught him. Simone was Judas as a man since childhood. Seeing his father as a superior being, and believe it as the top man in the world, he led Judah to embodying his own father, and make evolutionary apex of the father its evolutionary starting point. His curiosity was always satisfied. And the fascination he felt, along this evolutionary path, facilitated the apprehension and allowed him to go further and further, his father was like a light that illuminated his path, and he followed this light. He was more than convinced and had had proof in some events of life, where he could watch the behavior of the father, that her he was a super man, more than it had any father of her playmates, adventure, course, and his friends. There were many stories and events that put Judas in a position to explore his father's personality. All stories, that he felt from her father's speeches of past adventures and heroic stories as he lived. Judah understood that his father had, over a natural power that he used in the right occurrence in perfect condition.

Judah, he wanted to know more, even though it was still a boy, and manifested this curiosity to his father. Simone told him: << Judah, from the shape of our bodies, and our appearance, each animal is afraid of man, just to our personality that he does not understand who we are, and for what reason, we have two capable hands of everything. The animal is as fierce, attacks or fear or hunger, but before man, the first thing he wants to do is escape, good son know that the man is an animal, and in some circumstances belonging to worst kind or better, it depends. Certainly, a man must know himself, the measure of its strength, above all, what it is able to transmit to the next, that is cunning and courage, goodness, love, according to its purposes. Remember that man is pure evil, as if to balance irony, the absolute good. It depends on the circumstances, and its own evolution on the council if in opposites, and what and how it wants to be, and what you want in life. >>

<< Thou father you ever killed a man? >>

<< Yes, of course! >>

Tell me:

<< I can not tell you but I tell you I killed only traitors. But you do not tell Mom. >>
Judah learned the culture of his father who was also the Roman, that is, not to betray the traitors are killed. He absorbed everything that he could absorb from his wise father. Finally, believing that his father was a Divine being, asked him:

<< Father, you are the man superior to the world? -

Simon answered

- No! I believe that each and superior in his own way. You have to realize is who knows more of the old young. Apart from this no man I see more than me, though, remember that no one should be underestimated, especially "who" is apparently weaker. Superior to me there is only one God, the one God of my fathers, and my people. >>

Judah knew! Simon had his own strategy in life, and it was: Making sure that as a child he departed from in evolution where he "Simone" had arrived. Simone and so who worked on the personality of the child in order that he had the arrival evolutionary as its starting point. Simone was not enough he wanted, scholar and capable in everything, learn everything and enjoy what life had to offer him. He had to reconcile all things in himself, and this was a goal that he knew how to reach his son.

<< There are few beliefs, few ideals, or a few truths. There are millions, you have to believe in everything, and if you can prevail over everything, always believe basically only to yourself; in the end you have to be ready to believe in nothing, just so you can always make it, adapt and stay one step ahead of others. The What scares you in life, one has to face, fear serves but only if you have the courage to face it or go around it. - He said definitely to Judas.

Judah One day he asked:

- What is the absolute evil? -

He replied:

- The absolute evil is what they think they own the magicians, and give to those who believe they want. They think that it is so many men, even if they are not magicians. Even those who say that it has to do with the angels of evil, those who are convinced that he had given his soul to the devil, and believe they are well-liked of evil, this is the MALE Absolute. Therefore, you must know that the devil is every man. And 'well as the absolute evil, the one who knows how to present themselves before sending it to another man to be the devil in the flesh, is the one who owns the absolute evil, and against the men win, until they will not glimpsed a weakness. You have to be attentive to this psychological power, you do not use it against the weak and against the innocent, but only against those who believe they are superior to you, only with stronger you have to use this power, the day that you use it with the most weak, or against those you love, you autodistruggerai, you know why? -

Judah after hearing the good of wisdom thread executed by the Father asked:

- Why dad? -

Simon answered:

- Because GOD IS for real. He sees you, and if it intervenes, destroys your soul into this body alive, and nothing remains that the death of the body as punishing completion of the work of God. You have to reconcile the good and bad that life unfortunately brings to face and understand and by means of these two opposing forces have to live. So know that God and above all of us, so you always have to use common sense and justice that is within your mind, and you constantly speaks from the heart. -
The first maximum, the top tips, the first principles to be followed always, even unto the end of days, Judah learned them from his Father. Simone made him realize the God of his fathers and his descendants. Simon taught him well that:

<< No man is above you and no one can be as long as you do not underestimate anyone. Only I who am your father are greater than you, and no one else is superior to you than God, which is above me. Then you're the top in the world. When I die then, you'll be top of the world no man will be greater than you only God. >>

That his father taught him to Judas. Simone these values to Judas TEACH 'to preserve them in her heart like a treasure. Thus he grew up respecting always his ideal which was to: Give all of himself to the culture THE SUPER IO, that "this" Finally, it was the traditional Roman imperial ideology. So Judah became an admirer and good devotee of his father, and a servant and admirer of the God of Abraham, and at the same time continued the psychological road, which for some time had undertaken that led him to become (or to believe that, if we say), a demigod number oNE in the world. The personality and

142

ideology of his father came up to the soul; all that mattered as a philosophy of life, he had received from Simon, his father. The Simon's love, his consideration, protected him and was becoming stronger and stronger, more and more skilled, and more and more good in studies. Even in social behavior, it was admirable as it maneuvered and how seriously it was taken into consideration by the next. JUDAS understood that only God was above him, GOD After his father was superior to him, and no man could be superior to him. He became cunning in the arts, dialect, and could recite every part in any circumstances and in any environment, better than a great actor. It fit everything, understood everything, and as a divine gift, he could understand others in their deepest feelings. Judah had become perfect, in the civil dimension, a supernatural being. Judah did every kind of experience, in the house of his father had a great education and a great culture. He also learned the arts of Eastern mysticism, relaxation concentration, reflection, nothing left behind, he wanted to know everything and everything is left to drag until he understood. For this, even more followed the teachings of his father and told him what the God of Abraham, and pondered on this question, more than we can imagine and more than we can write. He Did Judas of age and had a personality, with a personal code on the world and on himself, based on his father's teachings, and the lessons he had drawn from outside the walls of his house. Its code was simple. You stay with your people. No man can be superior to me, until I do not underestimate anyone, Above me there is only my father, and higher God. Do not blame the weak, your life until you do not have removed always have time to treat it. Do not hit a woman. Do not hit the children. Respect your elders. The best defense and the attack. Never be afraid, and always be reasonable and brave smart. This was the personal code of honor of Judah, all based on the action, and the readiness to understand the things that are around us.

For this he had learned from his father, a form of being and personality, but also from the mother he learned other values, most contrasting but equally he could not create within themselves opposing conception, but it was all knowledge is an application to life conciliatory with his whole being. The father was more action, the mother more tolerant culture; mainly devoted to the good, moral principles; Lover of respect, politeness, honesty, prayer.

sociable woman and of good cheer. Above these educational influences he also had his personal data from the environment that he frequented, and where he lived. And then there were his idea and personal view of life and how to live it. Clearly its nature, inquiring, poses two questions: one was that the teachings of his father, he had the evidence and was convinced. The other that the teachings of God, had nothing but words. So he decided to find evidence for itself. I start talking to the father of God, and wanted to know everything that was possible to know.

In the end there was evidence that the teaching learned, they could prove, the entity or feature trying to GOD. He did not give up, had the basics, and began to think and find something supernatural in the ground, dimension of good that could represent the existence and part of the character of God and His creation. JUDAS began to dig it world, in people and within themselves in order to find a proof of God Blessed entity.

Finally, after studies and meditations, as if by chance, the music, that some were listening and through this were ridiculous grimaces and strange steps from sleepwalking, he wanted to listen, but without all these idiots attitudes. He wanted to listen to it with your heart and with all your mind. Here you feel inside when a liberation, as if his psychological stage, went higher and higher through sensations. And his spiritual self expanded till it reaches the top of the universe and the sky. All this made him feel happy, and his mind, despite the action teachings received from his father, became good, smiling and it seemed that he was at peace with the world, and he wanted to love everyone. When his cosmos expanded, which he was almost afraid; is awakened by meditation, and wanted to understand with conscience, what had happened and what was all this, realism within him. Judah realized that the music, the melody was a representation of the asset, and that it was proof of God. SAID between if- "Music is a characteristic of God, comes from God, we must know how to listen and be able to understand what makes you feel the sweet harmony of our Soul." Only then everything becomes clear in the emotional and spiritual state. Judah had discovered an evolutionary stage connected to CELESTE plan. now ivy knew certain of the existence of God. the exceed His father now he had identified a feature. he was pleased and proud of himself.

JUDAS alone had come to God, now believed in GOD, AND NOT ONLY More HER FATHER, but also in God, and we had arrived alone. In fact, I wanted to keep this secret to himself and did not want to share with anyone. And so it was, never shared the secret of a character evidence discovered was that understanding, humans evolved, the existence of God. A secret that, that brought him to the grave.

PERSONALITY 'OF JUDAS -P.41

Something had happened in him at an early age, (very positive); because he believed in friendship, to the point of putting the feeling of friendship, a place forward to the feeling of the woman or au pair. Judah considered the most important friendship feeling affection for a woman. Try friendship, pain and suicide; so he felt great satisfaction and great joy to be in company with friends. something innate inside him, an element of his nature that no one and had imposed or handed down, was like that. After all, the man is social in nature. Judah seemed excessive on this side, could not get far, the friendship

145

was more and more digging and the more cultivated. He believed in friendship. The evolution of the brain of Judas is really a mystery without, measure. Judas believed in friendship more than anything else in the world. It is strange to find this quality in a man of action but understandable given its dualistic nature and open-minded. His, psychological strategy was based on to explain as little as possible of himself.

Maybe he was jealous of his great wisdom, and did not share it. Understandably, many things he had learned, but many others they had achieved alone. So this, so that others could see inside him, in a profound sense, knew the mystery. As if he had something to hide. Or as if he wanted to dominate the world around them, and did not want the world to know it was in his deepest soul in order that no one could predict how he really was or how he thought, and so so on, how could he act in various circumstances in, according to the situation that life offered him. More than a strategy was his natural being. Everything came naturally to him, he did not need to strive for nothing was quite natural and spontaneous. His unconscious was acting like it was led by an instinct under control. Judas was always ready to work even when awake. So it seemed. SO 'Despite having fellowship with his peers many sports, cultural activities, he gave no space, or not open enough to put in the condition to others will be able to understand deeply and to detect, how he thinks and what opinion he had.

Hardly, this for anyone, it was easy to know him in the true sense. It was always one step ahead of the others. Certainly the habit to have anything to do with him, and the habit to see it, to treat it, put a; condition believe that you know, but in reality it was not. Leaving a trail of something, contentment, involving all those who interacted with him. Maybe it was her smile, which was always ready to cheer up friends and the friendly acquaintances. For this, the man could think to know it, for a number of factors of his personality, but he was suddenly

146

deception that attended it, and that Judas could well show up as he was suited to the environment, which from time to such was calling him. It fits, in a really incredible way. He could change its quality instantly. It could be good, bad, all he wanted, and so perfect, and in every art go where s'immedesimava, persevere to the end. He decided, determined, a man of action. This was always an advantage for Judah, adaptability. All with the utmost naturalness, and automatically his personality fit automatically, great reciter good actor, but not false, because in every part that s'immedesimava, there goes the distance as if that part was in him and he so he was identified. We know that he was moody and a great adapter. Good and bad. He performed all over in an instant, and everything done to perfection. In order to succeed in achieving and getting what he wanted just so he could do something, good or bad that others had not reckoned. He had a special magnetism, attacking, drew people to himself. As if leaving a halo of fragrant smells behind him, strange, who was in communion with JUDAS I could smell. A particularly sweet aroma. Being the perfume, JUDAS. His strategy was to understand as much as possible the next, and not make it clear that he understood, or at least if this is not really considered it necessary, he decided whether or how to understand that he knew.

Judas was a scholar of human behavior, a scientist, if we say of thought and man in himself. He had the ability to drill down deeply into the thoughts and souls of people. Similarly one would not know: something magical, magnetic, that leaves people thinking of him, even those they had known him for a short time. Attracted, he leaves its mark, and everyone had pleasure to talk to and get to know it. Great spiritual and psychological strength, a deep magnetism that: attracted and gave pleasure to be carried away by the personality of Judah, as if it were wrapped in an aura that gave pleasure and curiosity. Judah sent the next I do not know: something magical, a force that gave him pleasure to be with him. A magic attraction.

A real mystery, to bind people to himself, and make them think like him interested. The understanding, what are the people inside until the deepest secrecy THE IO, a real mystery. However he also knew how to respect the laws of the good. His acquaintance in of itself evidence of the existence of God, put him in a position to apply a sense of justice and balance to the next, both in quality real well, both as a defense. Judah had become a man, you really had to be forced to do evil to survive or to defend themselves, or otherwise avoided any provocation. Still he possessed his father's teachings, which were the ones who ensured the survival, through the strength and cunning, and go down to the comparison with others to determine who was superior. He possessed an understanding of the reality of God, and that put him in a position to reflect on each whatever it was about to embark, for worse. Desist and gave a regulative, each time, was to do evil. He had created a code, just not having Conflict remorse and to feel good about himself and against God. However he not if ever took with the weak and hated those who picked on the most vulnerable. Good for him, to be judged man or to feel that, certainly not required to prove to others that winning blaming a weaker than him. Judas had not nearly this kind of reasoning. He put it against anyone if he wanted one thing, if he took it, both belonged to the Romans or the Jews, was to be a dangerous and monstrous, but a code was created. A code of its own. A code that called his conscience, and he to its principle and self-respect could not and should not disgrace, that was his principle, self-respect. He even allowed himself to disobey him. His conscience was him, and to this, he had to give an account, that was his principle, to account to his own conscience whether you want to be at least an existing number, or six zero. A way not to be frustrated, was to be careful not to commit injustices. Judah thought itself: Make no mistake, not to scold his own conscience. For this he had his own code of honor, of

148

life, to be respected, only he feared himself. For, you can look in the mirror without having to repress things done heedlessly for lightweight or wrong, that they would have to commit shamed in front of him. Strict with himself was Judas, alone you and He judged himself was afraid. Judas did not accept to be wrong, he thought he was perfect and did not allow himself to be wrong. And its code was to benefit if I weave and served to keep ZITTA his conscience. One of the articles said: "Do not take it with the weakest." This was an advantage to the detriment of the weak and the strong, and the people that eat the bad, maybe; What was the other written in its code, we do not know, but that's what in our survey, and psychological preparation, together, me and you, dear readers, we'll find out. His psychology did not consider this way of thinking and reasoning. If it was necessary, he was the worst evil and if it was necessary, he was the best good. It was under too menate, was a man of action, and stand against anyone. It was really scary. No one wanted to against. But to win he studied in his own way and won. In an instant he believed in everything, and at the same time did not believe in, nothing. A monstrous council of opposites, with a cold check of the outside world, and with its code ordering him to leave the weak and innocent from, and not to involve them in its covert war, silent, dark, secret. A real murderess, does the fact believed, that he should kill. A real thief said smoothly. He had no problems, looked into his eyes a person and say, "I am a thief." No problem for JUDAS. It was a merchant. He bought the goods, and not paying. He sold the merchandise withdrew the money and not delivered the goods. Irony of JUDAS personality. Faced wretched people, as if he had not done anything, it was quite normal, and those who wanted the bill, do not know how happened, but he did not count, and it gave, and those also became his friend, despite not having against. JUDAS a monstrous, a terrible man, with a courage and intelligence, supra-human, took care secrets: his person, of his ego, the world around him, a true mystery.

He could not win against JUDAS and you could not have JUDAS against. It was better to have a friend. Outside of this, Judah also had a heart. A deep sensitivity, and like any man of evil life, he felt the mood of next to skin. The sixth sense I had everything. Instinct, and immediate analysis of a situation, understanding the skin of all that a person does in the brain that is before him. Computer of each move. Provident, analyst and expert. He Did Judas wisdom as to shiver the arch-wise, the scholars of science and most learned any. Judah a man who saw over the wall, without the need to go to see. Be a deep and sensitive. And all this was composing his personality.

He looked at the world, and sees it too small under his feet, the win and the habit of winning the apportavano this understanding. For him this was not fantasy but a reality.

When a man thought to frighten him, Judas suddenly changed personality treated him like a child without problems and if daring him, escaped went to look for him to give him a lesson, true. A brave man who saw no obstacles, and even embarrassment. A true man of action, with its code ever created by him, in order to respect the laws of God, that he did not want to offend. He believed in God, because the existence of God had included alone, otherwise no one could convince him, believed in nothing in himself and in his mind. And what with certainty included existing and real, he lent FAITH.

The create a personal code, in good standing in your opinion, to comply with the laws of God, made him affable and civil devoted to well with the material representation of the same right and under different conditions of their existence, he testified all its qualities. Just to be affixed with himself and with what he believed, evidence and comprovarle himself put him in a situation of right and good council with himself.

One of these rules or articles of your code was the respect of friendship. For this he, when he was a friend, he was a true companion. Unable to offend and to make a bad part or bad action has a friend. Absolute respect for friendship. He totally changed his being and his way to be against friendship. Happily became incapable of offending, rather woe to pick on a man of whom he was a friend, if this would happen, came a bad time for wretched people, was his bread. Judah sociable, hardly refused friendship, and to those who asked, and he looked the worthy. This is why many were, happy to make friends, even for convenience. He did not evaluate the opportunism of others, did not make him weight and was not important in front of him. The friendship was sacred, in his opinion, the rest was of little relevance. He is self psicoanalizzava in order to find the improvement of his personality and character. Was judged to be only occasionally, it was a car account of his personality and behavior. In compliance with this included, where he was making some minor adjustments to your image or your people litas, and where it was just him to go in his way of being.

It was psychoanalysis that he compieva on himself, which helped him a lot in his conciliatory evolution of inner opposites. Clearly in a developmental stage, gender, we understand that to get there he had to spend several hours in deep psychoanalysis of himself. In this way you were taught and educated self, alone. He used his brain, so climb. All that was examining, was drawn up. Things that were not respectable to his belief and his interest in the winger eliminated, and adhered to only pursue what was part of its creed and its interest. Everything was, however, with respect for the family, affections, relating to the rules of his moral code of honor and which nevertheless also required, respect the surrounding environment. Similarly he protected its center, not change stability and not to offend the moral, psychic from the other. In this way he controlled the surrounding world and his very emotional. To understand that his Sacred center was well protected, if we consider that he only believed in God, in his Father in himself, it is understandable that independent proceedings. Could not the outside world to influence him to the point that he could lend it faith to the next. For this it is argued that in the end he, confided on himself. For this reason I think that he had found out, that in the final stage of sleep, the dream in conclusion subconsciously sends the data on which it was written or there was suggested, the mood or the way it should have adopted the following day in order to keep his temper in touch, or in order to find solutions to the problems of the external world within himself. Clearly to achieve this would have to be able to carry part of his unconscious to consciousness information to be able to read and interpret them so agreed. Judas probably was capable of doing this. Surely in the final stages of sleep he was receiving messages from his unconscious, he read conscientiously, that indicated the mood or behavior to be taken during the day or in the near future, or even the unconscious, the sent data that he read conscientiously but they were news or practices used to solve problems and to protect its sacred center. Right of this type justify an evolution of personality and character so superior to peers of his time. Certainly Judas obeying the final stage of sleep, where the message was interpreted as: maintain the mood for the next day, he did not enter upon any one, and his Sacred Center remained in harmony, and in the same stadium remained in its wake . Certainly it would have seemed cold and detached in front of others, but I think this is an element of his personality, just to justify his psychological autonomy and his enormous knowledge without, in part have learned any education. Judas knew the secrets of the human brain, or otherwise could not be certain, of truth, then by other discoveries over time and with the help.

THE RETURN-P.42

The day came that his father, after so many years he wanted to return to Judea. Emperor Augustus was no longer in its place was succeeded by his adopted son, TIBERIO NERONE AUGUSTO The TIBERIO NERONE whose father was with Marco Antonio, this has caused many troubles besides the loss of his wife, who was pregnant of TEBERIO, he had been taken in marriage by

CESARE AUGUSTO Ottaviano, that: these also part of GIULIA CLAUDIA family. A family of origin SABINA. However the political changes and power laid the conditions, fulfills a wish of the heart by Simone; who it was to return to earth JUDEA. THE Judea, now became a ROMANA province, and was no longer a vassal of Rome. Everything seemed the realization of a distant dream. Judas knew of Judea and Rome, He was sixteen years old when his father decided to return to Judea Romana. Of what he had been able to hear from his father and from ROMAN friends of his father who occasionally passed to visit the rich father.

For this, only he knew the land of his fathers, what Simon had told him. Had the legal age, a little more than sixteen years old when he undertook the return to Judea with his father and his mother. Judah was busy with studies and other work. He had a self-sufficient and independent life well integrated in society and in the social environment. It was a destiny, be watching the road once traveled by his father. As regards the problems of SIMONE, The time had passed. In a sense, everything seemed normal. His past was obscured, buried by time and forgetfulness. The past was left only the shadow of a now fading fast, set aside and replaced by the new times. Renovated ideologies, and new, it was. Judas did not know who was to start a new life, all over again, and that some privileges and some social gains that owned the land where he was born, in Judea was all lost, you had to start from scratch. This for him was a real surprise.

Indeed, he knew who his father was, he had heard, of his old friends and starters. He thought that he had received a good reception, he thought that the prestige and respect for his father, had not been lost by his acquaintances and his relatives. He believed that arrive in JUDEA meant it was in a second home, and everything was the same socially and social status as his homeland, the East. Unfortunately, he had a surprise not very good. Old friends of his father, had died a few others, who also had been in the East in the JUDAS home, they pretended not to understand. The relatives then seemed almost annoyed by SIMONE old grudges still not completely healed. So Judas had to rebuild his life from scratch, and in the same way he had to be near the old SIMONE also protect the mother.

NEW HOMELAND - P. 43

Definitely come back to his country, it was all a start over again, this is normal for some men and some families. For JUDAS family was different, they were not emigrants in search of life and fortune, as happened then. They were members has an environment and has a high middle-class society, fell into their land and nothing else for Judas was not the most social ascent, now began the descent, both in the environmental field and in the social. There, in the East it was rich and respected, here suddenly became poor and had to work and work hard to live, a great humiliation for a man of his talent and of his reach. The descent, led him in the environment of the poor and of those who were busy to just survive, which was inserted JESUS '. Judah began the descent, where he met the Son of God.

For Judah, I start again placed him in a position to meet with some poor, even sympathetic. Those who have no malice, and are simple and fearing evil. Although this was a new phase of his life, and everything was experience. Thinking Com'era in its conception: everything goes to school and experience.
Until being logically Romano, the doors opened, slowly, slowly in the meantime, life as it should be had to continue. Have it all, stay well and a blow not to have anything for those who have never worked to begin is fatigue. And during the time between the open social doors, make order and return to have that place in society that it should for reasons of chaste, it takes time. Judah had to order, had a long way to go. Some old relative of Simone, looking for something to do to help him to the family. Matter of habit. Meanwhile, the relatives had found a home for them. Certainly a house comfortable, not the usual

luxury you had, but you had to adapt.

Judah was raised in a different culture, now he had to face a new world, with a different taste, a way of thinking to be discovered, a new culture, which he knew only from what his father had told him, but not so direct. For him it was all new. The start over in order to make their lives, randomly but almost obligatory must have had contact or meetings, or new knowledge of the environment of the poor, or those belonging to a social class inferior to hers, with a way of thinking and conceive life, unlike what he had been accustomed. Everything in front of his eyes seemed to be apparently lower than his.

JUDAS START WORK-P.44

Once he worked for the pleasure. Now he had to work for a living. He served working, now is very easy, even if it is bitter to those who were at the top being down, having to support their needs with a job not suited to the social status of belonging, to its evolution, it is not for nothing easy digestion. His personality will fit even the humble things. He knew by his own strength, climb the steps to bad luck had fallen. Hard worker, ability to always exceed the competitors had to do more and more, never wanted others to see that he had done less than another. More and more. From humble things at least, graceful him, it was to be the first. If one began to work in the morning, he had to start earlier. If the end of the work was in the evening, he had to stay until sunset. Incredible, but he always had to give more than others, a way to meet the teaching, and always prove to be in first place. This allowed him to climb and be considered very good and talented. A good name is a great Judgment and the community had for him. They made a reputable name with their own hands and their own intellectual nature. In less time than when a normal man he used to climb the stairs, and had become a character. Pleasing, considering Estimated.

When things seem to be affixed and all was well; was seized by misfortune, he is missing the FATHER.

Blow to JUDAH. Huge blow. He does not go to work, and he begins a life of gimmicks and the scope of its deepest understanding, to the meaning of life. A crisis that puts a strain. Judah no longer values life, and in it he sees only the dark sides. Starts to not believe in anything, and sinks into a pessimism that allows him to fail, respect the lives of others and of his. The sense, the reason for achieving a place in the sun, is not there and it loses value. See the dark world, in the end fails to social rules, respect for others and to himself. Start the journey of the deepest evil, where the man is the only guilty of being in the world to suffer and to suffer. Judah lost satisfaction, he begins to mature the idea that, even if, dies okay. On this way of thinking considers his life almost nothing, and the next less than his. Why risk their lives in all circumstances, he does not care if he dies. Eventually she decides to go against death and to end it.

After you think about this hypothesis, it realizes that there is still a feeling that keeps him in the world, and that of His Mother, this feeling him away from the macabre design. In the end the idea matures, under emotional advice, which leads me to seriously consider the possibility of returning to his native land, and leave all this pain and this disappointment behind. And 'tired, very experienced, although no work and lives by his wits. From morning to night after much consideration at all, and most of all his greatest feeling, that has vanished overnight. All these thoughts the hammer and tired. Tired and depressed. More tired, and less it seems that this macabre psychological work wants to change course. His thoughts, his emotional injury puts him to the test, you have more energy, get tired alone, and can not help anyone. Always tired and increasingly weary, from morning to night, again automatically, his brain still worked there, beating the same nail. Does not he leave her alone, she could not, and there was the most to suffer, Judah, get help, or else sinks into anguish that leaves no way out and you do not even know how to be ending. In a hint of glimmer he thinks about his spiritual teacher in China, and sighing understands that it is his lifeline, decides to return, only he can ease his heart and his suffering, and free him from the anguish chronic. The mother is with him, although painful for her to leave the place where he buried his great love, care and considers it its duty to think of her only son. Judah begins to make preparation and now is close to departure. A couple of days before he left, at night Mother, tired and proven, dies. Too much pain, too much despair, his heart gave out. JUDAS has a deadly trauma. Just like it was planned, can do only funeral for the mother, then after this, his anguished state now irrecoverable, makes him mature the final decision of his life. Now nothing holds it to the world. He decided to leave the life and let go. Judah is so vague that losing all respect and all consideration of himself. Living does not care anymore. When it has hit bottom, and holds only a thread of light, he decides to let die.

MEETING JUDAS AND JESUS-P.46

Imagine a man of action, who lives to win. Aware that a part of its evolution was connected to the plan of God, but we do not yet understand the deeper reasons, and who has one point in his life decides to back down and abandon all that he built, for reason of an emotional crisis of enormous thickness. The encounter with Jesus', comes at a time, that JUDAS requires a psychological stimulus, in order to divert his deep wound, and be saved from himself. He wanders the streets of the town aimlessly, thinking how out of the way and be done. While vague: He sees a man surrounded by some people. He does not care at all, but the situation and placed in its path. - A man, it is impossible to see, in his East from where he came, and even in the same JUDEA. A guy like JESUS 'not easy to meet; just for its expansiveness and His way of relating with others, serenity and tranquility that was conveyed to the people of great depth. JESUS 'put peace in the minds of men, gave peace in the minds and eased the pain to the next. It has an approach towards our neighbors, friends or strangers who are indistinctly, tender with enthusiasm, and with a touch of melodic harmony with his words and with his smile sends into the souls and safety, strength, PEACE . All those who meet him, are all pleased; as if by magic those penalties in the heart receives benefit. JESUS 'and with open arms to the crowd and smiles of joy and love. The people ask him:

<< Who are you now therefore, that with one glance and smile, students hearts and make us feel so much joy, happiness and peace? -

Jesus' answer:

- I AM THE LOVE. >>

In saying this looks at them with gentle eyes and a tender smile. And d they derive benefit. JUDAS, sees him, and a shiver catches him and fills him with new and old emotions that he was convinced that death and never would have been able to try. Hear this melody, that JESUS 'with his sweet words, his smile, his enthusiasm and his joy transmit to others, and it also receives Him emotions, that binds to the same, she felt when the musical melody I had connected the Divine plan and had made him discover, one of the characteristics of the entity from God.

He feels within himself a force that relieves deep pain. An effect that Judah needed it received from Jesus', a stranger to him until now. Attracted by this, he approaches to look on his face and in his eyes this divinity, in your opinion. When it is in front, he receives an effect similar to a stun Thunder: A blow that he would not have expected, ever, ever. A blow that rejoiced the souls and eased the terrible sufferings of his soul. Judah suddenly felt free from pain, as if by miracle, a negative energy within his soul would go out and freed him. He collides with the face and eyes of Jesus'. And 'it pervaded by a stun feeling that cancels every thought and fills my heart with joy. It begins like, hand to smile and his eyes become smaller, and begins to cry. Tears flow from his eyes and down his face, he can not stop them, they are not under its control. He let go; He continues to smile and cry of joy and happiness. And his heart is like magic freed from the pain and the anguish his mind. JESUS 'sees Crying, feels inside this strange deep pain, understands that it is pervaded by deep anxiety. Pity, he rests his hand on her shoulder Judah; He says with words from his sweet and affectionate:

<< Why are you crying my brother? Do not worry that everything Adjust. -

As if he knew your drama.
JUDAS, looks up looks him right in the face, his heart and relieves the comfort of love received and moves him, starts to romp freely crying all her pain. He was freed from a terrible knot in my stomach. Then he answers:

- I do not know, but I'm happy. -

Then he asks Judas:

- Who are you ? -

Jesus' answer:

- I am Your Brother Jesus, I love you, do not cry anymore. -

JUDAS, knows he is alone in the world; being called brother in a painful moment of his life; is a blessing that makes him touch the sky. This statement saves; feels the Love of JESUS 'that enters the heart; with a sweet smile responds:

–   Not after all he is happy; I met you, BROTHER, my soul is freed from pain and my heart is filled with joy. -

It was the first time that Judas called his brother a man perhaps; a word "strong" however, he felt alone in the world at that time but now it was no longer alone. JESUS 'replies:

- I too am happy to meet you. -

Judah looks at him in the face and smiles. It understands that Jesus' loved him even before I met him, he
 has always loved and was waiting for him. JUDAS stares into his eyes and realizes that the love of Jesus is deep, genuine. spontaneous; with all his heart, he embraces him as if in front of him had his loved ones, and whispers:

- Thank you. >>

Then, he greets smiling serenely, and heads home, with a light heart and an open mind.

THE ATTENTION TO JESUS-P.47

JUDAS, now feels that his life has a feeling and to be continued sees why! Inside his soul, and feel a fatal attraction for Jesus', requires "why", to see him every day, to be with Him and partake of his affection, and therefore also to deepen knowledge that gives the chance to climb a new degree in evolution. An essential comfort to exceed an actual lack of enormous importance, this is initially Jesus, then it becomes something even more important.

Most likely Judas reflects a lot on the account of Jesus and how man is his custom during the night, that man deeply navigating with the mind for more understanding, and thus probably in the days that followed after the friendship made with the Son of God Judah he thinks careful with His Brother "though spiritual but at the same time deep affection" JESUS '. So now it is no longer alone in facing himself and his life in his emotional solitude, but in something to believe in, that is, a feeling, that besides being this gives him the incentive to proceed life in a new dimension. Judah so it toward Jesus directs his thoughts, his thoughts, all his arguments, he focuses on the personality of Jesus in an almost automatic instinctive way, no longer subject to his will and his will, and that with time it is praise that happens.

Judas probably was believed top of the world. This is because his father was not there in life, and he had held the post. Only God believed to be superior to him, as only the Eternal Father was greater than his father Simon when he was still alive. So he asked: "Who is this man?" A question within himself, because it is this man who is able to deal with it psychologically and deeply and to give him the intellectual satisfaction that a certain intelligent, (this thing usual and for anyone human being), then for him as a man requires in order to feel satisfied and saturates the mind and even his person. So all could expect but not a person as Jesus was seen, could be just WHO would put him in a situation of intellectual satisfaction and to give him satisfactory psychological stimuli. He understands Jesus not as man is superior to him, but as a spirit, or rather intellect. Judah is clear then that there is something in Jesus' mysterious, something associated intelligent evolution of man, and this independently from the street and raised, puts him in a position to communicate and understand each other with our neighbor even if he does not It has the same culture and experience. Judah noted that strength, and that strength becomes within the Messiah who is able to embarrass the evolution of Judah in the intelligence that attracts Judas as a calamity, and at the same time gives the stimulus and satisfaction of interacting with this, new "Man" that is Jesus, whom he had never known of similar character invoice. Jesus from the teachings in the deep reasoning and all that appears mystical and spiritual, that Judas is astonished, because some things, he knew very well that you learn in life only if you follow some type of evolutionary path, a path that Jesus could not go. So Judah sensed almost immediately a profound evolution of the Messiah. He notes that the Master has a shocking spiritual sensitivity, and receives a warm feeling from this man that leaves him stunned and at the same time helps him in his pain and makes it grow differently, better. Judah becomes sincere and clean feeling friend, and Jesus accepts it as such, because it does not affect the intellectual personality of the Messiah, with its attitudes super man. Jesus therefore beyond the love that is has a deep culture of man, which is associated to the spiritual evolution own whenever he needs to communicate. All that His being is basically the same His creation, His creation this gives him a moral depth that makes The understanding of the next penis and puts it in a position to understand what people feel the suffering, and thus unable to communicate by helping and comforting the grieving people. His being puts him in a position to rationally analyze the life of his neighbor with all its tragic misfortunes. Analysis same as that shocked Judah, but not only in the spiritual dimension Jesus does this, but also in the material and practical dimension. Judas includes this being of Jesus and his esteem grows so deep, considering it a distinguished man, not conforming to the mass, intelligent. This was bread for Judah, that He rewards for intellectual needed to meet people of the Messiah measure. Judah at some point is mathematical thinking within themselves and DEMAND: This man how can have this kind of spirituality? It has so much love, and at the same time is analytical, practical; He is able to understand things that are usually only understood through the study or to a certain type of experience. Who is this man?

He asks again: Jesus can not having learned some notions of life, in this environment in which he lives, the spiritual knowledge, of creation, of the values of solidarity and brotherhood here in this Roman province, are destroyed from ancient times, in this place harbored materialism, pleasure and devotion to the immediate and instant satisfaction. Here in every mind of every man there is evil, there is no spirituality and no human value, because here everyone thinks to himself and to his own selfishness, how can this man possess values that no one has made up his mind? How can continue to live on a way and such an environment?

Who taught These Things? He is poor, education is the only the rich   have.   Who   is   it? Therefore, in the opinion of Judah, in reflection to the spirituality of Jesus, and his experience, this is a spirituality That can only receive and learn in the East and not quite so easy, and probably Judas car convinces, or has reason to to That think even in the East would sono stati easy for poor to receive education or learning an evolution similar to That glimpse manifest itself in the personality of the Messiah. this acute observation That leads him to want to know more about the account of Jesus', and blackberries Thus to study it deeply, up to bond emotionally and become just an NSAID of the Messiah. And this thing is really strange, it's almost impossible to believe That he could possibly happen to one like Judas, but definitely know happened, become a follower of a man, even though   he   was   the   Son   of   God.

A HAND LEADS THE DIVINE FRIENDSHIP BETWEEN SENTIMENTAL JESUS 'AND JUDAH, THERE IS NO OTHER EXPLANATION'! P.48

And he realizes it to be taken on the personality of the Messiah, and, Receives in himself all the emotions of the good, and happiness That JESUS 'the emanated at that time and, immediately associates; That His ecstatic experience he had time to back When He Recognized the musical melody, the celestial plane connected to the well and to God. All this is related to love, is created in the plane Celeste from God. God through music conveys the good and love and even blackberries. All this was felt in the soul of this cute, smiling and joyful character named Jesus That he did not know well, but he felt magically inside her like BE coming from Paradise. That Paradise That Jesus, being in communion with him, morally transmitted, and why He came from that place and to receive These emotions, you had to have Achieved a certain evolution on earth. Judas had! JESUS 'broadcast in the soul, to all Those Who Through Their sensitivity and Their evolution, they had come to the point in evolution Which places them in a position to receive all its light. His joy His happiness, and emotions were so strong, as to receive a celestial melody, but That only sensitive men and deep in Their perceived spirituality. Judah a shot feels disarmed by all its aggression, by all its force, from all its impetus, and no longer feels the pain inside him. The Same Thing That happened one time long gone in His land. He Recalls. A man of action who instantly Becomes happy and good as an angel, and in His heart feel relieve pain from taste of death: appreciate this miracle for the rest of His days. Judah Became a liberation from suffering, Became smiling. He smiled, and it Seemed That he could not stop His emotional desire to rise up and get rid of a burden through the smile of joy and comfort. Within himself he felt only joy and happiness. He smiles with pleasure and cries for the first time in His life, crying freed from Their penis. What strange miracle sent him this man; good from happy and smiling and joyous gaze called JESUS '. Suddenly, as if by instinct, it includes; here is the reason why His father took him to JUDEA. He thought he would not come to Judea without a Divine right, but now Understands That Necessarily Celeste as if to tell him. Judah had just as in JUDEA, was God. Who had guided him in His footsteps. Everything Became understandable in front of His Eyes. It Includes Because, to continue living. Now he start to think; despite All These and pervaded by emotions, he puts His deep intelligence to understand and to understand who this be

Divine; as it Has Been born on this earth bad something so beautiful? He includes in totality. Almost feel the fear That he might disappear at any moment and never see him again, and Began to tremble beneath this feeling. He did not take her eyes off him with His thoughts; and he Began to watch him and try him with all His imagination and his mind; and ask: where and in what ways review it and meet him.

He wanted to keep up at all costs closely, and wanted to see it, understand it without manifesting his enthusiasm either from him or even with the 'other, this thought. I want to know him as a man. Judah is stunned by the person of Jesus'. And continuing to pour him reasonings and thoughts, suddenly he feels within himself that: his fate was tied to this man and his departure is clear from Asian lands, and understands the reasons. It includes also the reason that it is so endowed with intelligence. Think. This has only been a chance meeting by fate, but driven by the Divine Hand.

He thinks, and is taken by all sorts of thoughts and reasoning about the Messiah, and all his mental energy as if by magic, and unconsciously turned to the MESSIAH all night and for many nights.

IN BRACKETS - P. 49

CAN we do not believe that Jesus has to tell a guy like Judah: I am the Son of God recognize me, and you stop azzannarti with men like dogs, and follow me, and you will save his life in the highest. It would be idiotic to believe that Jesus could have done this, just with Judas then. We may believe that it is Judas who confess Jesus to be the Son of God, this is logical, because no man on earth can be the intellectual dimension of Judah, it is the only one who has dealings, it is Jesus, but because it is right the Son of God, otherwise he could not even discuss with Judah, and Judah knows this truth, because it knows itself, he knows to be the number one in the world! No man on this earth can be smart like Judas, no one! So it's idiotic to think that Judas see the Messiah do a miracle and believe for just this reason that lies in front of the Son of God. Judas recognizes the Son of God in Jesus, even for those values that are within the spirit of Jesus , and for other things that we do not know, and perhaps also for the love and the feeling of friendship that develops between the two magically.

JUDAS IS BETTER-P.50

Judah, after the experience with JESUS ', he feels better her brain reacts abruptly. In the following days will start a new life for him. JESUS 'is stronger and safer than before. JESUS 'has made one of his Miracles, now Judah, may return to live and to progress. Back to work. It resumes its usual activities from the point where, by accident had had to suspend; with more force than before more courage and will. Return to review friends and acquaintances, and life begins again and he smiled, find new satisfaction for it.

In his heart harbors a desire to meet again with the man whose affection he still feels in his heart; know, deeply, the human personality that has given HOPE, became his main focus.

TIES REQUIRED OF DESTINY-P.51

For a reason or for a number of circumstances the two meet. As he had planned, carefully and tactfully he starts to make friends with his friend desired. They meet again in a place of work was just one thing desired by the sky, their becoming friends and know each other and floating in an environment of this kind rather than in another environment. They both do the same job, carpenters and wood for buildings. They recognize and greet with joy and affection. From this situation arises a new way to get to know, a mutual sympathy that both are likely to make it become a good friendship. From here the confidential situation, which ultimately prepares the way for a long evolution for Judah in the field Spiritual and JESUS 'in an economical work.

JESUS 'makes his knowledge, in a superficial form from his point of view, a case of fortuitous knowledge like so many others, but it is stimulated by the enthusiasm, respect and education that this man manifested towards him. Participates with commitment to the communicative confidence and interacts with more pleasure. The friendship becomes more and more beautiful and profound. JUDAS has only JESUS 'as affection and cultivates it with all his heart and his esteem. JESUS'. It has many affections, but by nature he cultivates them all without neglecting anyone. With the succession of more time in that place of work they speak and discuss, confidentially each reveals about himself and his stories. Jude tells her, she came from, and JESUS ', tells her. The naturalness of their interact portends a long and lasting friendship, full of deep affection. Judah feels affection and sense feelings against Jesus', in his heart is His Brother. He does not see a friend but a brother, a gift from God. Although dominates this enthusiasm and happiness in his heart, not to be seen too exuberant, JUDAS has feelings of this quality against JESUS '. The two spiritual brothers begin to see each other in different places of work, and even in a place where both year friends and acquaintances. JUDAS realizes that there is someone who wants to take His Brother game, but can not react, does not want Jesus', see something in him of not really very good and they want to impress, but throws one of those glances to shake and not being able to sleep for a night on the ground. JUDAS includes fine and delicate spirit of Jesus 'and does not want to ever see in action, for any reason want to upset him: friendship with Jesus' Sacred and is willed by God. In your opinion; "This is a feeling given to me by God and I have to take care of it, it does not need to see me in action." Judas calculates every move he does or should be implemented in the face of Jesus', He is the one and only family. By sentiment, Judas, unable to open up and give more confidence, putting him at ease and making sure that would open deep, too. Understands that Jesus', has evolved impressively Spiritual, he makes even cringe its masters of the Middle East. Understands that the environment in which it interacts JESUS ', is mediocre and profitable, and he can not have learned all these developments only by means of Celeste Floor: directly from God. How are the people, different, which is in communion and friendship; that JESUS 'is Divine, bestow something to the neighbor who know, love and mercy. Judah also covers a sad side of the world, that part composed of men who notched JESUS '. That decomposed side that is within man that makes fun of JESUS '. Regrets when he thinks that some, are perfidious, that behind the back cover of the image and its person of ridiculous, but does not feel they do not matter he is quiet can put them affixed whenever he wants. Although this does not like much, but it can not help it, he regretted it, understands that as we proceed, it would have ruined, and he can not stand with your hands when HAND see that your brother is corrupt acts in the dark and hidden without anyone knowing, he wants to protect it at any cost. Understands that it is surrounded by good friends, and even from false knowledge, and behind his back is dissociated from him. It seemed that she was convinced car to listen and to be near him, just because they knew him, and out of curiosity. Them uniformly shallow as to point to the next, and at the same time makes you believe in JESUS 'to be an interesting person, after which he was ridiculed behind his back and left alone. JUDAS understood all this, and judged this to some friends and acquaintances, coward, devoid of feeling, and honesty. However, do not consider them much knows that Jesus' side by if he has nothing to fear. He admires JESUS ', which, while reading in the heart of them, pretends not to notice, respect them and for all test the same estimate. JUDAS listen JESUS '. He talks about the good and all the Divine values associated with the item. JESUS 'does not say and does not claim to be the Son of God, even though with his talk revolves around us. JUDAS understands that it is not all that, however, says that Jesus' true and there is something that does not complete the speech. In your opinion missing something, there must be something over in this man; but he does not open and does not say. JESUS 'Anyway uses discretion and the defendant is not revealed; It is surrounded by beautiful and good people, and not only from those hypocritical.

Many are with him, and they come to him attracted by curiosity, and will remain so taken and fascinated when they return from him, and call him MAESTRO. JESUS 'knows how to use the right fit both with words and with the speeches, eventually let them in-concluded and causes them to decay, in order to be able to understand that everything is superficial, and there is no other. Judah knows that is not so, there's more to his opinion, but does not know what. Remain infinite or not finished speeches that eventually leave the void, though, represent great spiritual depth and attract interest and curiosity. JUDAS understands that its power to heal, is not fully represented by his speeches, there is something that Jesus' has to say but it is not yet time to do so. Think: JESUS 'This creates a balance between the opinions of others and its half to say, in order to be able to return psychologically, in perfect communion with others and with them not tilt relationships of communion. Does not want to create misunderstandings and conflicts in the social may remove the possibility of whether to participate with others and through others to the game of life and thus to sustain itself. JUDAS includes this farsighted way of acting Jesus', and evaluates it diligently. He understands that he is not only intelligent but also a smart computer, knowledge of the brain and human thought and acts intelligently. What's not usual, and as it is mysterious, because JESUS 'had not studied like him, and had not walked the path of wisdom as the path he had. This left Jude marveled. Had evidence that the formation of knowledge, wisdom, culture personalities. Etc. Etc. ... ... Do not depend only on the environment and the human study, but also depended from their thoughts, and their way of thinking, of understanding life and to reason. He believed that this was only an exclusive of her personal dowry and had not yet experienced that others could have achieved this evolutionary stage. Instead he understood that another man on earth, he knew what he knew, and it is real that humans can evolve and learn even if nothing is taught, using only his mind. From hand to hand he began to learn about family environment, work environment, and social development of the SON of GOD, and he pulled the evolutionary sums, and its spiritual evolution surpluses resulting from itself without any influence and teaching environment. Judah does all this work ignorant of all, it was just his being that was expressed and opened with himself. Judas reflected on the environment, where Jesus' grew. It understands that families are living the spirituality and mysticism, but it seems that it is not as profound evolution in it to justify the immense spirituality that transmits Jesus'. His ideas are always addressed to God, which he achieved through the evolution in CHINA has recognized identity. JUDAS understands and sure in JESUS 'there lurks an important truth, which is yet to be discovered, and wants to go all the way. Love for Him who always leads them to see in a deeper way into the personality of His Brother. Always listen carefully the speeches that make Jesus. He sees realism and rationality; He is thinking only about people of a certain culture and a certain kind of evolution. He ASKS many things: How does My Brother to talk about these things they can know them only those who have studied and those coming from a different background? He is a poor man, and I know for a fact that it is an inferior way my father taught me, that he was the top man in the world, who is it? Where is he from? JESUS 'knows things they know my teachers. My teachers are the only "in this world" can understand. He is a poor education and culture was denied, where he learned? Who is Jesus'?

Questions unanswered, but that required a careful study of the figure, the personality of Jesus. So Judas know that His Brother "spiritual like himself in the intellect" is the evolution of this dimension makes me proud and happy.

E 'proud that his brother "spiritual" is number one at that time. Jesus was a superior being in his opinion. For Judah have discovered Jesus, that looks like a casual acquaintance, and instead DESIRED from the Divine plan, it makes him feel happy and proud of his intelligence. In fact Judas, like Jesus, had an intelligence researcher, great, I could not to touch the ground, in the sense that He lived in contact with Jesus in psychological intimacy, true, pure, real, and that no another had this confidence but himself with the Messiah, it is this realism that makes him feel proud and suggests to understand the Divine reasons for its evolution. So Judas is increasingly amazed by the personality of the Messiah, thinking and reasoning all the time, and in the end you feel tired and confused. Watch and observe his Master and always the same question arises: How can? I see that Jesus is a man of poor and working people, I have known many, but why he thinks differently than how he lived? Where did he learn?

Judah began to study more and Jesus again, one day after the other is always in a deeper way, it is more I studied, the more it binds affection. It examines the childhood of Jesus', and includes many things including the Messiah, that; Jesus certainly suffered a lot, and suffered many privations. He wants to know him all the way. Judah want to see clearly about Jesus, and curiosity drags him to want to always include your new feeling and more of the time; He decides to be told how he spent the Childhood, the Son of God.

JESUS 'TELLS HIS CHILDHOOD -P.52

A troubled childhood, immersed in poverty and indifference, social. Devoted to his work and thought. Jude takes their sums and the result is always the same. He could evolve up to this point there is something wrong in his heart. JUDAS asked JESUS ':

<< You, as the fact to overcome deprivation, humiliation, social

171

isolation, poverty, certainly you have been injured several times in the soul, so how did you overcome and to win it all? -

JESUS 'looks at him with a smile then answers, but asking a question.

- Do you know how it overcomes evil? Do you know how to overcome the pain of the soul? -

- No! Tell me! -

AND JESUS 'replies:
–   The evil is overcome with a smile of joy, just so evil disappears and becomes smaller and smaller. -

- A yes! - Exclaims Judas, then continues - I have always known that the best defense is a good offense, but a man who has suffered and the wounded soul from where fishing the smile of joy and want to laugh? >>

Churches still Judah. And now and then he thinks to himself: The poor always have taken to the heel and sent down from the understanding of this and be demolished reason and psychology, as did Will have "Jesus" to overcome the evil of his own people? What evil is not considered because it intertwined with the feelings of friendship and family and which has always MALE? Little is also self countered. Mystery! And while he thinks, Jesus', he replied:

<< In his heart and in his mind reaches the strength to defend themselves from evil. The man just has to want it and listen to the music they love within our Spirit. Singing and melody heal the pain of the spirit. -

The music! This was to Judah, a chilling response, and at the same time the key to the mystery. Think: << The music and the

172

kind of melody that gives these vibrations, healing of the soul, and that they raise the mind up to the top of serenity and peace by putting the man in communion with creation and emotions of good, They exist only in the East, where he fishing this knowledge? Here are men devoted to pleasure and war. >> Judas, then asked again.

- How does the music you listen to? I want to hear only the melody. >>

AND JESUS 'sings with his voice no words but a sound, a melody, which transmits peace and serenity and elevates the spirit to the heavens.

MAYBE: P. 53

A melody of the symphony type. Men who still do not know, but will find out after thousands of years. Therefore JESUS 'already knew the melody that represented the good, the mosaic opera and symphony! Only this tune is good. But also the eastern melody is good. But Jesus is not the east. However, Jesus has the melody despite not having studied music, even not having studied anything because you, poor is not allowed to study, only the rich and the children of the rich. Only to them it is building a brain mass.

Judah is under emotional trauma. So Judas is one of the first men in the world who heard the melody of classical music. And this was Jesus' to make him listen not with tools but with his voice. Judah still dominates his emotions, and asked again:

<< Where did you reach this melody? -

- From God. >>

Jesus answered, '.

A melody that is not similar to his but that he recognizes the joyful harmony, and it is amazed. Judah begins to make its analysis. The evolutionary path that made him as can donated this depth, which draws on another street that I know well, that the spirit in communion with the universal love, there in heaven where everything you can only love. Judah comes a point of fixation and think JESUS 'that, there, has constantly before my eyes it also smells OF IO. Jesus on the other hand does not consider the interest Judah He is instinctive and full of himself. He wants others to understand and to study, is part of his being, a way of expression of His character and his personality. Judah also includes this character quality, and admires him because Judas knows that wanting to study others could also mean a way to do harm. Judah still spurs the situation, I attended because it is impressed and wants to fully understand how Jesus thinks and how he obtained his knowledge. Judah knows manifest with good manners and great ways he is an educated and good manners does not lack, and start on this basis to get involved in the way of the Son of God and Jesus in a cartel INVOLVE friendly and deeper psychological. With this fold mystical and spiritual.

Between the two there arose a profound esteem. A born feeling not only moral obligations, but also for reasons of intellect and human values. Solidarity of both did grow their esteem, and their arguments were always more constructive. The admiration between the two friends led them to a deep respect and mutual trust.
This gave birth to their collaboration in them an insoluble affection, from this came a venerated joy, and a respect for life and all creation. They shared a feeling of friendship become pure because their minds had purified him. Their emotional dimension, which to us still too human beings, is probably unknown. Together they have a deep pleasure to discuss, their

intelligence binds them together and to be together with respect and pride. The communion is indispensable for high-level intellectual happiness that is achieved and lived by the meeting and the merger of two top minds! So Judah and his brain is stimulated by living stimuli can no longer hold back must continue this evolutionary study that allows him to understand a new dimension of evolution. What it is where you least expect it, from "God" directly. Therefore JESUS " does not reveal his secret, otherwise everything would fall in front of a personality that thrives on stimulation and get bored easily, Judas there has to arrive alone to the truth, and the only way Jesus is believed to be the Son of God. However JESUS 'does not reveal its a priori entity and not even consider this realism of the brain of Judah. The Messiah is and remains sealed within him, without having it decided by strategy, but only because it is instinctive. But Judas as the days passed he realizes that there is something that does not come from the heart of the Son of God, and understands that the situation of the fellowship is not complete, this makes me even more to study and to want to understand the Master. So Judah over time increases the observation, dedication and commitment, in keeping alive and continuously, the friendship (watering the potted grow gracefully and education an attractive ratio of two superior brains), he arrives at a saturated information point of Jesus'. Then gently pull back from time to time to reflect and why he does not want to push harder the ride, in his opinion, he has enough information that we can arrive alone to the truth and to understand what is hidden secretly in the soul of JESUS '. What mystery encloses this man? A question that had to answer. At some point it would seem that they had nothing more to be discovered and to say to each other. Judah understands and avoids blocking, begins to talk about his evolution, and of his being, changing the subject. Though unusual given his character, but he wants to finish his research work, and he wants Jesus' somehow remains stuck to his person and so understands who he is and you get an idea and also have interest in him that this is ultimately more that binds two people in the esteem and affection. Judas includes a flight as a must do to adapt Jesus and how to be accepted by Jesus and how he should behave in order to avoid shocks and not to lose his friendship. It understands that the very mention of violence would provoke something in Jesus that he would turn away from him, therefore, avoids to speak and to reveal that part of him that is evil, and that it does, although it is necessary to live. For this reason, he balances his confidences. Understands that to be good-natured that he (Master) is, he would not be near him if he would tell everything about himself. At this point tells things half, or told in an engaging and fun way, they seem to be more fantasy than realism, but surely to raise his ego and make it clear that he is a man of great knowledge and culture tells of his studies and the arts (sports) where he has triumphed. Unfortunately Judah is limited to open because the distrust of Jesus (God The man bumps into violence and aggression) puts it in a position to reflect in every gesture and every word. So hand in hand also in their personality differences, both get used to being together, attracted by the knowledge, wisdom and mystical by similar way to identify life and its mysteries with the same judgment. What amazing and Divine in the opinion of Judah because despite not having the same culture and the same personality, sees things similarly and equally judge the mysteries of life. So even though they have little in common temperamentally speaking, therefore, have little to talk about, a mystery of evolution of the brain arrival, binds them. One arrived, where he arrived the other, although by different routes.

Of this notice it either. Therefore the Dell'amicizia feeling becomes just deep to the liking forced by communion that is born, respect and moral satisfaction give rise to a profound feeling of friendship ties, their affection that draws from each other in discussing, in being close; and it is in understanding each other that the relationship becomes more satisfying and more sticky, but without the same way become shocking.

Therefore, their bond is perfect, their friendship is genuine. The one is bound to each other deep in the soul. JESUS 'from the stories of Judas, includes caricatures of events and facts, and admires the delicacy that uses JUDAS in present them. Jesus within itself includes those who are Judas, she looks at him, watching him from head to toe, sees him smile, and says to himself:

"No joke, this man really did what he says, even if he speaks as a joke, but it will certainly have done much more."

However at the same time how much love he feels for him Judah, and this makes it easier to understand and pity almost as if justifying it. JESUS 'reflects the same way the man whose is giving friendship and confidence, and within himself feels, that you should not trust the way and says to himself: "Better that I have not told my secret." this is a normal attitude of the Son of God, he did not trust anyone and he could not trust even of Judah, else his secret would come out earlier than expected but not only, he was to be believed the Son of God from Judah, above all, and for this reason he could not confide; if he had done a lot, probably, it would not have obtained a deep and interesting effect.

REFLECTION! - P.55

Judas reflects its own IO, and understands that his supra-human intelligence must have a superior right, I guess with the feeling that this understanding is real and your head goes to Jesus' personality. Understands that Jesus has psychological, and certainly understood he says to himself: "And 'at my level, to communicate satisfaction." Judas processes almost automatically within himself every detail of the personality and behavior of this terrible friend. He in the cleavage of another's personality is practical, is coached by his oriental and spiritual evolution to do deep analysis. He finally understands how Jesus within themselves. It includes how to think, and how is your heart. In the end as to Divine inspiration, during one of his deep spiritual reflections, he says to himself. << JESUS 'DIVINE is a being, here! He is the top man in the world! >> Exclaims: "And 'the SON of GOD." At the same time it understands this, understands that Jesus does not know to know, but I know who is at the bottom. Judah says to himself:

<< But Jesus does not know to know the top man in the world so why not the Son of God was revealed in mine, if I had known I would have turned out for sure. >>

COMPREHENSION. - P.56

JUDAS now includes: Jesus is the Son of God but only knows him and no other person in the world knows. So God wanted only he knew this truth and no one else. << But he really does not know to be the top man in the world? He really does not know to be the Son of God? If he had known, I would have waved, and I would not be able to believe him because it would have prevented me from studying it, and therefore I would give him a madman, and I would not have followed. No. He knows that he is the Son of God. >> Then
 he thinks again. << No does not know it otherwise would have been a sly to make me arrive alone to the knowledge of His Identity. No! He does not know that the Son of God, is not a smart is a good and nothing else. >>

ANALYSIS. P.57

But why. JESUS 'is a feeling of brotherhood given to him by God? Perhaps ORDER 'did not feel alone, BECAUSE' after losing everything and all the relatives of his blood he lacked a sense to give a reason and why his life. Then he makes a reason for feeling that for Jesus, and he says to himself thinking:

<< Here GOD has given me the world's largest most handsome

brother so that I do not I stay alone, and that is His Son as my Brother. I am elected! >> This thinks Judah. He is convinced of this motivation, and pays no attention to his opposite pole, but understands that despite the diversity he is in communion with the Son of God miraculously.

GOD having established that Judas has passed the tests of respect of friendship decided to reward him. Tests Pass from Judah who during life has put in his path seems the LORD. God has rewarded this His emotional honesty, and he has not left alone. He in His infinite mercy, has given him a brother to Judas but greatly needed and his heart and wanted to have, and it does meet him at a particular moment of his life, in order that they appreciate the value. GOD HIS SON JESUS ', GIVES THE JUDAS AS BROTHER. A prize to Judas recognition to the devotion and respect of Friendship as a child that he has proven worthy in his heart. JUDAS follows is this realism that belief becomes clear in his mind. His analyzes finally led him to this realism: "JESUS 'DIVINE is a being." He sees something IO THE spirit of Jesus that strikes and humiliates, and likewise binds him, in a profound way. It born in his heart, that only death can separate, this bond Affective; and since SEPARATION FROM HIS BROTHER JESUS 'AND' SIMILAR TO DIE When Jesus died, he too succumbs within himself. But as a brother he believes that God has given him the task of protecting Jesus'. Probably for this task and he has really given. Judah understands this, otherwise many things of his life and of his intelligence would not have made sense.

However, returning to the earlier remarks, we do not know what he sees Judas in Jesus, and we'll never know. And God only knows Him, and in accordance with what he sees, recognizes Jesus to be the Son of God. A secret that only knows Jesus. Now I also know but Judas, Jesus' does not know that Judas has revealed His secret. This is the point.

SUPERB-P.58

The question that I pose to man, is this: How can Judas break the seals more secrets of the Divine Creation which allowed him to recognize Jesus' being the Son of God?

Who is Judas? How is it possible? has not grown along with Jesus', they are not lived in the same environment. disparate religions of the time, impossible that Judas has come to this. What mental and spiritual power, has achieved JUDAS during his lifetime? What kind of spiritual and acute experiences has JUDAS to achieve this power?

This is a power that is achieved through a pure feeling of affection dictated by a deep love?

Still in our age, man does not know these secrets of the spirit.

How did he do? What did you see? A secret that can only know God.

Now to know the secret identity of Jesus', it is only Judas and God, and no one else.

Here comes a man of another culture, and shortly thereafter he knows the secret bearer, here reveals it, and with conviction recognize it. How did he do? What mystery holds Judas within themselves? Who is Judas? We never would know, even as we might never achieve the power to know, we might never achieve the spiritual power of Judah; and we understand that he is with God, and is part of the design of God, and God and with Him as with JESUS '.

The dilemma that man will never understand not even if it was studying until the dawn of time, is: What did Judah into the soul of Jesus, to recognize the Son of God. And how did you see it? He will never know the man, and we will never know, too.

I doubt that Judas has revealed this secret, of what he saw inside the Soul of Jesus' to someone. Judah also at the same JESUS 'may not have turned out!

Judah now knows who Jesus is and we arrived alone, as alone came to a character qualities of God and shall demonstrate compliance with this Existence, and according to this he obtained Reason and Faith.

Jesus, unaware of the discovery of Judas on him, always has the usual attitude against Judah, but Judah not. Judah suffers emotional trauma and at the same time, spotlight all his intellectual superiority beliefs unreachable for a human being. Therefore the most terrible trauma for Judah is: stand in front of Jesus', knowing that it is in front of the Son of God, know that it is His Brother, why is this feeling he has with the heart, and not be able to say.

Judah shows a huge emotional resistance, and a deep control of himself and of his emotions. He proves to be a truly CREEPY Man: The smartest in the world after Jesus, and no man in the world may have, or may have had in the past, the intelligence of Judah. For this to pull the accounts men, all mankind will follow the judgment of Judah who says << Jesus is the Son of God! >> No man on this earth is able to oppose the will of Judas, no. The man is obliged to believe in Judah, but from himself! Judah is number one and that even if it were only for the fact that he had discovered the identity of the Son of God. When you encounter with Jesus: He knows he is in front of the Son of God, and yet manages to dominate his emotions. And even if his behavior changes a little bit, and JESUS 'notice it for sure, however, carries the friendship naturally and controlling his exuberance. We human beings at this point we know who Jesus is, but do not know who is Judas, and never know it. As He did to see that something in the personality of Jesus? And what he thought to recognize the Son of God? What did he find?

YET I HAVE COME TO MY LITTLE THEORY. -P. 59

One of the profound things - personal characteristic - that Judas might have discovered in Jesus, and that led in the right way to recognize him as the Son of God is. ... This I describe below.

the Son of God's greatness is his weakness.

You are now, we think that this weakness would put him at the mercy of others, we understand that he could not prove it to the man. Otherwise man he would advantage. The man gave his dark side, always ready to splash out at all times of interest, he would have suppressed even before finishing his journey. Jesus could not show up for that being too good and too weak that it was mathematics. Only a superior mind could recognize him and discover the truth in him. This was to be Judas. I can not say that Jesus actually it was weak, but I can say that it was because it was created by the Eternal Father. We can say that a lion is not a feline because it is a lion but because it was created to be. For this reason, some human characteristics, such as those of Jesus, are innate in creation. With this we can not claim that the characteristics of our creation will not change in us, because we do not know if our evolution over time will let us perform independently, but the reality until the changes are due to changes is not achieved, we are like born and created. So we possess the characteristics that are important to recognize and distinguish the one from the other, even as Jesus. So Heavenly Father created it with this feature so that He is for mankind a vaccine against evil. Then it is clear that Jesus, as his mission and the goal to be achieved, which in the end was that to be part of human history could not show his being fully man otherwise this could suppress it. Now is his exuberance, his joy, his happiness and contentment with life, put him in a lie, so sometimes find yourself out of love and joy in front of the man, sguarnendo its defenses. So the enemy, seeing his weaknesses and understanding that it was to penetrate the suppressed. Jesus is truly the Son of God because his size is in weakness. However it is amazing intelligence of Judah.

So extraordinary that friendship born in intellect suggests that our source is not earthly. This affection that comes through reason and intelligence is not an obvious affection as the one familiar to similar to that of friends who have known for some time, and have many things in common. Among Judah is Jesus in common there are only the intelligence and spiritual evolution that makes him understand things as they are the same way, because things are not for opinions but because they are so. And two superior minds which are different in every way they see something not according to their own personal point of view but for what it's really like that show that we are beings created from the earth but from heaven. The extraordinary friendship of Judas and Jesus, people so different and culturally distant from one another, we declare that we are not land but from another galaxy.

So that's true! We have the body borrowed from the earth but when this body dies, we are always ALIVE! Because we are SPIRITS IN LONG LIFE AND BODIES (which basically are) SHORT LIFE! We are not the body. We are SPIRITS: Only spiritual beings and nothing else!

Wonderful - P. 60

Judah From this trauma increases its evolutionary basis, going to evolve is larger which places him in a stage to interact with the Divine Plan and understanding of the universal laws, and understand the CELESTIAL plans. JUDAS is now saturated, its evolution has achieved a completion stage. It 'also has a family member is no longer alone, he JESUS' a feeling of great importance that gives a value to life itself. The trauma of Judah serves as a spiritual magnet, and places it in an affective communion with Jesus, in an upper floor, the Heavenly Plan; where only see each other and being together brings happiness and joy. For us it is inexplicable emotional depth.

In our human stage; because love goes into a spiritual state that you live only in the Kingdom dimension of God, maybe we could never feel those sensations of pleasure that Judas received to be with your Friend Jesus', even though we were with any best friend our life.

Both when they are together have emotions that they feel to be together in PARADISO, but they do not realize they think they love each other like brothers. Only two twin brothers can have this deep connection but they live it and, I am not studying just as wrapped in a cloud.

Two human beings who live the love and the feeling of friendship the same way that you live in the house of God probably.

We could never understand the depth nor the quality of their feelings but we understand that the end of the earthly life of one of them, can not allow the continuity of the earthly life of the remainder. The pain of life itself would become deadly.

All in Judah becomes within themselves revolutionary. If at first had a view of Jesus in a certain way, now things have become different. His entire being and his intelligence, he single-handedly if it questions. For Judah, Jesus becomes a sacred center and the thing that surprises his psychology is: the fact that he never would have expected to discover a truth of this thickness in a seemingly ordinary man, and that is a poor man.

184

Just an ordinary man, had to be superior to him, and not only; also he had to be the son of God, his brother. This realization fills him with Pride and Pride.

His reasoning was under the influence of a serious psychological trauma, that only profound evolution as its neither could get damage from such a discovery.

For his part Jesus noted this change of Judah. You feel more valued, more considered, and every word he says he realizes that Judah hears as if to understand everything; Every word that came from the mouth of Jesus, for he was now, word SACRED. This inner turmoil of Judah, although notable, does not place does Jesus have in the curiosity to investigate what had happened inside his friend. As he is wont to do does not investigate immediately and let it go, it pretends not to notice anything, for him is normal. The question we can ask ourselves is: What did you see Judas inside the Soul of Jesus to recognize the Son of God? I am still not able to understand it. Therefore it is so, it would explain his human intelligence over if not to recognize the Son of God.

As it would explain the emotional bond he feels with regard to Jesus, so deep that the disappearance of Jesus' life is death as the final choice. As it would explain the conflict with his conscience which led him to suicide. As it would explain the courage to go see his Master carry the Cross, as if to give him a final farewell, challenging in this way all Judea community and all the people.

JUDAS SPEAKS TRUTH '-P.61

JUDAH:
<< JESUS ', I must explain to you how you are, and reveal your truth SPIRITUAL, in my opinion. -

JESUS':

–   Okay you listening .

Judah:
- You are a man in his spirit thinks the WELL and then represents it. Your soul has been hurt by pity you feel for the next. You'd need to see the happiness in the world, it would serve to marginalize and heal the wound. You do not have the instinct of defense, and the only action to nature and to smile and love all living beings regardless you know about them or do not know you. You're defenseless anyone can harm you, you have no defense inside you, you can not hit, you feel pity for those who, seen by all men, do not need. Your love which accompanies the wound of your soul and so deep that you act in this way and you are so. LOVE that walks you really TU! I could take you and keep you always with me and not build yourself out of the house, just to protect you and to make sure no one comes close to you. So I can not do, would prove to be afraid that someone might hurt you, instead of this I am not afraid, I trust in God. Although I understand that, I'm worried, but I'm with you. YOU one of those good, that everything he possesses the gifts, although it remains FREE.
You are so, but yours, wound that is the pity, it's your own creation of Love. This love which pour out who makes you happily embrace whatever is around you, and cancels you resentment for all men, it puts you in a position, to be always happy and full of joy. You are HAPPY God is with YOU. And 'This is your harmonic creation is made and wrapped in light, and when you are wrapped, you feel, how you perceive that you really are, that is a Divine being. Therefore it is by means of your deep love that everyone can take Harmony and Peace and bliss of this no one is excluded. So for us men it is easy to feel that you are the Son of God, if we agree to see you in the civilian side and without bias of social culture that dwells in the hearts of all peoples. So are You the Son of Love, and you're in a pure state, such a sweet musical melody that lives in you. Of

186

this I also have spiritual visual certainties, but I can not express because neither know the words agreed to express this; but I know you understand me. >>

JESUS 'remains a minute to think. Then he says to himself: "We saw clear even if not all."

For the first time JESUS 'it captures the fiery spirit; that everything can: with desire stubbornness which is the fastest of JUDAS instinct to make him understand this impetuosity learning Spiritual. Then he says to himself: "What if he has safely spirit of Judah strong and impetuous." JESUS 'knows that Judas has hit the target and comments:

<< You are injured, this wound makes me the man when I see the evil that is the next, and my heart breaks, I feel a deep compassion that fills me with pain and hurt me until the Soul. Here is the man lives his material well-being, and indifferently observes his neighbor starve, as if this vision was normal. Normal that he lives in the well-being and normal is to see his brother suffer and die of hunger. The man is indifferent. This is evil. Because he does not understand that is not normal in his being of consciousness that others starve while he lives in the well-being, especially when believed to be so right. Meaning: It 'just that I live well and others do not! This is the evil Judas. >>

Judah then listen says:
<< This t'indebolisce, you may not be able to defend yourself to others, you should control yourself, or else someone might get hurt. He sometimes people live better if you know not.
Instinct and intuition they know better than us how to make us behave. Speaking of love and brotherhood can. However the man is not ready to understand this quality of love. -

Jesus' question:

- You you you put against me? -

Judah:
- I have a feeling in my soul for you, Special; You are the only

187

living being who can be offended at me all you want for good or for evil, and not incorreresti in my wrath. Would I be able to give an arm for your life, and kill to defend yourself, and now I can tell you: I'm a terrible man, I do not do anyone, and I have no problems at any level, but not with you I could never go against, I want you too well. >> When Judah had finished, Jesus' sighed and everything he said, he realized that one side: JUDAS was deep more than he could have sospettarsi. The other felt the impetuous spirit, full of energy, strong self, is confident, that JUDAS be manifested. And JESUS 'was a great evolutionary step in civil and spiritual dimension. For this reason, he began to show up and work on this spirit that Judas, had transmitted the genuineness because it was at its maximum concentration and in this circumstance, I looked into his eyes opening all his soul.

After talking all night, they managed to understand each other deeply. It was then, after having understood that they decided to take leave to go to each home to reflect. The one on the other's behalf.

SATISFACTION AND TRAUMA. -P. 62

Jesus and Judas were satisfied, had assimilated all the information they had exchanged each other, and now each knew a lot of the other. Their communion uniting even more their friendship, and grew more and more their degree of evolution. Finally the two friends greeted each other affectionately and putting off their communion at another time.

Judah had a psychological trauma for recognizing alone the son of God, but who can control and hide almost perfectly. Jesus, seeing his secret revealed by a man, who did not grow up with him, the recently knows, has another trauma. The trauma makes him ask a question: But how did you discover this truth?

The only I know, and no one has ever proved, not even my closest family members know that my secret. I am the son of God, but who is this man?

His trauma, which is the same way as that of Judah and places, to do a thousand arguments to understand who is Judas, and as he did, he discovered a closed secret in the center of his Holy Spirit.

At the same time of Judas, Jesus through this trauma, passes into a higher stage of development which puts him in a position to interact with others in a stronger, deeper way, different now know that there are men in its evolutionary psychological level, and at the same time refines understanding and even deeper divine affection with Judah. Therefore, like Judas, you are bound to Him, Jesus is fond of Judah in the same manner, and equally affective dimension. All this bond has competed by the fact that they can communicate together and eventually understand each other and understand each other.

The two communicate with a more genuine emotional and moral depth and their esteem and affection are becoming very strong, as to arouse envy to others.

They have an exchange of affection belonging has a heavenly dimension. They love one another as if they had known from eternity of time. Warning! They live a clean and honest sentiment that is almost instinctive to believe it was timeless. Theirs is a feed your soul just to serene things and with words not offend the sensibility of each. An affection cultivated by both. With respect, esteem, clean affection, sympathy and joy in being together, interacting satisfaction fellowship, understanding, they continue to occur each other. And this is what stood by their union and cooperation. Their friendship was based on estimation and respect. Even just seeing their souls becomes joyful and all that surrounds them, is transformed and becomes fun.

Within themselves, Jesus does not include those who are in the spiritual dimension of Judah, but he feels the spirit and his benevolent expansion.

Judas, Jesus is a friend of the heart with deep intelligent and of great evolutionary importance in socialization.

Judah, through JESUS 'he draws the spiritual saturation of his knowledge. Now he knows everything, what he lacked learned by knowing and discovering Jesus'. Its evolutionary stage, with regard to His mission and saturated, should only represent its mission, which is to stay close to the Son of God and to follow in His path.
In balance Jesus for Judas is not only a friend and brother to be estimated to have pleasure in being together, but it is the Son of God; no one in the head and put it and no one can and upbeat. Their friendship, their respect, and the habit of seeing and dating test themselves and they end up understanding each other at a glance in the eye.

From this friendship and emotional quest'apporto starts for both in almost the same concurrent communion with the Divine Plan design, it would be: the way of Jesus of Revelation.

NOTE. -P. 63

JESUS 'is the Son of God, whatever that men are believers or not believers; there is, and there can be, no other opposed solution. JUDAS, he can not be wrong about this field. Not a word was heard Judah he came from the mouth of Jesus, and showed him His Spiritual Entity. No one could make people believe something to Judas if not from himself. For this, we SHOULD FURTHER BELIEVE that JESUS 'is the Son of God: The FAITH JUDAS, also leaves no escape for those who do not believe and did not want to believe.

COMMUNION OF TWO BECOMES POSITIVE FOR BOTH - P. 64

This communion of character personality and thinking between the two becomes constructive for both. Each draws something from the other, and their lives begin to have a positive cycle, more constructive; both in the situation of work both in the psychological dimension. Judah becomes stronger psychologically and exceeds every adverse situation, salt an evolutionary step.

JESUS 'becomes more successful in work and climb a social ladder in business and economics.

For both miraculously begins a phase of prosperity. Quality of life becomes better, and some floor plans begin to take shape and to be implemented.

JESUS 'did all this social evolution, not away from God, and in the utmost for the good of others manifested His Divine Mission.

PLAUSIBLE DISCUSSION BETWEEN JUDAS AND JESUS '-P.65

JUDAH:
<< Why did you come the world? -

JESUS':
- Porto, faith, the word of God? -

JUDAH:
- The man already has this, there are two reasons for your coming. -

JESUS':
- They would? -

JUDAH:
- I was at the end of the world, or you have to show the way of salvation, in essence bring the compass and the men who are able to understand it and use it, can glimpse the path, then follow it and be saved. -

JESUS':
- I do not have a compass with me. -

JUDAH.
- They know you're the compass, you just have to understand the message of your words and your person. -

JESUS':
- This is enough?-

JUDAH:
- This is the Faith, Believing in everything you say imitate your behavior, which is to give all that you have, even having taken nothing. The universal law of love, feel the pains within themselves, that others feel. -

JESUS':
- Yes, I understand that we are all brothers and we are all made by his father, and when we walk, we carry within our bodies also the blood, the flesh of our brothers, and if we hurt, or we do not act to help others, we do ourselves. See Judah, when you walk inside you there is also my blood, and I when I walk inside me there's your blood, we are brothers, just do not know. The test and piety that you and I, we can try the one against the other, in certain painful precise and rejoice in others as glia other joyful circumstances. Probably port the compass, as you claim, but if the good is not physically represented and distributed among brothers, the compass is thought only to follow it, and it is not certain that you follow in the exact way. -

JUDAH:
- I understand you, see that you are the compass, m'indichi the path of salvation, and how I have to materialize it, it is I who possess the Faith and courage. You on earth harbors this. As the road that leads to the LIGHT. Now I understand, I understand your Truth! You have no feelings hurt that other years.   -

JESUS':
- So I do not do it with the intention of committing, it makes me so natural, just open my mouth, everything comes out automatically, and my heart I my being and so of course. I'm so, have done so. -

JUDAH:
- I know this is you! No need to explain to you, why you're the top of the world, for your of good values, you're always You. If they were not the values of the property to decide the degrees of evolution, in which we can understand the greater dell'inferiore, life would have no meaning and no future. The degree to which a person establishes his reflection, the law of good. Here we see the right degree of evolution and compliant in order to glimpse the way, you know that only indicate, and that leads to the LIGHT.

And you already own by birth this road that leads to the salvation of our souls. Dear friend, that you own is not for granted understanding, but for the Divine Creation. Are you the Messiah. You're a natural, in practice the salvations of the road is You, not the word, we must be able to recognize you, learn from you how to behave with others and follow your teachings, here's what to do to save his soul and have access at Paradise.

What you going to do now? -

JESUS':

- Talking to follow the path that I scored within the Heart. And say who they are when God wants. -

JUDAH:
- See, Master, You are ready to reveal Your Identity, to do so; as a personality agrees Master, but unfortunately you're not a social situation. Your do not have a home, you have no money, and the work apparently does not do much. The home is important, and must be Tua, but just Tua.

JESUS':
- That what you got to do? -

JUDAH:
- When do you start your journey and things are not as they seem, and as expected, but different because it distinguished the man as it appears that puts foul. Human behavior is sociable, you! It is true the man socialize, but also opportunistic and corruptible, this means falsehood. It is also true that man creates the group, is the company that does not give a chance to those who are outside. Dear brother, you have to make a reputation, that sometimes you do the others. The reputation you have to have it, with the sword, with the courage and the honor says Roman. You're smart, you're ready with the Spirit, but as a man you do not have a reputation and are not estimated, you're not a number, and you know others with what eyes see you? No! Brother, you may not accomplish the task that God has given you, no one is with you and you do not belong to a group. Dear friend if you do not protect, and you create a base of defense, now that no one knows about you, will not be able later when everyone will know you to do so.

When you need, it is just then that you will turn your back, and anyone though honestly want to be near you, be afraid of losing part of his reputation, so in front of you is one way, but behind your back is another. No! Too many enemies. Jesus, you become self-sufficient, independent. Achieve strength, defend yourself from creating you company a permanent economic security, job security that guarantees life, a place to live; otherwise, you will do little headway because my friend in Your path will find hatred and envy, and few will want you to stay close. As soon as you begin the journey, you lose your job, and probably some affected, which are important to you, even if now so you do not appear, unfortunately it will. Now, Master, You make the WELL pray the Word of God and God's Good and heal the hearts. You love Revealing Your Identity to human reason, and say God I'll communicate knowledge and you do know, and you will fulfill the God's will, but in the meantime some social milestones to be achieved are also truly necessary for defense against you do not accept what you assert to be and could shut yourself some leads of survival and employment in the face. Think about it, others are men, are not divine beings similar to Thee and Thy values, they even manage to think of them, they figured if they can understand them. You have to know that not everyone knows get Your Well; to understand, require time, and on this Tu Maestro, you have to be sure you get enough. You need the strength to complete your Divine Mission. This strength comes from the work, but at the same time you need the time to communicate well, and therefore only God can help you. - JESUS':

- I had already been thinking about all this, Dear Friend. I trust in the help of My Father I know that risk of being completely alone. I can also understand that the risk of losing many things, but the affects lose if smarrirò them, mean that they are the ones I've never really had? The affects are not an opinion, that friendship is not an opinion, but it is a feeling. -

JUDAH:
- The affects do not lose them out of envy, but in consequence of job loss. Who will work one who claims to be the Son of God? Nobody. You'd be embarrassing to anyone who would

lead the work. The work means money and forces to defend themselves. Remember that when you have no money and you do not work, friends can help and encourage one and two, but also; the trick of the difficulty which leads a man to rub first friends and then the relatives, everyone knows him, certainly not in your case, but explain to them will not be easy. You will be driven away, nobody will pay FAITH to what you say, you will not accomplish your mission, if you do not ponder the situation. You must bring order and prepare you in your life, you have to achieve the goals, until in the end you can talk and nobody has to throw down with a simple closing of the door. Dear friend the world revolves around this. Step after step, you will come to the point that you are socially ready to present the Word "in the world of" GOD. -

JESUS:
- I know that, and so I intend to proceed. With regard to the affections, you notice that you're cold and too pessimistic. Family or close friends has nothing to do with the money and well-being, I could have money and not give him, what difference would it have money or do not have? -

JUDAH:
- If you have money, nobody asks you for them, but everyone loves you for that. Your money in companies shows that you are a man of prestige and deserves respect, so he thinks.

Moreover, your friends think you, perhaps because you are good, as they imagine, and hope you can donagliene a bit ', one day. Etc. Etc. ... ... Who knows. Even this hope does not count in the final and misses. Unfortunately, it is also true that poor people are distinguished by the rich: the poor and the less money the more they loved you "if you are their rich master." In fact, the powerful maintain obedience keeping people in poverty. In fact, a people who are well in the end has the strength, and this strength can use it against the powerful.

196

Therefore more a people is held in suffering and best ensure obedience and respect. Their people, respect you, if you're rich from birth, or if they did not see you become rich, or envy has its cycle. And any man knows this, as anyone with a bit of intelligence knows that people in power has also love, such is life, and if not, it was not necessary that God had sent you, on earth. So you have to consider that the rich see it differently from the poor social reality and personal. These rich, if you are money and power, are not jealous of what you have, because they too have the wealth you possess you. Among them the rich always bring along somehow, oversees the rule of corruptibility among them, and solidarity but beware. The poor who see you become rich start to be jealous, and hateful as well. If God would not glimpsed the possibility to change the course of action of man through your teachings, he would not have sent you to the ground, there would be no reason for your coming. Rich and poor, the way they think and associate, is a man of character elements unfair, they have done so that you, now is here among us. For this if you do not the money no one asks you for them, and no one loves you. You know that in nature, the strongest animal mates more easily, in humans the money by force, not only for mating but also for the love of a certain degree, but it and the dimension of love that people are used to share between them. Everything is wrong, and you're here for. Therefore, in its universality affects are related to love, for this reason: Even people that you have brought into the world plan, try for yourself a minor feeling, just because he has no money, you are not realized. You are a failure this is enough to change their minds and behavior towards you, and there is no feeling that takes! It 's sad, it is painful, but slowly, slowly, unless you become strong in the human system, everything collapses on him even Heaven. It may be that those who turn away with their hearts, they do not know the reason why he loves you less, or maybe they do not want to know, but the reason is that you have no money six weak, and you are alone. -

JESUS':
- God is with me. Surely there will be people who will love me and will help me.

JUDAH:
- I have faith in the spiritual dimension I know who you are, and I know how you talk and I FAITH Master. Rightly as a man must have material energy, of emotional support, from whatever side it comes. love feelings destined to fail before they are born, and if they are only a thread of resentment remember, just because it did not work-force energy and money, and emotional energy to always lead them back and let them go. Necessaries walking together. So of course, if you have the attributes of nature and you're connected in the environment where they are appreciated, you can make a career. Dear friend possess something that is fashionable, contemporary to stay healthy now, this counts for men. In any given era, the money will come effortlessly, if anyone has any interest on you. Surely, enter the game of life, or of social taste, if something you can give, whether they like it BUT '. In this case the money you send them straight in your pocket to any request that you would do, and no one would not object because you'd be protected. So to get this, you should possess certain attributes targeted and specific, which always affect people and their way of thinking and living life.

Now it elevates you, gives you power if it recognizes in you a guide, something to follow, someone to whom to entrust their future, their security of tomorrow. To gain power, without any attributes and the wind that blows from behind, but by others that allow you to enter their group must let insert in their game, agree to become part of them, and like them. This is the game of the powerful present, at any time we want to see this, and what has always been, and so it will be at least as long as God does not intend to change everything. Unfortunately, it is inserted in the Game of the Mighty, requires corruption. And then, just to see your smiling face, everyone will be willing to give you the money you want, especially if you do not need. It is not man that the check mark to its value are other men who do ruler, you know, you too Master, that the mass requires a reference point and to entrust their collective will to a single character without even asking if he it is worthy or not? The choice of this guide is connected concurrently to the social position and dedicated representative of the power of man. Already what is inside, it is inside us remain. Man is a social being, needs a powerful guide that takes the socially united to the other, for better and Love, but who goes to power know this? Does this? No! In most of the cases. Those who could be and act as guide Right, is not in the environment. And if outside environment one comes forward because the right attributes is in most cases isolated or placed in a position not to move and losing support. The people no matter where it led what counts is to follow, it is hoped that those commands with their will the mass to be able to bring peace, love and prosperity.

You Are The Right to Follow, and I recognize that these qualities to have. God is with you. As I am. Therefore, to be followed, you have to defend themselves from competitors, by those who are to fly when trying to stop your flight, by those who are in the environment and are followed by bad luck or failure. You have to climb the steps, although not necessarily need to become too rich, but self-sufficient and do not need material of others, can be a great advantage for Your Mission.

JESUS':
- God is with me, and when, He m'indicherà the Way, which means that they are ready as are the men who will follow me. My will, My intelligence does not matter, in this case, and probably just as well that your accounts; what matters is the Will of the Eternal Father, just that you have to follow. You talk, reminders only your brain even if what he says is sensible, FAITH in God is HONORED, is His will must be followed at all costs, if God is with us, our social defeats, are always a way to

win . I will speak of My Identity only when God deems it's time, just waiting for that He let me understand. -

JUDAH:
- This is right. Why in the meantime and also right that you prepare. -

JESUS':
- It will always be myself. Inherit my house with the work I can do this and my necessities. -

JUDAH:
- What you say it is beautiful, much nicer than what I think. Even if I do not, for common sense I have to believe in what you say. >>

PLAUSIBLE DISCUSSION BETWEEN JESUS 'JUDAS AND WORK ON THE THEME-P.66

Judah:
<< If you want the job, make money by owning your own home, and even prepare a nest, you have to know all the people on earth, with a speech that reflects them all, and it does not exclude anyone. -

JESUS':
- A speech that reflects all men on earth, and that does not exclude anyone, difficult, you tell me. -

JUDAH:
- These are the lessons learned in the next way to essays, anyone I've ever said it to you, you reveal them. It is known in human and instinctive form in perfidy, where all men are identical, on this side of the world and of all races. -

JESUS':
- I listen to you. -

JUDAH:

- The action is: You see a man he demands something, is an opportunist. You will understand what the need, but remember that you request something, the exchange must always be fair and just. By but you have to take. -

JESUS':

- And what do you do if it happens to you, you have to give, but nothing that man to give you? -

JUDAH:

- I have my answer, and I do not know if I can, I make a small gift. But you probably smile and what you have, even more than necessary. So unfortunately, if you want to climb the steps and make sure the strength for the future, you have to control yourself. Otherwise you will lose your energy and comprometterai the mission that you have to accomplish.

Jesus: Do you believe that I can not complete the mission that God has given me to do? Judah: The men will not give you anything, and you have to fight to live, and to fight you have to have the time, and if this, it uses in a way, you can not engage him in another. So you have to really be able to gestirti in every sense, but above all the safety of the future, economically speaking, nothing else you can do if you will need to dedicate time to eat. Brother know that "those" who have written had the time, and so economic security. Know that though the trend is on the road and not within the walls of castles and palaces of the court, then know that win full even if you know nothing of science and truth of life, and win because they have the power and the time, and they are always teaching their culture to the new generations, although their evolution is minimal, and based on falsehood and unreality. So Brother You need to do a hard road because your wisdom must be pure, be imbued with the wisdom of the road and work.

Jesus: I see. God has put me in the street so I became strong, and comprendessi the truth of men who suffer evil, I understood the weak in their difficulties. However there are also weak who harm the weakest of them. But tell me the characteristics of which you were speaking to me.

Judah: Know, that a common feature of all men in the world, is giving and receiving. So if you understand, it helps you a lot in the work, if you respect your job and you check in donating. Respecting their job means to get paid when you do a job. -

JESUS':
- What do I need to know this? Whether in the practical, I feel sorrow? And then at the end of the gift that I possess? -

JUDAH:
- I see. This behavior in my opinion the way I explain: A poor man asking for money to the poor, because they see weak regardless of who wants them to return or not. Hardly she asks them to rich. This is nature. You must do the opposite do not blame the weak, you have to ask for a job and money to those who believe them rich, even better if they feel hostile towards you and maybe the six unsympathetic. And to them that you have to ask, are the ports that you must open. But you do not have these qualities, you do not know why I'll explain, however, defend yourself someone they can take advantage.

Jesus: I understand and I understand what you want to communicate. But I know that it hurts the poor the poor, I went beyond that. Sometimes it is not the welfare state in which an individual is changing the nature of man.

Judah: Well, since you know how to live and how the man then demand work. Secure your future, because no one will help you do not crews alone. Remember that after asking for work,

202

is honored in front of everyone. If you ask business to wealthy people, they naturally will rise up the plug and you earn good money, if you ask the miserable job, it will be you to take less, you'll be miserable like them, and your spine do not you take anyone for sure. You must stand with those, better than you on the socio-economic side; you believe: unapproachable, those who know wealthy and who are able to pay for the work you do; they'll take away the obstacles in the way of your journey; they are the strongest. You must, Maestro, win this thing innate nature, which would like to invite you to put yourself with those like you or inferior to you for the imagination makes you believe that you can win; (Opportunism deceitful means); is a great advantage if we exclude, because the energies coming from where we are, and you need energy, to spend time in the mission that God has given you. You have to be bold and daring to knock the door to who is better and stronger than you, it will be open. Work can help you buy the house, and to achieve the goals they need to live, and above all to carry out the mission that God has given you. No one will rent the house to a man who says he is the Son of God. Do you understand? Especially if he has little money. Jesus you have little time and you have to earn a lot in this short time.

JESUS':
- This is also right! I'll do the right, for anyone working. I admit, this is a vote for your good advice. Thank >>

JUDAS: (smiles happy that his Master made him a compliment). But Jesus compliments made them all, and was humble with everyone, and Judas knew this, and it was precisely because of his humble goodness that esteemed him and loved him more and more.
<< Very likely to You, Master, will you do just that. The right. -

JESUS':

203

- Usually a job who's boss, wants to pay for it all and honestly. -

JUDAH:
- It depends on who has the greater opportunism. -

JESUS':
- In every discussion with you you always end up in doubt? -

Judah makes a sweet smile.

Then begin again to discuss. Judah is happy to talk to Jesus', he never offends, and whatever he says listen, and avoid bumping his sensitivity with the contradiction. When something does not like, just he says, "Here we go again, back" etc. or some statement like, all under a wry look, Judas admires and loves quest'armoniosa ease.

JESUS':
- When you say I'm the Son of God, even those who pray to God, the religious community, they put against me. -

JUDAH:
- I think so too, Master. The moment you say that you are the Son of God, the religious community does not appreciate certainly a competitor came from one of the poorest households and more numerous in the country. You know that you have been marginalized, with your entire family from the beginning, how do you think will take it, the other to see an outsider who wants to know more and longer than them? They claim to speak every night with God, and now you tell him to be the Son of the Creator, this is good. -

JESUS':
- Certainly not good, I am more than aware. -

JUDAH:
- You will be despised more than they are now. You are

considered an inferior now, let alone when you talk that anger infonderai hearts. And perhaps you may not be hated by some people, but others when you show them to be what they are not able to contradict and prove otherwise I would have hidden enemies and deadly. Many "village" people will hate and despise you for your ignorance and stupidity "This lack of compassion that TU Son of God, now did you bring it to us all, and for lack of deep understanding of your Being." So they see you and look at you. Always judge you no differently than they have always judged you, even if you feel profound things to say, and for each one to his understanding, will understand that you are to hate, because you want your villagers that they change their minds about you; This makes him angry. Some who know you as a regular man, resembling those of the simple people, and that they have never visited you, and in you will notice quality superior to theirs, who knows what they will think. Now when you observe you, they will think much about you, and see you do the wise and the healer by God, you know some say they talk to God since the time the oldest, no title they gave you so you can do it , Jesus them get paid, and dearly.

Jesus: Lo or well!

Judah: To them God is an exclusive monopoly, but only them. They are convinced, within them, you should not be how you present but as they will have prepared the way, which is what runs through the poor, servants and slaves. I believe that much will turn the boxes, you will despise you and ruin your reputation, and if not everyone will be against you, a good portion of them will be safe. Jesus is one that has gone off his brain, probably someone will say that the guilt and too much poverty and misery in which you have lived with your entire family, but to laugh at you and always put you on a plane of inferiority and RIDICOLITA ' . Mockery to tell each other, that the trouble you have also ruined the brain, and your existence is considered dead and useless; and even before the light of

205

your life blood goes out, they will hit you and pull your hand back. In the end, when they will have demolished you and you can not defend yourself, they'll give you the final blow, and the saddest thing I saw you faint friends and relatives, someone will take advantage of you. -

JESUS':
- I understand the world. However, God is with me, why should I be afraid? God is God. You Believe Me? -

JUDAH:
- What a question, it would not be here! Imagine the chief priests and the elders who rule, when you say to be the Son of Almighty God they say it is for everyone, but they are only the ones who can communicate with him, you're not even a priest, why they should believe that God communicates with you, that you're a priest, rather than with them who serve him with veneration? They pray to God and believe that God is their monopoly. How do you think that will take? From time to talk to God are only the elect chief priests who say they do His Will. Teacher how do you think will take cues when you say this in place? -

JESUS':
- I know not all goods. God is with me. I was born this way and I can not help it. Probably God lost faith in man and it is for this reason preferred to send me to earth to do His Will. I am with God, you are with me? -

JUDAH:
- They, too, are with God and with You. So then how do we change your mind? They belong to another thought, and make Doomstriker judges, they decide who and what is a man, are convinced. Here you have to become strong, before you speak, and I say not rich but self-contained, so things will be a little 'different.   -
JESUS':

- Thou me, what do you think? Do you believe that I can achieve the milestones? Since hitting on the same question. -

JUDAH:
- I'm sure you do, Maestro. -

A woman can help in this project, remember that love helps more than you know. Of course you have to really love each other and not for convenience with the heart. -

JESUS':
–   That's for sure, I NUTRO OF AFFECTION of all the creatures of God. Even the women are creatures of God, I take from them the affection and love clean. -

JUDAS: (smiles, pretending not to believe, as a joke.)

- You, Master, you know what features common to all women of the world? -

JESUS':
- Here we go again, tell me by. -

JUDAH:
- Women of the world, have one or two features that are common. A frustration and suffering, that arrive when they go in conflict with themselves and struggling to do the prostitutes. Usually they choose a middle ground, a pair of lovers and some adventure every once and a husband who gives security and a stable affection. This regardless that they are in love with a man, or that they are not. The other, is that if they can win their inner conflict and decide to be prostitutes, they are all happy, because I'm always calm and relaxed. The other feature, and who need to be told I love you, and drive convinced of being loved is essential to their minds; so you must always tell her to love them, even if it is not, in this way you have peace, and they live well and serene, and yet another characteristic is:

they basically are not evil like man, are always good. The Woman at the bottom is a mother, gives birth to the Sons, gives life, not take it away. On this side they are all the same. With some exceptions, which I hope you will not find, indeed I hope that you find only the good ones. - JESUS':
- All nonsense. The good features are that the woman is indispensable. We need definitely the female figure, his warmth, his company and his love, however, we can not say that does not help it is easy. I dear friend I feed only of Affection, saying, God be all that I need. Whatever, and superfluous, if not blessed by the love and unconditional affection, I am uninteresting my Love, and in this way I want to be loved. You know that I have a lot of friends and acquaintances, among them many young women, whose friendship with them and exchanging affection, nothing, believe me I live and I have eaten of this GOOD clean and sincere. We then, Dear Friend, we must not and we can not judge, we must love in Universal so indiscriminately, all Creation, the woman is inside. >>

Judah and happy to hear those kind words and smiles of Joy, her heart requires to feel affectionate words of the good. Still he wants to tease his Master to make him talk fondly of beautiful things. He pretends not to believe with his attitude. So Jesus' is the game, which includes JUDAS has also calculated that.

JUDAH:
- Yes I know. If so you can find good, I recommend Master if the call needs a hand. Always tell her I love her, but let him feel inside that is not certain. The woman needs to uncertain confirmations. She feeds on doubts and certainties that want to verify. -

JESUS':
She smiles. "He asks, giving importance only to what He

asked."
–   You follow me? -

JUDAH:
- Because I'm not following you? Most of the time I call you Master. -

JESUS':
- Of course I realize that you have a lot of respect for me, which is basically what I too have for you. -

JUDAH:
- Yes, I realize. Friend will be with you until death. And if you die, I die too, so trapasseremo together. Therefore, we make the horns; I love you too much. - "Judas smiles amused" for good luck.

JESUS':
- What are you saying? -

JUDAH:
- It 's so I can feel it. - "They both smile doing their fingers crossed for good luck".

JESUS':
- We can also talk about work. Look, it's an important topic, change the subject. -

Judah looks into his eyes to understand how much desire he JESUS 'to talk about work, in order smiles.

JESUS':
- Why are you laughing? Look, I've always worked for me like. I know that you are the best I accept willingly this truth.

JUDAS: (laughs again) and responds.

- I know, that's the problem, I do everything. -

JESUS':
- Do not overdo it. >>

TWO FRIENDS-P.67

The friendship is made, the two have been dating, it is estimated that you respect, and being together is a great satisfaction and joy for both. Two friends meet and talk, and they love each other. And smile, nothing more and for a look at each other and smile. What melody transmitted JESUS 'in the heart of Judas, in order that in his face lights up more than a deep smile, and his eyes with joy become small and watery happiness? What sensations received Judah, this supernatural contact, which makes him happy and full of happiness and joy. And smiles JUDAH, the man of action who was, is transformed into a simple, happy man who loves everyone and smiles with everyone. Nothing more from the hassles, all love him, and cries of joy, and is moved by any sadness that known faces that pass before his eyes, or are there in the corner of the streets. Now JUDAS smiles, and all people, they make it. I see a boy biting an apple, and pity, he sees an old man with a stick and feel sorry, sees soldiers watch them, and they also make him worth; Jude enters a new dimension.

How much pity and tears come down in the face of Judas, that he can not stop his smile, and cries of joy, and her heart wants to embrace the whole world, and the whole universe. Then look in the eyes JESUS ', and his smile deepens as not being able to keep his eyes open, and the whole, the harmony of the heavenly plan and its melody JESUS' he transmits it, with the only presence. Emotions of the good that perhaps a few moments, are experienced by every man in this sad country. However everything will be broken by that something, that comes from those who are from another social part and although it has nothing to do, for simple and bad perfidy is interrupted.

POSSIBLE DISCUSSION BETWEEN JUDAS AND JESUS-P.68

JESUS':
<< How to have long ago, I understand that I am the son of God? Did not know me well, you're not grown along with me; how did you get this? -

JUDAH:
- We can talk about BASE, before discussing Te which are the Son of God, and as I did I recognize you, and eventually you can understand the emotional and emotional sense of which I rely to recognize a man in his Spiritual Identity . You must understand that I read within me all the next of the emotions that I receive from the contact. You with your transmitter to be me, when you respect me, emotions that I listen to the soul and I transform, I communicate to my brain that deciphers to the point that they are also recognized with the words. I read some other I can not understand, even though I live, but I understood enough to know you. -

JESUS':
- You read inside yourself to understand others? -

JUDAH:
- Of course, Master, is the most natural basis that there is in all of God's creatures, the difference lies in the fact that not all emotional messages that you receive, are easily decipherable, all in the light of developments, to the experience of a man, his intelligence, his sensitivity, experience. ... Etc ... Etc ... But after all this reading is set in motion unconsciously, and lives in the authentic realism, through dreams or visions, it all depends on what can pass from the unconscious to the conscious part. As all this work stands if the emotion are processed in their reality. Each element OF IO brain has to work perfectly, until what and feeling or intuition does not reach a clear and visible to

211

consciousness, every IO THE spiritual elements must work well and not make mistakes. -

JESUS':
- All right, but how did you decipher these emotions plausible that I would have sent you, so that simple just by talking together, and come to make a conclusion so deep? -

JUDAH:
- The whole becomes simple, for BASE. When a man knows the base, if you believe in God, and seeks perfection of God, with the Love mirror and its derivatives related to this force, you can understand and recognize the Son of God and others. -

JESUS':
- Tell me about the base, which you say, he made sure to recognize me. -
JUDAH:
- Of course this was one of the ways, it may be that there are several, but is quite a talk. How can it be that there are several others. However in this case we do not know. I speak to you of my way and my evolutionary sense that allowed me to recognize you in the end, for what the emotional level you have sent me, and my unconscious informed my conscience. -

JESUS':
- I listen to you. -

JUDAH:
- The BASE is: One of Plates or one of the forces that make up the evolutionary pinnacle of man, and understand that God, the love of God, puts men at the same level. For this reason a man follows when its apex connected to the love of God, includes as well, that there is a king, and there is no man more than another. Clearly if I meet a man and send me modesty and humility, I will be like him. If he says to believe that all men are equal and no one and superior to another, I'll be like him if I

feel inside me that is sincere. I'm right because I feel his emotions, be sincere and natural. I decipher which in my opinion is loyal is good they are with him. If he does well and lives these concepts of goodness and spirituality, I am with him. In sincere and natural emotional form, it informs dialect, transmits them with clarity and conviction that I intuit sincere: clear, at this point the unconscious with all this information and processes the result to consciousness. If consciousness is hard to understand the results for lack of evolution in a tie, the unconscious through associations of the dream or vision, sends the message of realism to consciousness in a more understandable way. Everything is including, from the beginning to the end. You are the Son of God. We have come through a long process and the help and the will of the Heavenly Father. He made sure that I understood this truth. -

JESUS':
- So, this might not be enough, the human side, but clearly God can help you achieve and to communicate to people the realism. -

JUDAH:
- Right. In BASIC, there is the other, and if I do not expose, we can not speak of the Son of God, even if the Son of God is You. -

JESUS':
- D'you listen agreement. -

JUDAH:
- You must know that since I am a believer, I know that in my evolutionary apex, the Son of God, must be a man of my size at all levels, otherwise, I can not follow him and not be saved by Him. The line draw horizontal and that I know of the existence of God. Among know the existence of God and know eXISTENCE of God's Son, there is easy to cross the border.

There is a gap to consider: The Son of God can not be

213

presented to me as a prince, or as one of the powers that otherwise occurs plagiarism, and would no longer be my choice, my natural form, my personal evolution to recognize it, to choose him as a friend, but it would be the charm or other, which in turn only excuses voluntarily or involuntarily to conquer.

My evolution must be necessary or otherwise does not make sense that I could make it necessary to recognize you, my king son of God, but without that you are superior to me, or else I can not accept you, you would not be in the perfection Celeste and my evolution would have little meaning, the man less than another would remain as a principle of creation, it would not be in God's righteousness, and you would not be the Son of God. For this reason the Son of God is to be a simple man, with no power over other men, possibly accept me stronger or bigger that's a saint, an angel, but not the Son of God, especially by law Divine must one day rule the world, does not want it more than me, the world must go in the hands of an OK. No MAN is to be superior to another MAN. Men who accept that they are superior to ME, at the bottom are the Angels and Saints, this accept it, but the Son of God, can conquer me only if I accept it, I have to recognize it and to understand it and understand that it has nothing more than a another man, and the Angels and the Saints are to worship him, because he is a man below them, like me, but he is the Son of God. This is rightly, the Son of God as Divine RE entities in the world, and not more than without the my self-understanding! The difference is that with him are always at my house, and for this to be so the Son of God, no power and they control, the only way I'm always at my house, because it is equal to me, and more, He knows no ownership, and even being more within in His house which is also my hOME. This way I conquer, but because He is so done. This is the basis, on this point to understand if we can speak of the Son Of God, what Te or else we can not speak even when delivered and reported to you. -

JESUS':
- I do not think, spinning a lot, I could be a higher being are the Son of God. -

JUDAH:
- You're higher, but you can not do you stay humble, your superiority is that you know get in smaller size to the next to feel comfortable, it makes you superior, and this is natural because you're so, you know born this way , you're done so, are what you are, otherwise you could not be so, cOULD pretend, but the fiction is not natural. You are normal in your humility, for this is You. You must understand that when I see a weaker man than I am, I have a man who has need, I know that he is represented by you, the Angels and the Saints know. This is one reason that m'inducano to understand, that if I do a lack towards this being and as if I did to you, you see it all, is part of the evolution that finally comes to the completeness of Love and its apex, His perfection in representing JUSTICE. For this reason my evolution makes sense, and that's what makes you superior; my evolution, becomes right, it reflects the truth that I obtained that is not only confined to recognize the Son of God, but also understand that He is always reflected by any needy and weak man Over Me. They will represent, and You REPRESENTING them everything fits.

I can not thank God the Father who has given me the right to put me in a position that you understand this; this is why the Son of God can not and must not be superior to other men, otherwise the whole thing would fall to the time and the love power limited, and distributed subject to the lower entities that are represented by these men. Instead your power is Jehovah thy kingdom is universal, and the Perfection and proven by the fact that within this dimension collect the weakest of the chains and they are up to you put in a position to interact with Your person at their level.

215

Takes the representation of respect for pity, for this demonstration of humility in the end it comes and it is Love, for all without distinction. These are the emotions that I receive from Your contact, so I decipher them, and that's how I think. Why are the Son of God.

You're an ordinary man in appearance, like all the MEN, and you're reluctant to blame the weak, and when they come close to you have confidence, even if you do not know you, you feel comfortable as if you've known each other always: but because the transmitter to be one of them, or rather a family member, although this emotional side will not include conscious dimension, in the way you transmit their act. Do you see that you are one of them, receiving this, and everyone or anyone has the courage to become familiar with you, because you did in a way that it is as if you had always known, and your friendship and your affection They've had. Do you understand that, the understanding of all this, makes evolution is sensible. Otherwise it would be useless to evolve, if You come into the world with all the powers, too comfortable. Humanity needs to be happy, and God through this You want to give. It would be useless, learn and go the stadium after experiences in order to achieve the universal sense of love and of what in is connected, if that would be contrary to how they really are and how Rightly Siano, under the Will of God. why does a man like me too, needs a long evolution to achieve something that you have since your creation. Therefore, this is also a way to be superior. A necessary evolution for humans to recognize you is to understand you. So not for you, you're already evolved, belongs to a communion with God. We are allowed to belong to a union with YOU. Through you, you get God. How do you see God did not choose an angel, a saint, a prophet, a prince or another as His messenger to be sent on earth but His Son. A simple poor working man, is a man of the people. Creating it with principles, which others need a long life lesson to understand them. You understand that in this way it reflects the perfection of God and of His choices. Proof that God thinks of His creatures equally and with equal importance. The special focus on the weakest and most defenseless creatures we have us men, we understand the value of love Universal, where inside is offline the degree of superiority or greatness that we men, unfortunately for involution, we try to achieve and we revere those who have obtained, even if this means setting us against our poor people, consequently against us and against the perfection of God. For this Universal Love and in the characteristics of you do not have to be the Son of God veneration of inequality. The creatures are equal in equal measure are loved. In order that this love is understood and that this is applied, the son of God for Divine Justice must reflect the Love. And the basic pinnacle of evolution that the man soon or later is required to achieve, and when will this include, the Son of God and the Universal Love that He is connected and in emotional dimension is given to men, in order that good triumphs, and there are more injustices and even pain for the next. This is the perfection, that man could escape, is obliged to achieve, otherwise than by the sword will perish SWORD. This is the BASE. Now if you understand the reasons why I recognize you son of God, if you want, we can talk further. Unfortunately, without this BASIC, we will begin to measure the size, and become devotees for greatness, or charm, or else, they would have nothing to do with the reality of God. -

JESUS':
- I have followed you, when you maintain compliance with the sentiment of pity, you could be more specific? -

JUDAH:
- Of course, you know I've seen him kill men, who at the first stroke of his sword, they realized that he could not go back, would not ABLE to heal the wound caused to their victims from their blow blow. In that moment I felt in their hearts they felt pity, despite this feeling he felt for their victim continued stabbing up to make sure she was dead. Strange thing in

human nature, you hit him, would cure him, but then the pain hit him again.

And in any death a part of you dies, the end so you're used to this that you do not realize that so many parts of you are dead you are DEAD too, just that you walk again. Here, you bring the possibility that man if he listens to you, can understand how not to give the first blow, but to try the mercy before the fight, and before hitting his victim. Through you Jesus', I realize that I pity before hitting a man, and I stop, so I think that the others if they learned to be near you as ME, would understand how much wealth there is in your heart as you are, You are the presence of God on earth, wonderful. -

JESUS':
- I will pass on this understanding. And how? -

JUDAH:
- Sometimes with words and your character, your personality, your own life, gives me this, speak to the soul, words are one thing more you talk with your heart, you have to learn to listen and have received the evolutionary grace of the good that helps you to hear the voice of your soul, the words of your heart; They say a lot of things and I listen to them, in every breath and every step you take. -

JESUS':
- You mean he does not listen to my word, and the voice of my soul, can understand God? -

JUDAH:
- Yes sure. Therefore, in life there is so much suffering and pain. Many men who suffer, many MEN who do evil. -

JESUS':
- I know even God, that he does not accept. -

JUDAH:

218

- Sometimes some people, suffer, because he had done wrong, and expect forgiveness. -

JESUS':
- We men have an obligation to forgive our fellow man, we sometimes help, even if a man has to learn through a bad away something that you need to learn only in that ugly way, we have to provide aid, we are morally obliged. God is pleased about this. -
JUDAH:
- I got that. However I agree, Just because we are sinners, and just to forgive. Certainly we do not know how he feels about God to forgive or not. A man, who did sin, this is something we can not understand that to forgive is in God judge him, we can not do it. The fact is that we human beings if we want to enter into communication with the plan of God and be in the arms of WE ACCEPTED THE LORD obliged to forgive the men. It also means that we have an obligation to help the needy. Rightly or wrongly, and without investigating what they have and what they have done in their past, or else the whole of our evolution and will lose meaning and value; we would do the right bad for not having done well despite having the power, even if we do not know whether the good we do we are making to the deserving or not people. We are bound to be compassionate and to dedicate himself to other.

Sometimes he minds his own business, in some cases, of course, is a way of sin and therefore to account for this to God and to their conscience. Why we do not care if any man suffers, and because it follows his sentence; good or bad, what interests us is: apply and represent, the law of love of God, which is to love and alleviate the suffering of others, and to respect the sense of piety, representatively, not useless pity if after is worth nothing is done. Besides, these are things belonging to Your Creation. For this I get through evolution, you are come because you are so done. And according to this love and deep Divine becomes one of many ways to recognize you. I know you. You are the Son of God, and it's my evolution that allows me to recognize you. A discovery my place after much study and not just because we have discussed. Or because I know for a specified time. Or why a particular TIME we hang out. I say this only bow to the needy bringing their help and need of that needing based, clearly each of us to his own possibilities, is a way of preserving a sound and rich our evolution, enriches the good, evil impoverishes, indifference, undermines and puts us in a position to be judged by God and by our conscience. -

JESUS':
- Right, good, God is pleased when we love even those who have harmed and even forgive our enemies. -

JUDAH:
- See that you are the Son of God. Only the Son of God could be capable of something so humble and respectful; how can you not love you and do not follow you when you lead the way, there is only the will to follow it. -

JESUS':
- I did not say just good because I wanted to buy you. -

JUDAH:
- I know, but you told me right and good, however; knowing that you're there and maybe you're already here in addition to what I say, it is done, out of humility, feeling, but why are you so fabricate me feel at home, even if they are at CASA Tua. And this behavior you have with everyone. Then when you get to talk to the others understand, that lent to education and respect for ear, because with your speeches, collect admiration and acclaim, everyone notices their authenticity. And they perceive the Divine value. >>

DISCUSSION BETWEEN JUDAS AND JESUS 'INHERENT TO GOD AND   HIS   COMING   -P.69

JUDAH:
<< How does God to come to us? Because in need of you, to come to us? He can also be reached without your service. -

JESUS':
- No, I do not think he would, even though I think he can do it. He comes to us men only if they believe and entrust ourselves to Him. I am here to present it, if you give him your hand, metaphorically, he is. Give the hand means to represent the good, recognizing that Love is God. The Eternal Life is God. We are made of flesh for a long time, but we are eternal beings, if we accept that God comes to us and leads to Paradise, but we have to invite him with our FAITH. -
JUDAH:
- God comes to us whether we recognize it, we accept it, and we   love   him?   -
JESUS:
- It 's right. Only then can God come to us, if we prepare ourselves to recognize it, to accept it, to understand it, to receive it, so I came to how to prepare the man to accept God, or He is not, I have the means to which humans can interact with God. Yes, of course, and goes against the suffering, his and neighbor. God has invited me in order that I would prepare His Coming. I prepare you to receive it. If you prepare to receive it, he is. If you prepare, you can not come, and we would fall asleep and men into eternal death and nothingness. Only God, the Eternal life. If I can not get in touch with God, my mission on earth has failed.

JUDAH:
- So far as man does not recognize the Son of God, he will find death and pain?

JESUS':
- Yes sure!

JUDAH:

- And men until you find that shows the way between them, they will kill, however, for any right or wrong, they make war, and never understand that in truth is biting each other because they have not recognized Thy be, that you are the Son of God.

Jesus:
- Yup! That's it. To always so happen to them, at least until they understand and will follow the path that I TELL them, and then it will not make war with each other, and not s'inventeranno idols, and false ideologies to be pursued and for them to die, they shall be always bogus.

JUDAH:
- Master, but the way you are You? Your person, your existence, your agree with your words but they are only an outline, it is your presence that shows the way, and recognize your identity, that will give peace to man! Because you're the Son of God, a part of the ground.

Jesus:
- Yup! That's right! >>

JESUS 'BEGINS ITS JOURNEY WHAT' YOUR DESIGN -P.70

JESUS 'began her journey and to speak to the world, after finishing   socially.
Judas, the friend remains, but prefers to stay aloof. He stand by and see what happens, it feels better. JESUS 'continues on his way. talk turns to the world, understands that JUDAS follows him in his own way and not regretted it. He feels in his heart that his friend is with him.

Judas remains Friend speaks meet are recommended, but the whole thing discreetly. JUDAS for several years has observed, to have seen, and now, in fact the analysis.

Judah finally decided to join his friend in his journey and follow him so no longer reserved but OFFICIAL until his death.

IS JOINS HAS JESUS 'FAITH WITH -P.71

Judah, despite being the first man in the world to recognize the Son of God, not joins Jesus' immediately but procrastinates, although it remains a friend. Probably Judas understands that for him work alongside Jesus' is not the same thing that is identical or similar to another man. For him it is different, and is aware of this. In fact there are so many Apostles joined to Jesus', but all in a way that can backtrack when they want.

With one foot inside and one outside.

For Judas, this is not quite fair play to the MAESTRO. He has deeply studied the situation understands that he lives in a non-decision, but fluid. JESUS 'does not decide the changes in their lives. It does not have the means, he glides on the bad or the good luck, without a word without opposition. It not has the means to follow the events. It understands that Jesus' is in the hands of God, in a sense, and only God is with him. He studied most of his patrons, he has understood the hypocrisy of some, and the feelings of others. He understood that they are psychologically human universe prisoners, which he knows like us, to be infected by evil and its derivatives related to it, one of these and the public embarrassment. For this he is different, it is different to become a disciple of Jesus' understands that humanity is against, is divided between, believers, indifferent, and enemies; for him alongside the Son of God must be a serious matter, a characteristic choice.

He knows that the enemies have the power and the means to put everything into question. His personality is different, for him alongside it means not being able to backtrack, it includes the commitment thickness

223

throughout your situation.

He wanted to return to China in his homeland, is now involved in the Divine Plan, has to choose a road that never would have expected to travel, never would have put in the account of his life, this circumstance and this entity. He is a character, and while staying and living in the middle of everything knows to be and to have some social relevance. Therefore justifies the reason of its supreme development: it is only to stay close to the Son of God. So Judah knows that for him things or have it properly or not at all. After all this travail says to himself:

If it is right that stream down my life for this man, this is the will of God, here I am, I will follow Jesus'.

But he feels within himself that for him is the end, even though he does not know how, but is convinced that having an adventure against evil is not easy. Now only two men are united against evil, and Jesus and Judas, the others are cotton candy on the cake. Judah does not hide like the other Apostles have strength and courage, and officially the world know that he is with Jesus'. What other one can only suspect, JUDAS is only clear security without fear without problems and with a LION heart; JUDAS, declares to the world that surrounds him to be: with Jesus'.
It 'clear that, since it's the Judas alongside Jesus'. The situation took another turn. Now JESUS 'is taken more seriously by both the friends and the curious. Now, you begin to realize that perhaps Jesus ', it is true that it is the Son of God, the character of Judas, it is strong and to keep up close, it means that Jesus' declares the truth. JESUS 'begins to be more respected. Begins a phase where no one can laugh more about him, at least not openly. If Judas and Jesus 'meaning that JESUS' he tells the truth, but it also means that we must be careful disrespect. The journey of Jesus' gains value, credit, and the right of respect. All this positive change he had he had thanks to confront JUDAH. Even the mad are more numerous. Why not just now

JESUS 'is heard by men, of any environment and social status. Both men belong to evil, both to right, now listen to the Son of God, and not with an air of mock him or consider him crazy, but with the interesting air and make friends. JUDAS created a huge upheaval. If Judas follow Jesus' this man is the son of God, there are no solutions. For those who knew JUDAS, See JUDAS that without fear or hide, or shame spoke and gave importance to Jesus ', this meant that Jesus' was the Son of God, no one would ever have thought that Judas went out of his mind, and knowing if it had anything to do with him; Because those who had been dealing with JUDAS, knew he was and how he acted.

JESUS 'makes the Miracles, and His fame to expand like wildfire. The increasing number of people come to him. Even his apostles feel more in a uniform body and all are near and follow him.

PLAUSIBLE DISCUSSION OF GOOD AND EVIL AND THE TRANSACTION SPIRITUAL-P.72

JUDAH:
<< What happened, why we are on earth, and God has left us to ourselves. -

JESUS':
- Probably a heavy fight between Angels who he has turned to God. -

JUDAH:
- Why does not God has destroyed them from the start, and the   story   ended   there?
JESUS':
- We do not know who was the Angel who has turned to God. However, we can imagine, that is painful injure or hurt they have their own creature, although revolts against. God wants us men we decide which side to take, and the only way to

225

isolate the rebel angel. -

JUDAH:
- You inside of you what you think of the choice of man? -

JESUS':
- God, I'm sure. This is the choice that man will do.

Probably, the time for words and deceptions and falsehoods is about to end, for this reason God is going to save those who believe in Him and obedience TRUST LAWS Love and WELL. -

JUDAH:
–   Even the angel makes love, even the righteous to evil love suffer, and many other things. -

JESUS':
- Yes, of course, but they are in a continuous vortex, where love, suffer they hurt and ask for help to God, rightly the evil in the end Angelo is not able to manage and help the creatures that followed; and these when they arrive at the height of pain and suffering, seeing the Angel of evil has no power to help, and to help, asking for help to God. God, is called to the rescue by us men who have mistakenly followed the Angel of evil, and then we realize that it has abandoned us, and is not capable of taking care of us, this misjudgment made us become mortal and suffering. Our pains become so deep that we recognize evil as a deceiver, and turn to God to intervene and forgive us for having followed the evil, and save us. The Angel of evil, thought to be able to give you happiness from God in heaven but what he has managed to give is always a pleasure, but failed to sacrifice Eternal Life; and take turns to each one gives painful penis. Those that bind to the end he remain a prisoner in the vortex of the penis and the eternal pain, and when you have had enough of suffering here; They turn to Heavenly Father, let alone the evil that gave only momentary happiness and apparent, and did not relieve them from pain. Clearly God

226

appreciates those who refuse the evil, and it does not eat, and if you now want to seek God and His help. Clearly those who suffered harm and it is nourished at the end when he arrives in pain, we do not know if God agrees to be searched and called only in extreme times of need. We do not know how he is GOD. we can not expect to rely on the bad for pleasure and in sorrow seek God, whether it is right or wrong, we can not say that our judgments are of God. We can refrain from speaking of his laws and follow them, to represent His will and his doctrine, but we can not judge and say that we are judges in charge of God. we may think it's fair to seek God when we are well and when we can be good and we find the strength not to feed us harm, even if we are tempted. This way we are sure that in time of need God be ready to support us and give us the happiness of eternal LIFE, love with a beautiful woman and the inner wealth, we just have compassion for others and do good, and seek God above all when we are good and it is not we need, too comfortable look when we are wrong and we need help. When we feel pity at that time, we have to do something, we do not do any good feel pity for others and staying with their hands HAND, that and how to commit a crime, as well as JUDAS You, I think, that you both agree on "this," I say? -

JUDAH:
- Yes! Sure! -

JESUS':
- So God can give all the pleasures that we believe, give us only the Angel of evil, only if we recognize the good and represent in a material way. And trust in Him in His love, and we recognize it as our Creator God. Clearly you have to behave according to the observance of laws for the common good, not necessarily deprive yourself of unnecessary things, is to be considered or to be taken as a sacrifice, but this is to be considered as the beginning of the Faith and devotion to the common good.

Man has not always wanting more, in this way following the wrong things. Peace is also nell'accontentarsi. You can avoid to be with the angel of evil, and not fall to his temptations, we must maintain a spirit of sacrifice and to enslave the less fortunate. In this way, what I put in the pot the angel of evil is always less than what God puts into the pot. If the angel of evil to be below gives a nice pleasure. Noting that God does not follow; trust in him and in good, even if it costs a little bit of sacrifice, in the pot puts an ever greater and more beautiful pleasure. >>

WICKED MEN scheming SON OF GOD-P.73

From that Judas was joined in JESUS ', now things are no longer the same. Its popularity becomes more consistent. The men who hold the keys of power in the hands come together and start discussing about him, and agree that his work upsets him constituted religious dictate. They decide to find a way to get rid from him. He has become too famous and cultures are overwhelmed by your thoughts. And 'His power to heal others, for kicking too many people. This is serious, they say, they feel threatened by your popularity that is gaining increasing consistency with the added beside him Judas. They fear that their influence on the people you always drown out more with the passage of time. Further agree that the popularity and power that would come from the Son Almighty, over the years, would seriously compromise their religious power. On these considerations decide to physically get rid of it. Thus, and for these reasons, in these terms they discuss among themselves:

PRIEST ONE:

<< We must get rid of Jesus', he with the passage of time will blur definitely our power and our influence over the people. -

PRIEST TWO:

- This is a task that we must, with due diligence, to carry Roma. And for this we have to talk to those of SANHEDRIN. >>

 SANHEDRIN. - P.74

PRIEST ONE:

<< We must get rid of Jesus' and the sentence must make ROME, we can not put our hands and our religion there prevents it, and do not want the people to have a part, we've wanted to get even. -

MAN OF THE SANHEDRIN:

- I'll talk with Pilate. >>

PILATO MEETS TO DISCUSS ABOUT JESUS 'CO PRIESTS OF THE SANHEDRIN. -P 75

PRIEST OF THE SANHEDRIN:

<< Pilate, we'll bring JESUS 'in court as a conspirator against the religion of Rome, he claims to be the Son of God, and our religion is a dangerous blasphemer. The crowd gathers to His call It seems that Men Faithful to Him has increased. In Particular There is JUDAS Side, SIMONE Son, Roman citizen. -
Pilate:
- And 'dangerous, it could lead to a riot. This JESUS 'is very popular, you can ensure JUDAS on your side? -

PRIEST TWO:

- We must study, a plan, but this sentence has still to be issued. -

Pilate:

- I understand, but we Romans do not mind, this is your problem, I'm in a bad situation. If I do condemn to death I take a pleasure in ROME, ROME but then how he takes it? If this happens another revolt among the Jewish people and ROMA, CAESAR this time will have my head in the past warned me; you remember your addressed the busts of emperors that I did bring in your town? He did a revolt, Caesar has not taken it very well. -

PRIEST TWO:

- Yes sure. So this time is different. -

Pilate:
- That was a mess, though ROME dirty their hands the blood of the Messiah, and he was born a popular uprising, CAESAR will have my testa.-

PRIEST ONE:

- If for us to study how to make you condemn without their born a popular uprising, you'd be more comfortable? -

Pilate:
- In this case, I might think about it! -

The priests go away and study a cleaner way to get out. >>

OBSTACLE. - P.76

Judas is an obstacle. They decide, after considering numerous, sending the Cat and the FOX inside the JESUS 'environment in order to investigate, as they are located together and to report every detail. As well as investigating they had to get into the good graces of the disciples and become familiar with them. More than any other the main purpose was to become friends reputable JUDAH, whatever the cost. Even if it had to buy his friendship and his affection; for them it was absolutely necessary to become affectionate and trusting friend JUDAS. JESUS 'realizes that within their circle there are new faces. Therefore they had the sweet face and the innocence of the boys; their minds were presented good and sincere, unthinkable for the Son of God, their real intentions. So good they showed that it was difficult to learn their backstory. JESUS 'realizes that they addressed many of their friendship attentions of Judas, Judas, and it seemed that the match willingly, indeed, I was pleased. These, with their gentle ways, become friends also JESUS '. So they could disguise, through their behavior and their affection, their true and sinister intentions. Everything is normal in the eyes of Jesus' and its environment. They spend a few months, and the plan of the enemy takes consistency. Through the cat and the fox JUDAS they are conducted in front of the religious leaders. Among them JUDAS befriends and becomes familiar. Religious leaders do not understand JUDAS their real intentions.

After that friendship takes its course, and the affection between them becomes more consistent, harmonious and predictable, the priests decided to take action. One day Judah, through the cat and the fox, is called by them. Judas goes to them, as it did a few times in the past, normal and quiet, thinking that most likely had the job of assigning tasks. M just reached them speak anything but intense activity, they say:
RELIGIOUS: ONE

<< Jude, you know JESUS 'a long time since he like? -

JUDAH:
- A wonderful person, talking about God helps the poor, He is the Messiah, I believe in Him, is a true friend.

RELIGION: TWO

- We know that He with His Identity Son of God, has turned against the religion that TIBERIO order to worship the Spirit of

AUGUSTO. -

JUDAH:
- We have our God in Judea, and there's always been allowed to worship the God of Our Fathers. -

PRIEST ONE:

- Yes, but it seems that his fame has come up to Rome, and it seems that Rome is conditioned by this. -

Judah:
- We have our Faith, the Romans have their beliefs, everyone lives for himself. -

One priest:

- Rome has instructed its provinces worship, Imperial Tiberius wants to be revered the spirit of Augustus but now you can feel threatened if the reputation of the Messiah has come down to Rome. You know, as we all know, that Rome maintains, balance his empire by means of their religion, when this is undermined, ROMA runs for cover. We know that the soldiers soon ROMANS, receive the order to capture JESUS '. And only a matter of time, it will stop and may He was born serious problems, and we could not save his life. We are against the death sentences, but if you are there, I deliver, we can talk to him and explain the whole thing to intermediaries through SANHEDRIN with Pilate, in order to avoid causing a bad fate. You know that if Judah ROMANS decide to take it, and before we arrived to Him, we at that point we could not do anything to save him. If He gives himself to us in his will, we can fix it, and put all affixed with ROME, through our who are SANHEDRIN, we can talk to Pilate and intercede for him. ROMA has no interest in going against us, Pilate, He does not want to have problems, just us, if we deliver the child of God, we can save his life.

JUDAH:
- I do what I should do? -

PRIEST TWO:

- We would like, question him, so to see what he thinks, to understand how things are, to try to save it.
We would like to listen to him and ask him about this, nothing wrong do not worry, you have to deliver to us if we want to save his life, and he will not do it, but if you are with us, then we can take it, you just have to lead us to him. -

JUDAS understands that the situation is delicate. He does not want problems with ROME and Justice ROME He is half citizen ROMANO. It remains to reflect.

PRIEST TWO:

- Judah, do not worry, nothing will happen to your friend, let us occuparcene, lead us to Him, and you will see that things will be alright. There are other solutions if we are to avoid intervening Justice of Pilate, and you know how he is evil and against us. >>

Judah, he faced the cat and the fox, which agree with a nod of the head that you need to trust ARE friends, and priests to God's service, and there is nothing to fear.

Judah then decide.

JUDAH:
<< Well I do not see where the problem is to take two and call it interrogatelo talk, he has no reason to refuse, it does no harm. -

233

RELIGIOUS:
- We have searched and did not find it, you know where? -

JUDAH:
- Of course I have to see him now, come with me and I will show you; but be careful, you have to follow me at a safe distance. Who will approach me, and will exchange kisses greeting us in the face, you'll see, it is Jesus'. I do not want you arrive along with me, I desire that Jesus' think ill of me; even if what I'm doing and just the only way I possess to save his life, does not want him to see that I was the one to take you from Him. This is why this I'll show you, you will wear it off at another time. -

RELIGIOUS ONE:

- On accordo.- he said to Judas. Then, turning to the guards continued:
- Go with JUDAS, see who is JESUS ', camuffatevi so as not to arouse suspicion, we will decide later when to pick it up. -

Then, turning again to JUDAS said again:

- For your trouble you keep these. >>

The priest gave him a bag containing the money. Judah accepted unaware of the seriousness of the situation, and leads with her characters to show them, your Master. Unaware that and I was delivering. Unconsciously they were afraid of him. Judas did not know what they were afraid of him, why he does not understand that he was involved and an obstacle which was, became permissive let go.

JUDAS MEETS JESUS-P.77

Judah comes to the garden, where, he knows that in that place

234

is usually to meet his Master. Behind him he has agreed distance are the guards of the priests, dressed in the usual way and the normal to avoid suspicion and be as unobtrusive as possible; with posters and attitudes of foreign nonchalant and disinterested gentlemen, they speak and discuss about their business peer with sinister glances from time to time to the Son Of God, trying not to attract the attention of those present to them.

JESUS 'and together with two Disciples. Judas and Jesus' meet and greet each other affectionately kiss. The priests men see the scene. Now they know who is their goal, and discussing each other move away without anyone being suspicious of their presence. JESUS 'has a serious expression on his face, with an almost sad tone, as if sensing a dark omen. Judah tries to have a serious and casual demeanor; but despite the effort it makes to suppress his emotions, there completely fails and the same part of the evil that surrounds him in, evades. Appears aloof, self-conscious, as if to hide to be deeply troubled. The effort that is trying to hire an appropriate demeanor in front of a friend has a thickness of Jesus is huge. To Jesus does not escape this unusual temperament of Judah, he is lacking in spontaneity and purity. The gaze of the Messiah does not miss a thing. JESUS 'feels within himself that Judas, and in the throes of an anxiety that can not hide. Is struck and saddened, to see so his beloved friend is a fact to what shocking. They exchange a few words. So even though Jesus' wants to talk to Judas and understand what happens to him, Judas is elusive. After that: JUDAS moves away, providing reassurance that all is well, goodbye. However JESUS 'warned the painful anguish of Judas. Begin to think and slowly, slowly, he begins to hear Him even into the depths of his soul. Begins to have a sense of foreboding.

The guards have seen who is JESUS 'and noted that he had company. So they refer to the priests it's seen by the situation. They decide to send along with them, to withdraw JESUS ', a dozen soldiers. The same evening he goes to pick up at home, many.

JESUS 'then includes the anguish of Judas and thinks that he is involved in his arrest. Automatically immediately he understands that the anguish of Judas is to be associated to his arrest.

He is led by the priests and no longer return.

JESUS 'combines the anguish of JUDAH to his arrest, and when Judas includes this JESUS belief', reached the height of contempt for himself. JESUS 'within himself becomes convinced and understands that Judas betrayed him.

Judah becomes involved in a situation of no return, and without being profoundly account, the blame of whatever would happen from then on to the Messiah, he would have been solely responsible. The sky fell on him. A process carried out with time, and with feelings of friendship called into question by the sending of people who gave their affections, collecting estimates, but with the purpose and deception in the soul; with the exclusive aim of reaching to have the Son of God through Judah. A diabolical ability to pretend to have FAITH and not have any. A diabolical ability to pretend to love, when in fact there was only contempt. Pretend to be loyal, devilishly keep a diabolically planned behavior, alo order to make believe in true friendship, but only to interest. When Jesus' begins to slow, it becomes known that he had been led by the priests; some of his Apostles and family come to ask him. Simon, he sees the seriousness of the situation and if before asking for Jesus', now says he does not know him and to be there, to ask Him to order and on behalf of others.

PRIESTS-P.78

The PRIEST ONE:

236

<< Now! The Messiah we wield, thanks to JUDAS there, it gave him up without being aware of our real intentions. Now we must act quickly to do so to prosecute and demand his death sentence. -

PRIEST TWO:

- Of course, we have to do it before it wakes up from JUDAS blow, and he realizes he has been used, and that he discovers the deception of the Cat and the Fox. -

SACERDORE ONE:

- Yes, everything went according to plan, now we do condemn, and then we will see what to study with JUDAS PRIEST when he discovers the raggiro.- TWO:

- We'll tell him we tried to save him but we did not succeed. -

PRIEST ONE:

- What shall we say to her relatives, if they found out everything? -

PRIEST TWO:

- That we were not able to save the same things that we will say to Judas. Chased, they will know that Judas was to bring him to justice, and the blame will go only to him. What are the family relationships of the Messiah? - PRIEST ONE:

- Jesus is the heart of his relatives, but if we act quickly and we get his sentence without spending too much time, will all be blown away as it will be Judah. We will see the result after the sentencing. -

PRIEST TWO:

- When the condemnation of Jesus will be done, now for them to take any action to save his life will be in vain. Time will prove us right; Judah shall be guilty of the Master's fate, and he sold us nor subbiamo, nor are we completely off, we are not responsabili.-.

PRIEST ONE:

- The information we have gathered about him, are clear, around Jesus there are men who live under the rule of fear, fear for their lives can not act in time to save the lives of their Beloved. Solo and relatives can get organized, but our action will be so rapid that neither will have the time. -

PRIEST ONE:
–   This is true of his relatives are not able to organize themselves in a short time, at least in appearance it seems obvious that they are not, this gives us free continuation of our intentions.
In future we should not suffer retaliation. -

PRIEST TWO:
Judah shall be guilty of treason, his guilt exonerates us from any kind of retaliation, the evil will turn against and toward him. -

PRIEST ONE:

- And yes, they will never understand that behind all this there is us.

Family members and close friends will understand that the fault is one of Judah, and we will stay out and we will come out with your hands pulite.- PRIEST TWO:

- Judas without realizing remain treacherous and guilty of the death of the Master. Now we must warn the Cat and the Fox to stay away from JUDAH, not to show around and to maintain an attitude equals that of the Disciples: vanishing. They will have to come out, after the death of the Master, and the first thing will put out the word of the betrayal of Judas, with great discretion, to be the people to condemn him of treason without knowing which is the direct source of the information. -

PRIEST ONE:

- Of this I'll use it, know how to lead them, everything is clear. -

PRIEST TWO:

- Right, well said, that way you will have to proceed.

Later, when Jesus' is dead, the blame will go to Pilate in front of Rome, so we would also clean against Rome. We would also be cleaned towards his friends and relatives, who will blame to JUDAH, and pronounced him a traitor. Us if they would be questioned, but I doubt this will happen, we will say only that: "despite having done, we can not manage to avoid him the conviction." So we would be freed from any kind of involvement and suspicion. Our strategy is perfect. Then we will see what to study against JUDAS, but this at the time. If necessary, we also rid of him physically, basically this will be just what he expects in the future. -

PRIEST ONE:

- Right this is a smart move. So before you get rid of Judah, we should let people know about his betrayal just so everything will match. We must wait and make a move at a time. -

PRIEST TWO:

- Of course, this happened after the sentencing, it will be the Cat and the Fox, the solution of this problem; They will make sure that other, in clever way, know the betrayal of Judas. -

PRIEST ONE:

- Now we have to proceed. -

The SANHEDRIN and with us, Pilate will have to carry out the sentence that suggest, or otherwise will turn against us and knows that is not convenient. He knows that we can make it a problem. Caesar does not want conflicts and unrest in Judea; among other things he should agree to the condemnation of Jesus', because he is also against the Imperial religion. -
SACERDORE TWO:

- Of course let's get a move on, we think about the rest later, close any link with Judas and let's get going with SANHEDRIN. A Judas We must not give them time to reorganize ideas, otherwise we could be a problem to be solved; if we stay on time, he will come later to the understanding and will remain guilty of treason. -

PRIEST ONE:

- Only the declaration, his betrayal becomes our filter, our shield, and this will avoid any retaliation or revenge from anyone. -

PRIEST TWO:

- For the moment, Judah will stay good, will expect that we save your Venerable Master, for this good and will stay on hold. He trusts us, there is delivered and is involved. His reaction before the Messiah's conviction, is not to be put into account, the story ends here. -

PRIEST ONE:

- Unlikely JUDAS include, before the Messiah's conviction, which we used and we involved with cunning. You're right. JUDAS for the moment is expected of us the salvation of his Master, so remain calm. -

PRIEST TWO:

- But we are the ones that we do condemn. We will find out, but it will be too late for him and for others. -
PRIEST ONE:

- Do not believe that we have done everything possible to save his MAESTRO. We understand that, we had to save it, we are the ones that we did condemn. -

PRIEST TWO:

- Yes it will take time to understand this, the right time that is realized our plan. -

PRIEST ONE:

- Will include our deception only when he sees his Master carry the cross to Calvary.

PRIEST TWO:

- Yes, I think so. However you need not worry; we have the CAT AND THE FOX on our side, have become very good friends, something we will study through them. You will see that we also get rid of Judah, and
even then it will come off without trouble and with clean hands. So before cunningly, they will have to reach the ears of

the people, the betrayal of Judas.

PRIEST ONE:

- They have to do two things at once. -

PRIEST TWO:

- They would? -

PRIEST ONE:
–   One is that it must stick to Judah, to calm him down and to control his intentions, and the other to
 run cunningly betrayal voice of Judah. -

PRIEST TWO:

- I know! Everything was perfect until now, it's everything is in our plans. We will think after this. -

SACERODOTE ONE:

- Yes, of course we will study later a plan to suit him and the circumstances, as we have done with his Master. -

PRIEST TWO:

- Sure. For now the involvement of Judah was rehearsed, can not harm us, and what we are implementing is linear, we are is we are not the SANHEDRIN, but the SANHEDRIN is with us, is the sentence will declare the Roma. -

PRIEST ONE:

- Right, that's true, it takes its time to understand, and to come directly to us. -

PRIEST TWO:

- At the end we will find the well rid of him the system. - A
PRIEST:

- I know that with this move, there we are already liberated,
must first heal the wound, and not only him, but also friends
and relatives. -

PRIEST TWO:

- Sure. First, to come to us, you will have to find a way to
overcome these blows: Death of his friend, our deception. And
then he will also have to overcome the blows of the people;
we'll see his reaction when they hear say that "it was Judas to
betray his Master, and 'he is dead because of him." We'll see
what will think of doing and how the take. -

PRIEST ONE:

- Yes! And 'all clear, for Judas is over. >>

PILATE AND THE SANHEDRIN-P.79

PRIEST OF SINDRIO:

<< Pilate, you have to question Jesus', and its examination will
understand that it is against the religion of TIBERIO, and is a
blasphemer, these are reasons enough to put him to death.

Pilate:
- I can not condemn this man to drop the blame on Rome,
when the people rebelled it goes in my head. I would not know
how to get out with CAESAR, though here comes a new revolt.
Among the people there are supporters of Jesus'?

SACERDORE of SANHEDRIN:

—   Few. Because they were afraid, they were recognized and also put them under arrest, for this reason they are few and maybe none.

Pilate:
- Mandate among the nations of your trusted men, and say to ask for Barabbas to be released.
PRIEST OF THE SANHEDRIN:

- What did you have in mind?

Pilate:
- I condemn the people, I will come out with clean hands, and you too. >>

So, they asked the people if they choose JESUS ', or Barabbas to be released. The people choose Barabbas, and the condemnation of the MESSIAH.

JUDAS IT MAKES STATEMENT deception P-80

Judah begins to will reflect. He understands that he was approached and has been used with affection and feelings of friendship. He begins to see the beginning of evil, think CAT AND THE FOX. Then he thinks that enter into friendship with priests was only one circumstance. It is convinced that the CAT and FOX, are missing. In the end, his head still goes beyond the Cat and the Fox. He sees everything, right before his eyes. They realize that they used to get to JESUS 'without having it against, and without that they could have retaliation. It understands that in the end the blame would fall all over him. Begins to change opinion. Clearly it understood that it was not a circumstance, the meeting that enabled to go in confidence and sympathy with the priests and to become their friend, but that was all designed and programmed by forfeit. JUDAS not by peace, asks: - How did I get involved and let me rub this way? Not only step traitor for having given me the DA Son of God. I can not fight back, they ripped me fooled me. They have used only because they were afraid of me. Guide includes everything wants rearrange ideas. Therefore, it hurt the thoughts, come to thousands He becomes the culprit of the death of his Master, and Best Friend; He does not accept what he did and what was left to do. He reproaches himself.

JUDAS wants to talk to the priests, to stop this criminal machine, but apparently it does not find anyone. He can not find even the CAT and La Volpe, it remains alone. Think of talking with Jesus' relatives, but they do not speak shall release they are far away and terrified. They are afraid, do not want to learn. The rest of the Apostles, he went into hiding. Judah seeks help, but can not find anyone to support him, all those who loved her MAESTRO hour of need have disappeared. SIMONE Also, do not expose it to him prevent other family members. Meanwhile time passes and JUDAS unable to do anything for his beloved friend.

THE CRIME-P.81

Jesus spoke with God. We can imagine that the offense was challenged Jesus has other could not be said to be the Messiah, the Son from God. The sentence was death is only given for this reason. When Jesus was condemned, and has been written here dies the King of the Jews, this means that:
Perfidy manifested itself, not because Jesus claimed the King of the Jews, but for the fact of banter, as if he, in the opinion of the priests, the wanted to know long. The blasphemy of Jesus consists only in this, said to be SON OF GOD?

HOW WAS THE ENVIRONMENT FAMILY OF THE MESSIAH JESUS '? HOW YOU ARE INVOLVED THE COMPANY 'WITH HIM. P- 82

Before the rooster crows you will deny me three times. You dear readers really think that to deny the Son of God, were necessary to wait for the cock could crow? Therefore, since Jesus' began to be revealed to the world those who have not, have denied there were definitely in the fingertips. Then imagine those who would follow a man who says he is the Son from God. Therefore, on the one hand, and did not not care to anyone what he was saying and what he preached, on the other side those who knew him was rather embarrassed that around you know he was his friend, or that he was one who followed Jesus'. Therefore JESUS 'was denied by many, and not surprise me at all if he was also denied by the immediate family. Unfortunately this is the sum. Free access, the priests, the freedom to manipulate the realism, to say I was with Jesus' death occurred in, it's all an element that is inside the evil nature and evil man. Judah also becomes the victim of a diabolical plot, those terrifying, because he remained a traitor of the Son of God for eternity. I think that the main problem of Judah is not to move from a traitor in front of humanity, but is to move from a traitor in front of the SON of God. Only he has this matter and nothing else. We should just ask a question to Jesus' and tell him:

<< Master you think in your heart that Judas has betrayed you?
-

The Master does not respond. Unfortunately this is the question that Judas would do to Jesus'. We can ask another question Jesus', and ask:
–   Master you when you saw Judas at Calvary for you to believe, looking at him, you thought that he had betrayed you?
-.

Here is the MYSTERY!

Because this could be the realism in its purest form and the explanation of many questions. If Judas warned that JESUS 'knew that he had betrayed him, Judas seriously he was saddened, regardless of who was or was not the traitor! One thing is certain that Jesus' was not wrong! Otherwise we would not be here talking!

THE CALVARY-P.83

How you can end a friendship so? Friendship wanted by the heavenly plan. It can not end a friendship as well. It can not end like this beautiful friendship. Too beautiful to be over, it's not right, it will never be. An immense pain. The two friends who cross your eyes, one under the cross on his right shoulder, the other standing at him, and both to stare into her eyes, with a broken heart. Both fell into a deep mortal anguish, even before his last breath felt the horror of death. can not happen something like that, it's not right, was not to happen, there is no forgiveness for what was done to him, there can not be forgiven, even if they were to ask this for the same JESUS '.

All that is given to men on earth everything will be taken away, you can not kill a man like that, is not a condemnation of Jesus' in this way.
He repeated to himself if JUDAS: "There can be a way to believe what is happening, but it is possible that IS going on?" It's impossible to believe that they are doing! What, do they fulfill? And yet they are doing it! It 'com 'is that they are doing? you can not kill a man like that! With broken my heart, and tears covered his face, JUDAS told himself the same words. "you do not kill a man like that!" his heart did not respond, his mind bursting. He could not, and could not accept a GOD SON reality that was under the cross ready to be killed. Unacceptable cruelty, suffering, that his master was going to try. He was to be killed and only realizing that he was dying inside, like his Master. Judas realized that it was over, his friend was killed and nothing could save him, and 'it was too late to do anything. all their affection , he was now separated from disgrace, and it remained only a mortal pain. A terrible tragedy, this was happening under the eyes of Judas. A tragedy, in understandable, and crime took place, and Judah had seen in

person, crossing the eyes of his master, all the pain and sorrow of his master. Through the Master's eyes, he included in its intensity the anguish he felt and the consciousness of the fate that awaited him. At that moment he felt within himself deep inside that Jesus' thought him guilty of his death sentence. Judah at that moment she felt die, even more evil pervaded the spirit, come up to stun him completely. Judas, filled with heavy anguish, which closed the life of the soul and the breath. His heart was broken. What his eyes had seen, what he has had the courage to see, what he wanted to ascertain the person had killed him inside. The thoughts, the pain, did not give him peace of mind. It was wrapped in a death grip, which gave him no more reason and way of living. Judah, I realized that, it was also dead. Within him he had died. The pain had become great, you did not hear him anymore, he felt only that he was dead. Only the meat was alive but he felt dead. A dead man can not live only because the flesh is alive, that this in the end succumbs without the spirit light up to lose his life. Including that he had died. These are the words that can explain the terrible feeling of pain and how he felt at that moment Judas.

Live, now, did not make sense. The pain despair came to him so deep, that there was another way, that commit suicide and die in full, because a living body when you're dead inside does not mean anything. In a glimmer of conscience he understood that he had been cheated, and felt a great humiliation. This humbling feeling was the straw that broke the camel and he troubled decided he could not go to stupid. So Judas, He took what little life was left in his whole being, and that it was placed only in the body, just because it was breathing. He decided to hang himself as a protest against himself, against man, against life, against the tragedy of existence against sin that men were doing to Son From God. Judas knew that committing that offense meant, that man the challenge hurled against God. He knew that with that gesture the man sanctioned the covenant with evil, there was no hope for man. He   had   chosen,   and   had   decided   on   evil.

Was over salvation of life, had ceased all, the man was with the evil, were fighting against good and against God. This was one of the many plagues that led Judas to suicide.

PLOT: - P.84

JESUS 'was the cross on his right shoulder. He was coming from the town. Around if anyone, the people that went back and forth as if he were curious and some kid, a young age. It seemed that the people to follow him there was no one, perhaps no one wanted to see the tragedy that was taking place. He wore a tunic in one piece, light brown. Long until, almost at the foot of which were completely bare. The tunic had no belt was a unique and free.
His hair was graying up to his chin, brown, like her eyes. With a line in between. The cross was about two meters thirty, from end to end. The width of the planks were about twenty centimeters thick, about ten or nine centimeters and weighing about thirty five pounds. With a wooden board of about one meter and forty nailed to the center, forming a T-cross, and projecting above a forty centimeters. The color of the cross was light brown or hazel. He paused for a second, turned his head to the left to look around him. His eyes interbred with those of JUDAH. Judas was dressed in a tunic, all of a piece of gray, and had his arms folded. THE eyes stared at each one into the other's eyes. Then Jesus' looked away, he looked at the sky and saw the dark and gloomy as his heart and that of his best friend. It seemed as though, gives a little later, it was to start to rain and continued his sad ordeal. Their anguish passed from one to another. It was the last time you saw him, and for several seconds stared into his eyes, as if he wanted to forget and never to part.

Life is a mystery, and men do not know that this land does not belong to him, and do not know anything on this earth belongs to him. All die, and even alone do not have to kill, each of us has the right to make their own evolutionary cycle. All we are passing through, it is useless to stop or prevent the unfolding of life to another person. We are, all of the Moors, it is only a matter of time. For this you do not need to create pain, death is our life, as much as it is life itself. We died sooner or later, no one is excluded, no use getting hurt, and give pain to others.

Both realized that they were dead, either. Disbelief almost, of what was happening, but the pain and the anguish had, of them did, the same victim.

Judas kills himself. The priests, celebrating, JESUS 'died apparently the culprit has committed suicide, he could not get any better than this; no reprisals, no revenge, the culprit of his arrest has died and the story ends there. Therefore, for the Jews, the story ends, but for Romani who have stained their hands of the DA GOD SON blood, their story begins with the death of the SON OF GOD.

THE SIGHT. -P85

Judas saw the herd that broke in pieces his Master. The flock of the poor, who enjoy doing evil under reporting or command of a wealthy chieftain. No maybe just like that, but almost. Already the poor who kill in a pack and follow the orders of the rich that they are keeping their hands clean. Already the dirty work they do always do the poor. Judas saw the herd. The stupid pack and without reason that kills when it can not be faulted and can not pay for the crime committed. The Pack is a coward.

The pack that broke in pieces his Master, and that no one could stop now, even if he had ordered the same emperor, now for Jesus there was nothing to do, perversion chain of evil had invaded the minds of all the poor, Judah saw this and realized this.

Jesus saw the herd, which broke in pieces, and nothing he

250

could do to prevent it. The flock of the poor who amused at him, and only when they were in the group were so ruthless, brave. Then their skill ended, already because the group is not reprehensible crime, and does not go to individual evil. Already the poor who kill in packs, are always good and not executioners. Poor people who are strong sets and then they cry when they are slaughtered (the laws) by the rich. Already the poor are dangerous when they are in groups, because they have no head and they enjoy hurting, it is unleashed. Jesus saw a BRANCO MURDERESS. This was his last clear and clean image that he brought with him in heaven. A beautiful memory of man brought to Heaven, nothing to say.

Already you have poor likes making war especially if they are convinced of winning. For this reason they sing in chorus hymns of glory, MOVING.

JUDAS SUICIDAL-P.86

The wind was light announcing that the storm would arrive shortly thereafter.

JUDAS brokenhearted, sings a lament of pain accompanied by tears. His eyes full of tears do not give more water but blood and his face are all wet.

JUDAS complains aloud his sentence, as if the painful wounds in this way can break free and express themselves. Only wind ilo listens to his gruesome wailing.

Then he looks up at the sky and shouts: "My God, I have done everything to save my brother." There've done, forgive me for betraying your trust. God! They killed my brother JESUS ' WHY? WHY '! Judah said that! he puts the rope around his neck, complaining of pain with the wind, the only witness sole caretaker of his words, and to him and his eyes to heaven and said: "FORGIVE tHE LORD." That said, he let himself go between the arms of death.

Here Judas' suicide is characteristic proof that Jesus is truly the Son of God. Suicide makes sense, in whatever side we wanted to investigate: repentance, error, remorse of conscience. ... Etc ... Etc ... The ultimate gesture says:

<< This man is the Son of God is I try through my painful choice. >>

Suicide as ultra confirms the reality seen by men who followed the Messiah. Jesus the son of God: the suicide of Judas, painful act of repentance, test action.

Man's consciousness understands this reality and communicate it to the world. Therefore man communicates to the world the betrayal of Judas that these means as well: "Jesus is the Son Of God." How to say "Yes"! Judas kills himself because he betrayed Jesus, but it is also true that it kills because Jesus is the Son of God. To betray the Son of God can not stand in the Soul. This becomes an action that do not forget easily. There are two reasons that go together. Two reasons why commit the suicide of Judas. These two reasons explain the suicide of Judas, are:

The betrayal, the identity of Jesus. Another proof that joins other motivations which together feed the beginning and the continuation of the Faith would be:

Judah through suicide launches two messages to others. A: "I'm sorry, forgive me Lord, always I know you're the son of God." The other: Jesus is the Son of God my Suicide is the ultimate guarantor of this profound truth, because I do not accept the death of Jesus, in protest at this act, and dissociation to the fulfillment of the humiliation that I suffered, I'll kill myself; because it is too painful this fate, what happened exceeds the extreme pain.

A profound grief, anguished, a spiritual wound that disturbed the conscience, decided the protest, suicide, against injustice.

See Jesus carrying the cross, and everything else, is the straw that broke a vase already full.

GUILT AND CONSCIENCE. P.87

<< Dear Brother: I do TI 'final farewell and I come with you. >> It would be a decision made even before Jesus died, and implemented its own hot from his Master's death. So in this case Judas kills himself before the people would owe him the finger and declared a traitor of the Messiah.

However Judas grows into a mindset where his father kill a person, it can have an excuse, so not all murderers are condemned, judged, and unforgivable. Judah grows in an environment, in a mindset, especially his father, where betraying a man, does not excuse, and betrayal only draw with death.

The BETRAYERS KILLED. -P. 88

In fact, he knows that the traitors can not be forgiven and therefore be killed. This concept HIM taught since childhood. His father can not not having explained these beliefs, because Simon was a killer who killed for commission and on behalf of the Romans. Mathematician who equalized Judas betrayal with death, with no exceptions for himself.

The evaluation of Judah toward the world and religion are that man can not sin and must not sin. So, probably, there is no forgiveness towards some deadly sins or serious, but only to a minor sins, which unfortunately does not expect the selection to us, so we can guess or imagine what they are grave sins and which are not. A sin of a certain size can not be forgiven, only death can do it. This tells Judas to humanity: << Do not sin must not sin, forgiveness is not sin. >> This man says Judas.

BETRAY NOT, AND 'THIS FORGIVENESS! - P89

In Judah there were all human failures that has spent his life in the period of Jesus without doing anything positive to ilo Son of God. So Judah with suicide has downloaded all the failures (THE BETRAYAL) man against the Messiah. Adam did nothing to repair the damage committed by him to repair and therefore did sin all mankind.

Peter, did nothing to repair the betrayal he has done in Christ, He just waited for the forgiveness of Christ; but Judah did the best work for the man leading him to Christ, and downloading all human failures, through his betrayal, leading humanity to Christ. Therefore all human failures, he led them to Christ and at the same time, he is the one who has led humanity to Jesus. The work of Judas is the strength that He gave Jesus in support of its mission as a human figure , supportive and affective, and his complete suicide his positive work towards of God, which ultimately serves to man, to walk the path towards Christ recognizing him, (initially) the Son of God through the betrayal of Judas. Suicide is like consciousness Soul screams of Judah, the sin that he has committed is the friendship of man for failure work of the flesh, and he has downloaded the betrayal of one who loved most in the world; destroying the betrayal by the Act of betraying those who did not deserve it at all, and that the more the way he loved, and with the action of his suicide, he declared to the world. << Jesus is the Son of God! >>. In fact, he threw the money, because he won the man's betrayal, and himself.

The Jews bought with the money Judas, Judas cast them in the temple, so defiled all mankind, and his betrayal is the betrayal of ALL MANKIND '. Therefore, 'Judah is all of us!

MY LORDS! JUDAH AND 'THE ONE THAT HAS BROUGHT TO CHRIST! HOW CHRIST AND 'THE ONE THAT HAS BROUGHT TO

GOD! P.90

The mentality of Judah is the one that the traitors should be killed, because if he had a communion with his father, it is clear that Simone has explained that the traitors should be killed. So Judah grows with the conception that a man who kills has a reason to do so does not need to even the score "in most cases." But a man who betrays into the match, only with death. Judah respect for the personality of Jesus, which is against violence, not telling him a part of his being which is this:

"The traitors are killed!" So many things about Judas, Jesus did not know them.

ANALYSIS OF THE NOVEL-P.91

From this novel we see, Simon, the father of Judas, who believes in himself, and only himself. This is a feature that a father could give an inheritance or transmit temperamentally a devoted son who loves his father and follows the examples and teachings. So he wants to absorb example, the personality and instinctive character. ... Etc ... Etc ... And I want to show to the world, by becoming some of his personality traits and part of himself.

Why Judas sees his only father to be superior to him, and no other man except God. And in accordance with, this concept is evolving, think, learn, and study the world and life. Be sure of his social class meant that the people respected him, and he did not find many obstacles to achieve the objectives of life. The class of membership gave social benefits and also considerable evolutionary, to men who like him and belonging to the same social class, were seeking to realize and evolve as much as possible.
By analyzing this novel, we notice that Judas did not grow up under the influence of the environment, where Jesus lived, so it is not corrupted by the environment, or at least not of the

kind of Jewish environment, even if they knew, and they knew informational characteristics and customs.

Judah has evolved, in another part of the world, its evolution and divided between his father's teachings that is devout Jew in Rome and therefore feels the Roman Empire, and the teachings of the society and the environment that are of another world . When it comes to the lands inhabited by Jesus, he does not even know if there is Jesus, I do not know, much less one dreams of meeting him, is already an adult, according to the custom of the time, when he returned with his father at home. Therefore, he knows who his father is, as it was before his Father and what social hierarchy occupied, knows: if it suits them said to be foreign, unknown if it suits him to be what he says is the blood of his father , this in order to be able to adapt and interact in any environment he wants to integrate or want to have to do. We unfortunately we would not know ever down that kind of culture and inner evolution Judah has assimilated in those days behind the world. Judah is distinctive in the way that Jesus has to undertake. Judah is a characteristic element for the project of Jesus and is part of the project of Jesus who is prove to the world.

So before you work with the system and with the house, then she began her journey, what God had marked. Also because I believe that claim to be the son of God, it was like saying, do not get me more work, and do not give me more like a home, to live. This is why Jesus is the obligatory steps in a personal evolutionary scope of work and economic stability, even if we can assume that social relations, and given his manifestation to the next, they could help in some way to be able to earn some money to get by on living. Before you start talking to the world, we know that to devote himself to this divine mission, he should not commit his person and thoughts of survival techniques, why we think something up and she did or would not otherwise have been able to engage in God.
However we may also consider that Judas as Jesus started on

his way, has a bit 'pulled the plug friendship, just because he has a double psychological situation. A: is to have to do with the environment and the world, and proper to maintain a certain reputation, probably with Jesus, as the enemies who had judged him badly, he could compromise it. It is part of life, that in order to fulfill their social ambitions, you must make sure to stay in a group, or in a social situation, so we need to make sure that you do not say something to read against it. And, the other and the one that can not come off completely to Jesus because it is linked within themselves, for sentiment, friendship, sympathy faith, wonder and so on. ... It would be painful to see him mock and not intervene. Therefore he wanted to be free in their actions, and not forced by feelings or by a packer or other. ... Etc ... Etc ... FREE to think and act without feeling compelled by feelings. However, Judah, not to see this double situation that embarrasses him in the choices, still managed cleverly to dominate the world around them and did not make it clear within himself his thoughts and his reasonings, dominates the world around him, and he studied the way of being, both of the one part, that the other part. To realize that the claim to be the son of God has embarrassed the family, the brothers were slowly, slowly isolated and work not nobody gave it to him and gave it to him if you took advantage of it, given the situation, friends they walked away, he had created a hostile world around Jesus and those around him. Judah does not could afford it, not in fear, but not to go backward in accordance with what his hard work had achieved. He had definitely constructive plans for his future and could not expose himself too much, but he did not move away from the son of God who had just recognized him, why he had to play his cards well to keep both ideals.

We are in a position to understand the air you breathe at that time. Jesus' apostles were angry, because of him were isolated from the Jews. Friends had left did not want problems with the priests, and Judas kept her eyes open. So all those who were around Jesus were curious, but not the official supporters. On this basis of this environment, and you could not spread the word of God. Recover survival it is the first of all thoughts. It may be that both came into play a split in the environment of religious after the death of Jesus, in conjunction with some ROMANS become FAITHFUL. In order that the religious cleavage occurs, here, in the novel do get the CAT and FOX into play. They came with treachery and deceit, but in a later contact with JESUS 'has left its mark and broke away from religious bringing with others and have gone over to Jesus'.

ANALYSIS MORAL -P.92

A man capable of splitting the personality and characteristics of the other, and according to this information to predict the future in principle, must know himself deeply, and also possess excellent balance and self-control. Ultimately though Judah believed that Jesus was the son of God, and that Jesus was, and 'is really the son of God, there are different solutions, and some doubts in this reality. Why two different people but bound together in the spirit, and not only that:

<< The intelligence, superior intellect noble class, artistic, civic, binds them more than anything mysterious. >>

Both possess: the intellectual culture, spiritual evolution, wisdom, ARE these things, which merges them with each other, and links them with the most wonderful Feeling like we can imagine. And for understanding and achieved stage of development, they are estimated, and they love each other. This is real! The supreme knowledge:

One is the son of God, which by its nature knows who he is.
The other is Judas, that its evolution has come to God, (who is the same God and Father of Jesus), and as a result, has put on its own evolution in intellectual terms, to recognize the Son; which is JESUS '. Why Judas manages to recognize Jesus the son of God, had come to the understanding of the Heavenly Father,

recognizing the Son was an evolutionary consequence of the Good, acquired, through an evolutionary path, we say a road, but we do not know which way is that taken from him. We can say that he had come a certain stage of evolution, but neither know the instructive path. This is a mystery that knows him and God. This was the truth that united Jesus and Judas deeply each other; Therefore he made them brothers in spirit, regardless of which were different in culture and mentality. However for certain that if, Judah recognizes Jesus as the Son of God, and that is in Jesus as we do not know and will never know! Jesus to bind him, a man by the stamp of Judah must have indefinite quality that normal men, common, scientists, scholars, academics, will never comprehend and understand, only Judas could do so only he knows everything! Nobody would have been able to recognize and to discover the extent of Jesus none! Jesus has something inside that only Judas knows, something incomprehensible to humans. Returning to the speech, as above of Judah and in search of his mystery, we say:

Of course we do not know and will never understand the Evolutionary Road which Judas path to reach God, but we know that only God could recognize coming from the Son. This is the only logical and rational view that we can consider. Then we men scholars on our own we can suppose the way that Judas has traveled to recognize the existence of God and to discover the characteristics of the Good, and therefore understanding this puts him in a position to recognize Jesus. We think that it is that of music . We not, however, know how and where he thought turned his thoughts and his inner thoughts. Therefore, if God allowed Judas arrangements achieved this evolutionary stage there must be a characteristic reason. The reason could be that the path that Jesus had to make, it was necessary that he had a man near her to believe in him so deep. And 'indisputable by psychological characteristics of Judas, that the man was really him. And what better way exists only to understand yourself with your own research a truth of this thick? FAITH and continue on it can make getting a Divine of Good understanding. Understanding of Judah proved that he had a deep faith in God and knew the value of good. Here is the reason why God allowed Judas to achieve what developmental stage, Faith. Judas must have been chosen by God as a helper of his Son because he has shown faith. We do not know, but we can assume that God has put to the test Judah, and having seen that has overcome, allowed that he met and put to the side of His Son. Strange truth. Conflictual our teachings, but plausible.

However E 'From this truth that was born their affection, esteem each other, the pleasure of being together with a big inner contentment, which saturated the mind when they reasoned together and indulged in mystical speeches and endless. The knowledge and the satisfaction I felt when debating were unparalleled. Their spirits for evolutionary stage achieved or achieved jointly held them together in life and inseparable from death. As brothers in spirit belonging to the same spiritual dimension, although unrelated, and several taken in the civil dimension, one of one kind one to another, however, they died together. While not brothers, they died together as two real twin brothers. This is the material realism, not denying what I was born to that realism is fulfilled. Only this realism can put together two people of different social customs and environmental mindset, in communion with each other. Must share something deep otherwise there is communion, and the thing he had in common was their supra-human and boundless intelligence, the esteem for them, and love for God.

MATH-P.93

We know that Judas was linked to Jesus, and had intelligence that made him self-confident to the point of believing that only God could be greater than if no one else. We know he was in relation to Jesus, and to bond with the emotional depth, means that he believed Jesus to be the son of God. A man who thinks in this way, and at the same time believed to be the most in the world, means that alone It included a spiritual truth which is that of Jesus. If includes a spiritual truth of this magnitude, meaning it has the power to read and open the camera of a spiritual human being. If you have this power, it means that God allowed him to have to recognize Jesus as the Son of God and to follow him in his hard journey, in order to help him. Judah certainly if for any reason, it fails in this Divine design assigned by God, clearly his conscience asks the account of a failure, that a man of his reach, absolutely can not afford a failure. From here you can be born a judgment against himself stretched that leads him to condemn himself to death just to even the score, which the Creation. For this inquiry and for this reason we can not consider the rumors that caused the suicide of Judas, in the same way you found them men, we can not. We are different and we see things in many perspectives, and the teaching of religion teaches us to understand and forgive. We can understand that Judas had the grant made to him by God, of human intelligence over, in order to recognize and perhaps to stay close to Jesus, probably to help him in his task, until his death, there are no other reasons they can be. The failure to do this may have caused the suicide. His intelligence suggests that he was aware of this task assigned to him by God. And, Beyond the bankruptcy, the death of Jesus, automatically removes the purpose and motivation given by God in the life of Judah, and he may not know this realism. Dying Jesus, Judas had nothing more to do on earth. Unfortunately, the situation of earthly ambitions and the realization of a social position sometimes distinguish man from his duties to God and the tasks assigned to him by God. So even for Judas, He was on earth for a specific task, accomplished the task, there is no reason to live. His intelligence would not be served to anyone. The proof of all this is that binds him to Jesus, and this can not be a coincidence, but it is a fulfillment connected to the Divine Plan, as evidence remains, which by reason of its intelligence, his choice to die. Now fate has a way to materialize almost obliged to go. I seriously doubt that if Jesus had revealed to Judas, the Son of God, he would follow him and would believe him, to the point of suicide. Jesus Turned out to many and no one has thought deeply, because Judah should have been different? Nobody believed in Jesus to the point of risking for him a small part of himself, as a small amount of their qualitative. No one has followed all the way, over Judah. The reason of the suicide, the result of a guilty conscience and un'autolesione sentimental in the affective dimension, or otherwise remorse of conscience does not get to determine a car punishment by sentencing a suicide. Suicide was born to kick of his own conscience, it makes us understand that the basis is a deep brotherhood feeling. The deep feeling of brotherhood between two strangers has a way to go to be born. The situation stands and it makes sense if you think in a waxed manner. This is the way you should think. Judah recognizes Jesus as the son of God, without which he reveals himself, because: It has an evolutionary power that allows him to see into the spirit of the Messiah.

By understanding and receiving within themselves the Holy Spirit of the Messiah it includes the amount and the identity of Christ. In this way Judas sees the type of representation of the Messiah. Judah sees what is the Messiah, what the Holy Spirit does in the ground. So the Holy Spirit which is the same Jesus, surrounds and penetrates the hearts of men, like that of Judah, in order to be included in your being. In this way His Revelation comes to occupy place in human history, with the aim that "THIS" follow the path indicated by the Messiah, to save themselves when it happens that our life on earth ends, and to save his own soul when he comes the end of the world. Judah also understands that the power of the Spirit able to see every act performed by men on earth and therefore the truth of every human being, for better or for worse. Judas to arrive at this understanding and to receive the Holy Spirit of Jesus, it means that he has evolved willed by God, who understand the good and the evil, to listen to their conscience, and to separate good from evil. So Judah to be reached this investiture made only by the Eternal, which then allows him to break the Sacred censorship that man has within himself, means that it is ready and worthy, for reasons unknown to us, the engagement to be close to the Messiah.

- God has His plans and we are not quite understand but Evolved from time addicted when the light illuminates us, we can understand them with His permission. -

This God has allowed to have. Or else the bond can not be born in a depth that can lead to suicide his break; This regardless that there are other causes that might act as an excuse. Finally They died together, just because he kept them together a Divine Design, connected have a deep feeling. Against this reasoned realism with the brain and balance; The result in death in one way or another is not relevant, and much less could be for one or any reason. As the same way we can say that it is right that the man they make a right, this is part of its developmental stage, but can only be an excuse any means for the right end. So we can pay to the FAITH Scripture asserting something which scholastic doctrine, and reflects a realism, that JUDAS was one of the most indoctrinated disciples of all colors that followed the Messiah. At the basis of this they continue to evolve the arguments in order to prove that what I have written, with the Divine Inspiration men, are sensible. This leads us to criticize and judge ourselves. Us if we are in a stage of evolution be supposed, that gives us the understanding and the right not to take to good excuses that cause action, when we know that there are greater reasons that are responsible for an action that we have committed. And that fate one way or another had to be implemented and for this to materialize, however things sometimes happen. We should just discover the reasons why things happen. We should work with our reason to coincide with our rationality and practicality. Our balance scale our understanding. Our balance is head of human nature and of Creation, and the same reason.

On this account we should do to find out things as they are. At the base there is an emotional bond that the breaking of it, may result in pain which does not allow us to foresee an action of us, man under the painful flow of his own soul, so by the beloved disciple, in Cross was a man, and this is the same thing. Therefore, Jesus dies. Automatically Judah has no reason to follow his life, by reason of the Divine design, demonstrated by his intelligence that stops having reason to exist not having steamy and discuss in a size that could have only the intelligence of God's Son of which he also harbored affection. By reason of the affective dimension that is of great importance, this could be enough to us, if we consider Love as universal principle. emotional destiny connected to the feeling of joy, the breaking of it, each individual acts in his own way, not really predictable.

Judah, destiny, had to go with his teacher, did not make sense to live without his master, because he was born to be with his teacher until his death, this for some time he had understood and accepted. To feel and do not rule out that, although there had not been a betrayal or a twinge of conscience to give birth to death inside him, we can not know if the pain or else he would not have killed him anyway. And 'mathematician. Inwardly He can only repeat: "You should not kill a man like that, I do not accept, forgive me Lord." Birth of a judgment upon himself. Ripe to himself: "How could I, rub me!" A man who lives by the spirit and mental power, of course, civil his opinion, has little, and can not accept that he did cheat, to the point of letting turn the evil, which is the fault of the death of the Messiah, against themselves.

IDENTITA'-P.94

We have said before, that we will never understand as Judas did to recognize Jesus being the son of God. We will never know the vision that Judah had to arrive at this solution. If you have had a vision, or if included with its evolution and intelligence that reality. We know that: To recognize the identity of a man we use the name and surname and the rest and we know who Tom is and who is Caio. Judah must give an identity going beyond human this custom. Therefore, we assume that we have not an earthly name, but we have spiritual identity. As it does, Judas to get to read the spiritual identity?

Let's say that our identity is made up of two sides: those created by two actions, and these are performed to distinguish ourselves. The first is: the thought and action of our thoughts and our beliefs, and we say that it is a mental action. The other action and what we do and we prove materially to the next good or bad. This two actions are our identity in the Divine and spiritual dimension.

- These two actions are also our identity in this life, except that the diabolical part of us, sometimes hidden because it has no interest in being recognized for what it is, at the cost of denying the facts and allocate them in diabolical way, to other . Even this man can do it, every individual who commands creates his doctrine to his advantage and his proteges, or cronies. -

Judah must have seen the mental action of Jesus, his thoughts of the good or bad they are. The physical action of what he physically represented at the next. In my opinion only in this field Judah may recognize Jesus being the son of God. Only in this way he can discover the secret hidden by Jesus. This opportunity this inner understanding can only have received it from the Divine laws. So how has materialized within him this understanding?

The trauma that Judas undergoes when he recognizes the son of God, binds him more and more affectively. A bond so strong, leading to choose not to live, can only give it an equally strong knowledge of the personality of an individual, who can not forgive human error. If you imagine that Jesus is the only one who knows the truth, feeling unravel a secret, it may have caused an emotional bond flow similar to that of His Disciple. We can imagine that Judas believed to be the top man in the world and has to change his mind, and besides that he must love his antagonist, because so says the heart, his whole being and developmental stage should be questioned if not shattered. And the same thing for Jesus', believed to be impenetrable in His secret hidden and guarded by Divine seals which makes sure of himself to the point of knowing that God's chosen, being in front of a stranger, it draws its evolution, also this may be because of a slight injury, which basically always feeds more an emotional bond.

The two are overwhelmed by a destiny that binds them in spiritual and places them in an emotional dimension of a certain thickness and a certain quality, that we men unfortunately we can not fully understand.

THE PATH TO JESUS 'AND PROVE TO THE WORLD-P.95

The affection and esteem of Judah damage the urge to say who it is, and to speak? Surely the consideration is an incitement, an encouragement, but to say that it was characteristic, it is not plausible statement. Surely, the Heavenly Father has always been close, and the Holy Spirit has always accompanied, on this basis JESUS ', would have the same run, His Mission. All life is an event boundary, dictated by reason and free will of man, but that would not affect that much, in the mission of the Messiah.

Betrayal. ... Etc ... Etc ... Innocence. ... Etc ... Etc ... Etc ... Remorse of conscience. Etc. Etc. ... ... Warlock. ... Etc ... Etc ... Crime against priests. Etc. Etc. ... ... hate. Etc. Etc. ... ...

What we're part of the turning world, elements of the struggle of the invisible GOOD and EVIL; the reality, this is supreme, can not be other, which determines an action and a reason for an event, JESUS '' brings us the anchor of salvation by FAITH. The WELL albeit painful, has triumphed.

For this during the tortuous path, there were friends and

266

enemies, win-win situations and less proud; element factor of the life of each man. Therefore the Mission has succeeded. We humans can save us if we follow the FAITH; His sacrifice is evidence of the forgiveness of Our Sins.

ANALYSIS OF DEVELOPMENT IN COMPARISON-P.96

Judah had an action mentality, the fact that he believes only in himself and only his brain does understand, that you could adapt to evil and do MALE if they thought was right. You know as I do that even today the underworld men believe in nothing, or at most only in themselves. So if Judas was action, he did not believe anything but only in himself, and God was the only being that he had understood, superior to him, we must understand that with these features if you do not do the evil life, the underworld where fear . He was to achieve a stage where he had to believe in Jesus, she walks alone in this truth, no one can teach something has a brain of this inclination, it was absolutely necessary evolution of the property on one side. Similarly, to believe in himself, when circumstances considered appropriate, be able to act as if he did not believe in anything, the stage of development achieved through a road of evil where he has really evolved in this direction. So in a sense, it has wrongly believe to be perfect as the Son of God; by means of this belief, in harmony with Creation. Of course we know that is not so, there is no ambivalence, or you are on one side or the other. This ambivalence it conditioned the well: he decease thing to be, it could be what he wanted it all depended on his will, and what he believed. Therefore, believing in himself, also means being a man of action who can think for worse, if he wants, even if: his spirit has achieved the Divine of Good understanding, and able to think even in the good. However, it is always an ambivalence conflict. Clearly, at the base of this nature, had a code of honor and relied in this code in order to be able to look in the mirror, and not having to reproach for an action committed or improper behavior, the code as arbiter of himself . She is analyzed and judged by himself.

This was a custom for excessive man or one who does not want to rely entirely to chance. One way to avoid conflict with himself, or not to be embarrassed with himself; Only of himself had probably fear. For this he was strict and serious: both in front of the world, both with himself, both in respect of its code of life. He wanted to be perfect in its own way and knew how to be in its own way, this conviction put him in a position to refuse life lessons were taught by himself; At the base of this complex personality to feel that while believing in Jesus' and while following it, that linked him to the Master he could be a deep affection and a warm esteem. Finally remained a man who had only about himself, and if he had the pleasure of something good if he did not have the pleasure he did not care. In any case, the link with the Divine Plan and with the Son of God, he has changed a bit the character, in the sense that I, did go up one step higher to others towards good, and perhaps a touch of unarmed of malice, he did not escape the situation from his hands. Still, it was a terrible man, or else the priests would not have needed to involve him. Sure he has had some importance: In an environment where you were trying to hurt him crazy people and give the show to the people, the friendship of Judah could make a difference.

Or someone might ask, what they have to do together, are two completely different people. Curiosity is a key to the approach and the survey. Certainly seeing Judas so taken by the personality of Jesus remained stunned and we wanted to see clear, this put them in a position, to try also to see Jesus with the same eyes that sees Judah. From this psychological situation arose new friendships and ties. However over the years, Jesus has come an evolutionary stage, where he also manages to impose his personality, not in the manner of Judas but fails, and from hand to hand becomes more evolved, until that arouses wonder for anyone who has to do with him. concerns for the enemies. Hence the idea of denouncing Jesus as a blasphemer, but in the same way by someone to put near to Jesus to bring Judah. Perhaps to somehow get his consent, or the assurance that was to step aside, if they wanted to give a lesson to Jesus. Surely, they will not reveal their intentions to Judas to the end. The will said he would only spoken and the thing would have ended there. Surely friendship given to enemies and conspirators against the Son of God, have weakened. Proof of this is always suicide. One thing is Certain that Judah knows that they had to argue with Jesus in a rather serious and heavy, a man of its thickness may not know this, but I doubt that he was aware that they would have arrested him, and then the situation has deteriorated until determine the man's death that he knows, being the Son of God. so understand that he was deceived, and in a sense the feeling of friendship that he so admired in which both believed was what I weakened. There is a certain confidence and a certain rip-off: We know that if a man cheats, and with a kiss, closes the betrayal, is aware that he is making a deadly betrayal and the kiss shows that the betrayal is happy and content, far as he any form of repentance. These factors are associated with treachery, Judas can suffer, but has no reason to try it for the Master Sui. Probably some of the CAT AND THE FOX, two jugglers just JESUS 'committed suicide, have walked the hand to remove therefrom all forms of involvement. We can not exclude that later, for remorse of conscience, they have become, good Christians and they asked forgiveness from God. We know where it passes JESUS ', somehow makes its mark; we can not exclude that they have not left a mark in the soul, that they have seen, over the years. Probably have become dissidents and integrated, to the Apostles of Jesus. However everything is plausible, the story as far as you might think closed by their enemies, was not locked; He remained always open. What does the text, and that is in balance if we were to draw a horizontal line, we see:

Pilate washed his hands, just because Jesus had not committed a crime. The fact that Judas died, in fact is that the priests, the people and all the conspiracy that cheered his death, washes his hands, saying he was sentenced because Judas betrayed him, and the whole the blame goes to them, and they feel exonerated. Therefore, we know that he was sentenced, as a favor to the priests of that time, and people leaped to his conviction, on the advice of the leaders. We know that friends and relatives of Jesus, could hardly see him condemned, for fear that someone said, - we saw it together with Jesus, - This could bring an upcoming death sentence. Therefore, none of his friends or relatives was presented to Calvary. Only Judas could have the strength to stand at Calvary and no one else, and so it must have been, or could not take the painful spring that makes JUDAS victim and executioner of himself, under a sentence dictated by himself.

The mystery remains to be understood that the enemies of Jesus, when he dies, feel pity and regret the death of the Lord. They recognize a child of God. How this could have happened, we do not understand, but it's a real mystery. Were injured by pity, that basically was at the base of the wound Spiritual JESUS ', which is Universal Love Daughter.

PSYCHOANALYSIS OF RACISM SENTIMENTAL MAN. - P. 97

The will give him the weakest, with morality, reproaches, always trying to put him in the minority and persecute demonstrates the spontaneous racist feelings man. The man for the racist sentiment that applies to the weakest selecting and targeting it to a bad future to live, run at no charge to the annihilation weakest subject, and does so with the consent of the community, because this is also trained in select individuals and materialize through a certain behavior, the bad fate that the dominant subjects, with their judgments and their malicious schemes have allocated. This social behavior due to the annihilation of the weak people, made so by the community which turns right or left in obedience to the instructions of the people in sight who have social voice command. Throughout this process the man run into almost natural way and with the use of reason and the consent of the majority. Therefore, the remorse of conscience is limited in man who judges and prepares the fate to others because it has the collective consensus. With this behavior the man shows that for interest manifested again the bestial part of his being. Therefore, even if the man's bestial side is dominated and often the man dominates with the use of a thermostat that does not exceed the bad or wrong things, when it comes to their own interests or to fulfill its envy, or to show their supremacy, he does not dominate his part bestial, though it should.

THEREFORE 'A PERSON HELD LOWER THE OTHER, IS RUINED. HIM BECAUSE OF HIS APPEARANCE, OR FOR OTHER REASONS, IS FROM NEXT PENALISED. HE WILL 'SENT BY COMMANDERS AND BY THE PEOPLE OBEDIENT MASTERS, A LIFE WITHOUT SATISFACTION. Who will judge him 'will pick'. THIS PURELY HUMAN BEHAVIOR DEMONSTRATES NASTINESS RACISM AND UNPRECEDENTED, MA that goes unnoticed. MAN is EVIL AGAINST HIS SAME SPECIES. MAN AND 'THE SOCIAL, THE CONFLICT AND SELECTIVE contemplate!

THEREFORE 'FOR A MAN NOT temperamentally AS MOST E' RISKY. THE COMMUNITY 'HOW MANY TIMES EVEN THE FAMILY, NOT ACCEPT IF TOO MUCH DIFFERENT. IN THIS WAY HE WILL 'ELIMINATED, OR WILL BE' MADE IN CONDITIONS to self-destruct THROUGH ISOLATION AND EXCLUSION. HE WILL 'SELECTED AND TASKS ADDRESSED TO USELESS AND DESTRUCTIVE.

CONDEMN A PERSON AND 'ONE MODERN WAY TO DESTROY IT. KEEP A DISTANCE, AND WHO 'WAS SELECTED SO BAD, AND' a manifestation of racism. UNFORTUNATELY THE COMPANY 'AND' SELECTIVE, AND HOW THE 'THE SCHOOL, AND' THE MAN FOR THIS flaw INEVITABLY WITHOUT FORGIVENESS. THEREFORE 'UNTIL THE MAN' IS NOT TEACHING AND DOMINATES ALL'UTORITA 'DÌ CHRIST JESUS' WILL 'ALWAYS EVIL,

RACIST AND WILL' EVIL EVEN WITHOUT REASON.

It happens in the family, the victim of the moment. The weaker relative or stranger is slowly selected and abandoned. It is mocked or marginalized in some way. Certainly, he does not miss him with the feeling of pity, and the moral always him. Notable, that sometimes the feeling of pity praised by man, strangely makes it not pitiful, but more merciless times. This transformation of self-interest? The interest exceeds the worth of the piety that in conscience burns us and calls us to the public spirit and the presence of God? This is a situation that is part of human nature, for centuries. As it happens that, in a company of friends there is always someone to mock, and to feel different. Clearly, we can say that there are these subjects, and are consequently treated in a certain way. However, I think that these subjects if there are people who create them when they live together in a situation, family and even when living in a social situation. Therefore, it would seem that, a communion of persons, have affective bonds, and create, in a subject with a psychological and behavioral state, different from them, in order to have a different between them. However this is something that is part of human nature and that man from this deviation, it must be said, he has not been able to heal. I could deduce that Jesus', in a sense lived in a stadium like this, just do not GLI was expressed directly, but suffered almost unnoticed by the company definitely, and perhaps also by a part of the family. The mean, that claims to be the Son of God, it is strange, maybe it's crazy. This judgment made in advance because some, deride him, others despise it, others can not stand his exuberance, or simply can not stand and that's it.

This sentiment proves, against the Messiah, because they think they are with God and have to deal with a braggart, but in truth they are not with God, God no longer has confidence in them, otherwise, why would send His son for this delicate mission? They are enemies of God, but do not know it consciously, but unconsciously they are. So they take off on your own, so much evil they have inside that fail to do so. Returning to the way others see Jesus, we say: Of course this type of situation has worsened to the point that resulted all in a collective mass murder. Clearly the sentiment of contempt and being collective oppression, does not place the man in the singular sense to take responsibility, such as kill or suppress a man, being a community choice, is not a guilty act, and almost both action right. So this eventually determines the will assert that Jesus' died to save mankind. I would say as well, which is always a way to declare the right and a collective murder punishable determined in part by racial nature sentimental man, against a person of the same family or the same people. A manifestation of evil in association chain, not punishable, according to the man, because of the numbers of people participating. Clearly, it is more than noteworthy that Jesus' was killed by a sense of contempt and collective emotional racism. It bothered him not, because he prayed, or the fact that he claimed to be the Son of God, let alone to some opinions that could express regarding the company and the problems then. He bothered him solely because he was ALIVE. BELIEVE JUDAH, we would have understood. It remains that his suicide is proof that he dissociates himself from this form of human thought, because he in his code was not angry with the weak indeed, defended them. Virtues very rare to find in a man even in our times, where many say petty, not to say, SCENTINO, (I'm far if no m'infetti); and many are merciless. Clearly humanity after consuming the mass murder against the SON of GOD, includes, strange but customary to man, that he was wrong and what he did and more bestial than human. Therefore, in the same way for community reason, pleads innocence, and guilt he goes to JUDAH, indicating he as the cause of death of the Son of God for having made against him a plausible treason. Clearly the death of Judas is becoming this slander, the more engraved and free without obstacles opponents contradictory to it. Therefore, most likely, however: JUDAS is one of only men, who like Jesus'.

JUDAS dissociates from being like other men, suicide is an act of protest, action demonstration that he does not think like the others against the Son of God. Suicide is an act of deep pain and anguish. Suicide answers the question save my MAESTRO? - Can not do that, I was left alone, and everything runs fast. And I'm the next to be condemned, everyone knows that I'm with him.

However heal, perversion in collective chain of evil within him, is a way to follow God, and choose God. JUDAS had cured this disease this form was separated from the community, living in the midst of the melee, but it was not like the crowd, it was autonomous and his brain was acting under his influence and that of the ETERNAL FATHER.

He chooses to be with God, regardless of man's judgment. Of course with this we do not know how he is God, but we are satisfied, to understand moral realism in association with the truth Representative in material form, to cope with the moral truth and painful for others and the character in question. Not having had the time to do something to prevent the crucifixion of His friend, he makes him desperate.

WHO 'JUDAS? -P.98

We know that Judas betrayed Jesus', that there was handed down, and on this we have become judges. Judas knew that if he would kill the next condemned was he? In my opinion, yes! So Judas who betrayed or not, he was sentenced the same time that it was his Master. We inherited a judgment. Judas betrayed for thirty pieces of silver, he bought some land and then committed suicide for repentance; in this respect we know it. Therefore, our ancestors have handed down even the intelligence of Judas, he said that he believed the less perfect than his MAESTRO.

Therefore, we have a man who betrays, buys land has the courage to go and give the last comfort to his Master on the way to Calvary after which it kills. In practice the intelligence of JUDAS you end up in all these acts? - A preventable hiccup? From a man whose intelligence is also manifested by the ancients, we could say Yes! If he could do something before the arrest of his Master.

When a man makes a deadly betrayal and accompanies it with a kiss, did not have any kind of remorse or rethinking, it expresses a hatred in its purest form, apical. - I think JUDAH with his final gesture, (suicide) does not reflect this case; (Evidence) that they had a lot of remorse. JESUS 'was the victim of a conspiracy, it is certain.

JUDAS, did nothing to stop the conspiracy, we can not say it, maybe it does not have the time. Man Action which he had, if he had delayed the sentence for a few more days, we can not know how it ended; considerable speed in issuing and executing the sentence against his Master.

Considerable courage to go and see his Master carry the CROSS; What could it mean? Go see Jesus carry the cross means something, but what? Usually those who have the wet coal, has little desire to face a truth of which she is the main cause. Where did you get this courage? How can betray, have a guilty conscience, and the nerve to face a painful reality, which has been the architects! Mysteries.

<< We know who has a guilty conscience, for any one thing that he has committed, he loses courage, become SMALL, SMALL AND MORE AND MORE 'SMALL. Up to hide. >>

Mysteries of the Faith. What To believe, to what has been said on the account by the ancients, or to our conscience? He admitted that in this case we had a. The head atoning Judah will be the truth.

- Considerable courage to commit suicide.

-      The difficult point to solve and if he could do something before the arrest of its MAESTRO;

- If he could not do anything because he too was a victim of a conspiracy of another entity but of origin by the very nature or by the same source of origin which ultimately is the one who led his Master before Pilate.

-

Jesus' twelve apostles. JESUS 'has done miracles; Thus it is known, he has done good. In the Calvary road where they were? Why they were not there? An inevitable hiccup? No! I do not think, in danger of being recognized and put to death.
He died alone, and in the hands of his enemies. Pity for Jesus' had the only part of the Roman soldiers, a PART of the nations at that time presents. Later, some are joints, the women of the family and the mother.

Possible that a legal sentence as unjust both makes men, all innocent and everyone with the right to play in them without feeling guilty?

Therefore, the other part of the people who loved Jesus', can that it was all hidden?

Perhaps he could not believe the event fast and amazing. Taken by surprise, this is reason for the absence. For this, the plan of His sentencing is devilishly studied.

I doubt that Judas was able to make anything out of that to pass for a traitor.

MY PERSONAL CRITICISM-P.99

However, not wanting to compromise the evolution of an apostle which is believed by historians of great intellect; on this point I agree; But I stick to point out a feature of reflection to what the negligent character in question. I suppose he had to know that the man before you travel to a place; imagines, by means of its sensitivity, WELL integrity and in any contour. Even if this place had to be bad and painful; the man by means of his imagination imagines, situations, cheerful to live in that place, or that specific adventure. This is proved, too, by the fact that many men go to war singing hymns of glory to then, however, the reality is not represented as they imagined them, but it is far; as in this example, which is the most dramatic, you can be considered disparate examples with different situations. And 'this leads in many circumstances of human life. Finally, through achieving a certain stage of evolution, man should not fall for his fluctuating imagination but should measure the realism is, the spiritual soul is in the body material, and through this understanding dominate the imagination and suggestion and, to understand what kind of situation can be found in a place to visit in the future if it makes certain choices and, by means of this consideration to understand what it might feel: happiness or pain. This is an element of human nature, and especially this element acts when the man is about to do something wrong; He receives a sort of inner conflict that ultimately can give imaginary perspectives to what debatable, but it can happen that the imagination wins on realism and the choice could be the wrong one believing that it is the right one. Then of course the contact with reality could be anything, and show that there were errors of assessment. Man, it is sometimes inclined to play with your brain; It is one of its characteristics. What I Act of psychological neglect of Judah was born from a reflection: the supernatural An intelligence like that of Judas as he could not understand the reality of what he felt in his spirit in his soul to act accomplished? A supernatural brain, you have not understood a priori, that the death of Jesus', would make him feel dying, in psychological dimension, even to him?

A supernatural brain as that of Judas, it is possible that he did not know to love the Son of God, as himself to the point of not overcome the trauma of passing? The death of his Master,

277

would take away any, purpose, every reason, every life satisfaction, the most beautiful and the most important thing had happened was to become expert of the SON OF GOD, it is possible that JUDAS underestimated all this has influenced the the point of committing horrendous action bringing harm to his Master and himself, irretrievable, and correctable only with his own death? Everything leaves me astounded.

Judas must have been shrouded by the halo of light harmonious, celestial, the Son of God, as he said, in tears and in desperation: "You can not kill a man like that!" We can think about: How is it that, JUDAS, could, be defeated by personal duality and make a choice contrary to what? Unfortunately the man is not perfect.

REFLECTION-P.100

In this novel we do not take into account, the MIRACLES, treat the subject as if they were not fundamental in order to help him continue the road of His mission and its perpetual pursuit. Although we know that is not so, just because the theme and a fantastic address psychological and historical; we we stick to the exclusion of these events but not to their denial. What was fundamental was the Faith, of Judas and his apostles, who laid it in the Lord, and God the Father Almighty.

Therefore, the fact that he made of Miracles was something that was an addition to his mission, and it was a sign of love that God through His Son manifested to those in need of benefit from it. Therefore, your journey and its continuation were been supported by affection, by Love and Faith that men of Good Will, they had! And by God.

SOCIAL CONFLICT-P.101

I wonder how it can be a merciless society that has received the Miracles and help in spiritual and psychological sense, from a man who has only Represented good? How can a company be complicit in a conspiracy made by a few people, and demonstrate contempt, hatred, cynicism, perversion and evil chain, in front of a man who has done nothing, absolutely nothing, only good.

The remarries might be: the collective evil.

Therefore, the only ones who had mercy, excluding close friends and family, may have been people among the nations and some Romans.

AFTER DEATH-P.102

To Calvary to be present and to give comfort to the latest SON of God none of your loved ones present. Completely abandoned. The fact is that probably there have been painters who then drew the whole thing. And 'this is an art more evolved and customary in the soul. Pilate, he did not condemn Jesus', he did not want to give in to SANHEDRIN. The condemnation of Jesus' had been decreed at the table even before he was put before Pilate. The SANHEDRIN had decided the death sentence of Jesus' even before Del prosecute him, it was just a false and Pilate knew it.

Rome did not want to stain a crime against an innocent. TIBERIO, had removed VALERIO GRATO and in its place put Pilate, but brought many problems and many political conflicts between Judea and Rome. Probably the power of SINATRO, was strong because TIBERIO had decreed, that no matter what decides the SANHEDRIN, Pilate had no power, nor to oppose authority. And if the first Christian probably were mixed, Romans and Jews. After the death of Jesus', Pilate is called to Rome to TIBERIO GIULIO CESARE, and he was sentenced to death, and he preferred to commit suicide. Tib had sent Volusianus, in search of Jesus' because ill, and he was hoping to be healed. Veronica went to Rome to confer with the Emperor and to tell him of what had happened to SINATRIO regarding the Messiah's death. CESARE, for this reason Pilate wanted to punish; in your opinion and what he had told JESUS ', he would cure him.

The situation is coming to the end in order to understand it: surely some ROMANS, have had to complain of the SON OF GOD death.

Probably TIBERIO, pretended to have contracted an evil and to seek JESUS 'to be healed, he only wanted justice, and Pilate saw the executioner of the innocent. Underlying these vendettas Transversal, to feel that the early Christians were the Romans, in conjunction with some Jews. Most likely Pilate kills himself, at the same time that repents and chooses to believe in JESUS ', just because he too saw Crucify the MESSIAH not recognize it, after death, SON OF GOD. We can not exclude an identity collective recognition of Jesus' in those last stages of his life, in almost MIRACULOUS form.

Repressed OF ROMAN CULTURE-P.103

FAITH that CONSEQUENTIAL ROMANS, is achieved by repressed. In their culture, and in their religious rites it is notable that they inherit, manifest, and leave a legacy to the prosperous merciless. They demolish or repress compassion from their inception, and their religion, this feeling does not express it and not consider it. HONOR, FORCE, however these are feelings that they have merits and value. For this, a repressed feeling, just waiting to explode, and was released in the circumstance of the Passion of Christ, and they wake up in all their consciousness and discover they possess a feeling of profound value that places man in front of his consciousness. This internal process has led to the consciousness of spiritual values. And of me, of which culture: religious polita of Rome he did not consider, not sought and excluded totally.

With this we can also understand the reasons of imperial

persecution that made against the Christians. As the Jews were persecuting Jesus commanders' belonging to the same people; the same way the Romans were persecuting the Roman commanders who had become Christians.

THE FAITH OF THE ROMANS - P. 104

The point is that the FAITH Romans lead them to investigate the life and history of Jesus', this could justify the delay of the writings on the Life of the Messiah, and try the FAITH of the Romans, to coincide with the Gentiles and the local characters .

For this, to feel that ROMANS believe and have FAITH in JESUS, we tried for realism, seen and experienced with the Messiah; and although reported only in the last moments of ACTS and IT life. Essentially they have FAITH, because I have seen, and included in his condemnation, and have recognized the SON of GOD alone, without anyone and did not require it. At the base of the FAITH ROMANS towards JESUS ', thus: There is the determination of the GOSPEL which should serve as a convincing direct, educator and stimulator. There is a genuineness of FAITH achieved for direct understanding with the MESSIAH. To believe that at this point the ROMANS would still believed that JESUS 'SON of GOD and, regardless of whatever they would have written the EVANGELISTI the account of Jesus and the life'. The circumstance in which ROMANS, investigating on behalf and on the life of Jesus', in fact so was born the GOSPEL. These were not half as to achieve the FAITH for ROMANS, was only half to find out MORE 'by the man she believed to be SON of GOD. Therefore, under the ideological profile, FAITH, is right and the basis for this reason to believe that it is related to the PIANO CELESTE. FAITH in JESUS ', comes from having CONSIDERING the SON of GOD in FACE, and physically from having lived the last acts of living with it face to face.
This makes PURE and genuine. The Gospel makes as delicious side dish. The CRISTINI, have caught the genuineness of the

Spirit of Jesus', something made possible only by having received an inheritance integrity and spiritual authenticity, from their ancestors who have seen it during the Passion, and through this occurrence I 'they recognized for what he claimed to be. Christianity by these ancestors has been able to inherit the character of authenticity SON From God, and I was able to reserve the spiritual integrity; representing it in His authenticity. All this shows the Good Faith of them and the genuineness of their Religion. This is what is right to the Light of the investigation. The fact that you can criticize the story, and intravvederne in it some facts not realistic, it means nothing and gives no conditioning the FAITH; as anything he wrote the Evangelists, they could not affect the FAITH, achieved with the direct contact with the Messiah during the PASSION. FAITH is Strong, is sincere in consciousness; fair because: it is anchored has a ANTENALE realism (from ancestors), the firm has historical integrity, genuine, and the Spirit of Christ; that! Who! Has transmitted integrity and authenticity Spiritual, saw his face, this makes him invincible, the same way it does visible to his heirs, because God that was in Jesus' was present before their eyes; It remains intact and this before the eyes of their heirs; This is your strength! This and authenticity! This is the integrity Spiritual! There is always the presence of constantly GOD. This is the Will of the Eternal Father; to this I think. The proof of what I say could be that: The Calling it does become a minister of God, man is born from the feeling. Solely and exclusively by the FEELING. This is the force; germinated before the Life stories from Jesus'.

HUMANITY ': WHAT DOES THE COMPARISON OF THE QUESTION -P. 105

Faced with the question of which is almost an integral part of the theme. Humanity has two versions unconscious and conscious. Conscious version says: JESUS 'is the son of God, suffered the Passion to save the man, but I betrayed Judas, and I think that is the Son of God, because that is, for others because, and especially why did the mIRACLES. The other version is conscious and always humanity that says, always in his mind and makes a car unconscious psychoanalysis. I know that Jesus' Son is God, and the reason that we believe, and that Judas committed suicide, clearly after having betrayed him. In the second statement psychoanalyst humanity it adheres to realism. The suicide of Judas is the only tangible proof of which humanity relies in order to have FAITH and to believe that Jesus' being the Son of God, but Judas traitor. Alternatively giving something in exchange for another. The testimony of Jesus and His works benign "Miraculous companies," are the most tangible evidence; although in this book, because the subject is inherent in another situation to describe, so for this reason we talk about it, we all know that JESUS 'He left a legacy through the Gospels and Acts of the Apostles, His IDENTITY ', very clearly especially by the Miracles. In religion factor, man, you've gone days, believed and worshiped a God that he must see and recognize exceed! Therefore, it is clear, he was worshiped JUPITER and other pagan gods in their superiority, fascinating, in the sight of man, superior. Then they love the children of the gods allegedly, be men. Finally they adore RE, Lords and Emperors. Clearly, religion, whatever it may be and in whatever address is being envisaged in worship, should see in it, someone who reflects or references to it be considered to be higher, Divine being worthy to be worshiped and served. To say that Jesus' Son of God is both Giusto is this is true. This man must suffice. God of compassion, and for man's understanding of his being Divine brings the good and FAITH on earth, through His Son.

So, who he is also a man, who called with their own pain, God, Father. Compassion and respect, are two characteristic virtues in FAITH brought by our Lord, that finally and with all human beings, without distinction has compassion and respect for all of us. God knows how, man must endeavor to become worthy of the Kingdom OF Heaven, and through His Forgiveness save his own soul; just wait for it we become men ready to understand it, and then He can show us; it is each of us takes it in the right time. However going back to our main question is that of the character of Judas, humanity thinks that he betrayed Jesus out of envy. This is something that I do not share, because Judas was not in the psychological conditions to experience this feeling, with this I do not say that he can not receive a moral shock, do not discuss his feelings, but he can feel envy to its levels really stupid to think so, and if you believe that he may have been envious of the Lord then it means that we have understood nothing of the work of the merciful lady.

HOW WOULD THE RELIGIOUS SPEECH IN HIS REALITY '? - P. 106
-

The point is that before the coming of the Lord, the man has a God punisher of his people, even a God able to order and to destroy sinners and disobedient, and entire nations. A God too severe, in my opinion. Instead, Jesus introduces us to a God who has compassion for all humanity. A God who manifests the universal love, and indeed does not judge the man marries his due, then his sins, that is, assuming the ills of all mankind, in practice if they charge, and through the Cross suffers the weight and the death of sin and misery of man, and that is the Cross that he carries on his shoulders, which spiritually is used to destroy the sins of mankind. In this way he is reborn in man a new awareness of mercy and love that leads him to God, then to the truth of God is unconditional love for all living beings, as salvation through the sacrifice of Jesus is for everyone . Jesus through His sacrifice want to show that the way of salvation is love and mercy, neither the judgment nor punishment, but only love and forgiveness. So Jesus does not discriminate in those days, which was a period a part of humanity was discriminated against, then he goes against the culture and religious beliefs of the time. Him instead, to "those" who are believed devoid of grace, speaks to him and brings the word of God, and does not worry about being laughed at or judged. So the God who makes known to Jesus is a God of love and forgiveness, and not of wealth and punishment, but at the same time, because of these revolutionary ideas for that time, he attracts to him if the disapproval of religious, that time, who do not think like him. We now know that for these reasons he was opposed to all and only enemies could attract to himself, since upsetting the whole ancient belief, and the current one. Judas pulls in all the enemies of Jesus because he is with him face-up, and is the only of the apostles who has the courage to do it. At this point we see and understand that the God who brings us Jesus is a God who understood how difficult to live "for the man" with the meat. Or better to say that humanity which manifests itself in him with sin, indeed it is sin because man. So for humans it is to deal with his own humanity that is difficult. Jesus understands this truth, for that reason knows that man is sinful from the outset, it has since its birth v. Because of this truth He brings to all mankind, the Way of Salvation, which is God. God loves us. He understands us. We must overcome our grief and at the same time to marry the difficulties of our fellow men.

Through solidarity between us demonstrate to represent the ideals that the Son of God has led us, then we become worthy of pursuing the path of evolution that leads us to the light of God. But it is just this kind God who forgives all mankind and he loves all that does not please the religious of that time. This God who brings Jesus does not like. Because they believe in a God who punishes sinners, free with his sword, his people from the oppression of foreigners, continues to test his creatures, speaks only with priests, entrusts them power over the people, and especially the of cursing, and apparently the punishment and the threat and its best weapon to subdue the people; always all in the name of God. The God that brings us Jesus is different. Jesus presents us with a different father, that of love for all and forgiveness for all. This however does condemn to death, and who loved him, honestly, he goes after, "rightly or wrongly" as Judas.

CONCLUSION OF THE CHARACTER OF THE NOVEL-P.107

Probably the situation was very underrated by those who were against the LORD. We will not know the way that end realism that escapes our grasp; which it is the authentic reaction of those who loved the Son of God, after completed act. This is a huge dilemma. The conclusion in respect of the character in question, be: JUDAS was the victim of a scam, someone's opinion corruption, not debatable, however, is clear; Of which he was to put this to the condition it; He chose to respond in a certain way; for reasons unknown to us; This is bad. Of any entity other than by his Master but: from the exact same kind as that which hit your MAESTRO; as already stated in the preface and throughout the novel.

BUT ACCOUNTS "UNFORTUNATELY" TO ME, NOT AGAIN! - P.108

Why JESUS 'has been deleted? If mathematics is not an opinion, it was deleted because he spoke ill of the religious, and certainly, his words could not be against the laws of MOSE 'since MOSE' has banned the sacrifice of children to God Malok. Probably accuses the religious, not to follow and do not serve God. Likewise I can not believe that He disturbed Rome, much less the Imperial Religion seen and because it was considered a fool, and no one took him seriously. Because Judas committed suicide? Because he has betrayed the Master? Thesis is not rational, whatever he had betrayed, that his suicide is not determined by the betrayal! Let there be something else, it can not be committed because he betrayed? No! He does not stand. Because he killed Judah? Because the environment would have laid the blame from traitor to the Son of God? No! Judah recently considered the opinions of others, he believed in himself too. So it has nothing to do with his final act. Because Judas committed suicide? The answer is obvious, because he believed that Jesus' burdened the guilt of His Crucifixion. Judah understood that Jesus' believed the traitor, Judas committed suicide for this reason there is nothing else behind this extreme act. By suicide just I wanted to respond to

Jesus'? Maybe! How to say:

<< JESUS 'you're wrong not center anything with your sentence! >>

Only way to give him this message was suicide? Maybe. NOW IS STANDING! Judah, when he went to Calvary to see his Master carry the Cross, in the eyes of his Master he reads the guilt that JESUS 'skirted him, his capture and his conviction. This JUDAS could not stand that his Master had understood or believed? And it is probably for this reason that he committed suicide? So Judah did not kill himself because he had betrayed His Master, but because his Master gave him a traitor. JESUS 'sends a message not with words but with the mood and through the eyes. As if to tell him with her eyes: << betrayed me! >>
This Judas did not stand, and tells him the only way left to him to communicate, which is to take his own life. So Jesus' died knowing that Judas had betrayed him, and that Judas has understood, and it is for this reason that Judas took his own life! Now we finally clarified an enigma. We know that Judas betrayed or his Master. And I'm sure that he committed suicide because his master knew of his treachery, and automatically has laid the blame of his capture and his conviction to the Crucifixion. How did Jesus' learned of the betrayal of Judas? The answer is obvious. JESUS 'knew that as long as Judas was with Him, nobody touched him. And he understood that to be arrested meant that Judas was no longer on his side. For this reason Jesus' believed the traitor, and he made it clear that he understood this, when you are seen to Calvary.

So, ultimately, Judas kills himself because he understands that Jesus' has realized this, and, arrived at this conclusion. This reasoning Faith, repentance and sorrow are the tragedy. What Judah can not stand, you know that the Master understands that he is the traitor and who believe in this. For what it believes and is the Master that he commits suicide. We are required to have FAITH: Judas is the betrayer of Jesus'! We could say that he killed himself because Jesus' believe him this, and Judas had understood.

ASSUMPTIONS. - P. 109

We must start from a logical reasoning. Judas died almost simultaneously to Jesus, he could be excluded that the world, after his death, telling him to be a traitor then the cause of the Messiah's death. Rightly it is correct to think, after his death he was declared a traitor from the world. This behavior might be questionable, but we must say that Jesus believes traitor and Judas knows this thought of Jesus, otherwise "if you do not know him" his suicide, which has many meanings, it would lose one, and it would not be fair, since it could say something to Jesus, in my opinion.

So if through Judas's suicide wanted to send a message to Jesus? We are not able to decipher it, while seeing and reading it, but Jesus yes!

The enemies of Jesus are the same as Judas, and if both had been victims of a diabolical strategy? One killed and the other "best friend" guilty of treason, and then only culprit and cause of his death?

If we analyze that Judas through his conquest of wisdom deep friendship with Jesus, we must also consider that he is sure that Jesus can decipher its message, otherwise, Judah, would send it to him, if it were so. Therefore it is logical to think that in this respect Judah to win the friendship of Jesus face deep reasoning. These in order to to show his teacher that is really wise, as well as be able to understand his mind, so it can compete, reason for which Jesus becomes the only man alive who knows profoundly the heart of Judas, not the place and some experiences where he has been formed, it is right to give him a little 'privacy, but I know enough to understand the

288

significance of the extreme action of Judah, and Judah knows. So Judah must open more than it has manifested itself with other glia friends. If it did not, he could not impress, become interesting, and then not be able to get the right account by the Master. I think another way has not exhibit their inner values, and may not be able to send a message that Jesus alone can understand.

So Judas gives him permission to enter his heart but just to make friends, in fear of losing his esteem, love him and want this profound intellectual and spiritual sharing with him. So the affection afterlife and the feeling of friendship Judah has no material interests to make friends with Jesus, at least initially, even if we wanted to believe traitor. So his feeling toward his friend is sincere and honest, then he strongly believes in the feeling of friendship. This makes us realize that reaching out for Jude is something that only those who truly loves and esteem, since it is a reserved type and too many things to hide. So this logical realism, makes us understand that Jesus is able to decipher the message of Judas, because he knows well and knows how to think, and Judah, through revelations and openness, which put him in a position to understand it deeply, therefore, able to do so to read his message, whether suicide is. So Judas is open in front of Jesus, but only up to a certain point, that is just the human one, and just enough in the spiritual dimension to put in conditions the Master to understand his every move. So no one knows Judas as Jesus.

OUR LACK KNOWLEDGE NOT JUDGE ALLOWS. - P. 110

So if suicide was a message; Jesus alone can decrypt it since and sent Judah, and he knows it, and understands his heart, and no other man on earth knows him, and he may be able to understand it like Him. So whatever we were to say, on behalf Judah, we could only go wrong, but Jesus no! He knows how many ways and manners Judah can act, and the message still manages to decipher only Him, for only He has been sent, humanity, myself included, we are excluded for the time being in this communication; so it's just a matter of communication between them two, and all of us are cut out of it, and made only between two of them. So Judah through suicide, says a lot of things according to a broader point of view, but above all send, directly, a final message to his Master, and only through suicide can send it, has nothing, and does not have another way. So if this was a message, in my opinion, it would be - D 'HUGE IMPORTANCE! - I'm sorry that we can not decipher it, because it is not sent to us, but to the Son from God. However, this makes us realize that Judah, who is or is not a traitor of Jesus, it is not for us to decide because we do not understand what is the his suicide, as well as a declaration of defeat and betrayal, and because deep down it has committed as a practical man does things if you come to something, so only Jesus is the understanding, we have no say in the matter, since his suicide it completely cuts off, and does not allow us to understand clearly the truth of his intentions.

NOW WE KNOW WHY 'JUDAS COULD have committed suicide!

In truth, That's My Opinion. - P.111

We hold for a moment this in mind that I declare in P7: Jude loves Jesus in a natural way and pure, to be compared with the feeling similar to what the Angels try to Heaven together. From here I can formulate the following.

P8: He committed suicide because of Jesus is God's son, he would not do it for other reasons and other ways to tell us than to dimostrarcelo through his extreme action.

Indeed we hear this from Judah, even though we do not know, and we believe that Jesus is the Son of God. Why is Judas who is said so then and there it goes on to say still, and we we hear all the time that we remember his desperate act.
I think that he speaks with the voice of his act, and we know not to listen, but not only listen but also believe, and without

knowing of knowing.

MY OPINION "NOT JUDGEMENT" BUT ONLY OPINION.
-P112

My personal opinion I can now express it, because after the whole study I did on this case, they are in the express conditions. Therefore, I declare this: JUDAS could not live without his best friend and only feeling which gave him a reason to be alive; he loved him too well to Jesus, but of a good that is supernatural and that we can not even imagine. Therefore he was very sorry for all the experienced during the life of Jesus, that he knew him very well, so too grieved to see him sentenced to death, and carry the cross. Why he killed himself, he knew he was the Son of God, and had proof of this he alone and not mankind. And if Judas says that Jesus is the Son of God, Jesus is really why Judas can not go wrong, because he KNOWS EVERYTHING!

PERSONAL CONSIDERATIONS – P.113

Therefore he saw the Son of God kill in the name of God, from "those" waiting God to deliver them from evil. Instead, God comes to marry, through Jesus, humanity by giving love and mercy to all without distinction, and they were crucifying. Judas knew ever since that moment this truth, and it was not easy to digest that Jesus be killed in the name of God when he had the proof that "He" was the Son of God. The situation was really horrible and drama exceeded the apex.

Judah excluded that Jesus saved us through his crucifixion, according to man, or if she had known, maybe, would overcome the trauma and would not take his own life.

So at that time judged the man in the name of God, but anyone who came to hand in the wrong way, and decided the priests who should receive the Grace and who is not, even he was convinced that there were men who would never have been able to receive Grace, they did not realize they had replaced God and everything we thought, according to them, was God and that he had communicated. Through this belief was then teaching "and perhaps in some ways even now", and this was a way of making doctrine which subjected the people because God was presented as avenger and punisher of people that if marching and did not think in a certain way was damned without remission of sins.

Instead Jesus brings to us a God who is completely contrary to what they expected, and they preached the priests of the time. In fact, He brings us a God of love, forgiveness and gives grace to all also to "those" who are judged, man, devoid of hope and salvation. This is the God that Jesus makes known to us, that God punisher, and judge of man he is presenting it. Therefore, his doctrine is contrary to all the priests of that time, I mean everyone not to exclude anyone, preachers, people, including relatives and people. Therefore, Jesus was alone, completely alone. Only God, Judas, Marta, and another couple were with him. I only repeat yet only a few were with him, otherwise the enemies would not dare to attack him. However, the power of good has removed their consciences and this was characteristic for the man in order to lead it in His way. Amen.

MESSAGE TO US! - P.114 -

Judas kills himself, and in his act tells us: << This is Jesus the Son of God, follow the path he has shown us. >> We judge Judas a traitor and at the same time we understand that this judgment covers what we understand by his gesture. We understand with his gesture that Jesus is the Son of God and we believe, the facts speak. >> This is the message that Judas from us and that we do not know to listen, and in a sense to obey, because too busy to cover it in the sentential form there is, and that ultimately is one of our characteristics and our nature the judge, and then, the sentenziamo a traitor for not understanding that we are following him and that we believe, for he killed himself because Jesus is the Son of God! Otherwise he would not.

WHAT IS THIS SEARCH? -P 115 -

This research I have conducted on Jesus and Judas, and to become more and more "wiser" or rather "be among those" who hold to absolute truth; but where it led me? And where it will lead other men? A nothing! Everything is silent and still the same. So just it has to be this man's evolution, which is always a becoming projected into the future with a creative energy, bursting which is the same powerful life in its revenues, which basically only served to remain what it is about anything else It serves. So a creative energy that is becoming and you can not stop in a continuous evolution that serves only to remain what it has always been far from our creation, now also made to me to the same effect that ultimately makes all. This is a full circle, and always turns tirelessly to infinity, that it is only because this keeps him alive, the infinite. And we men keeps us alive this incessant evolution that leads us to stand still. Therefore remain firm, we must accept ourselves for how God made us, who is love and we love as it is Him and if we do not accept this reality we can not understand that our evolution, "which is always a becoming" really just want this get us, and when we got there, only then we will have peace, and we will understand that all of our evolution has brought us to what we were already since our creation. Thus the various struggles will not cease until we will not get to this stage. So if in the beginning we were children of God, we get them inexorably. This is why He says: As in principle it is now for ever and ever Amen centuries.

THANKS FOR READING MY BOOK.

GOD BE PRAISED!

I was born on a Sunday morning, to MAZZARINO.
Province of Caltanissetta - 04 – 02 - 1962

I am the son of G. S. Farmer, C. and F. housewife. I am the fifth of eleven children. I spent my childhood in Sicily, and later in northern Italy, where I trained and I have completed my studies. Fifty years he started writing professionally. I started writing so amateur as a boy, in 1978 approximately. Many writings missing, and that I never published, because I no longer find them. I drove my life in the work, and study. The study followed me everywhere. During my life I have learned many trades: some professionally, others less, so my experiences are varied and wide-ranging. I've been in the military, where I learned many human values that added to the experience they gave me a good luggage to understand life in society. Destiny has made me learn along the way the value of existence, respect for all the differences, the importance of love as a principle for all types of cohabitation. My conceptions, religious, social and economic they always push to the search for truth and the revelation of the mysteries.

During my journey into work, and in the meantime that I devoted myself to serve, I have formed culturally in various ways: some intellectually and completely independently, and partly by studying and interacting with others. I traveled a lot, and I have had many experiences in the social and labor field. I also had a troubled life romantically. These have marked me, but at the same time have made me strong through the tribulations.

I still work, write, and study the mysteries of our life and of Creation. They are deeply religious, so I believe in God's Love. I also believe in benign and intelligent man. I'm interested in, not deeply, politics; most are deeply attracted by the social issues. I like to inform me of current things, I am interested in psychology and literature. I dedicate free time on volunteer services. I love nature, art, music, traveling, and I live a deeply spiritual life. I am a person, sociable, enterprising and artist, in the words of the other, in my opinion I am a free thinker. I hope you like my books and I hope you find them interesting. I extend a warm greeting to all readers. Thank you!

Casteggio PV

16-12-2016

in faith

SOTTILE SALVATORE
OTHER PUBLICATIONS

Non-fiction, Spiritual, Philosophy, Psychology, Religious
.
1) The sagittarius; wise

2) The woman promised by God; Novel

3) Light. Wise

4) The Pink Swan Novel

5) Holy; wise

6) Hope; wise

7) Thoughts and poems; prose

8) Judah Psychology

9) The breath of the soul; Psychology

10) I will love you from afar as you do with the stars. Novel

11) What to return the DC but with renewed men and young people; Politician

12) Dc the triumph of the people is the knowledge; Politician

13) The appeal; Politician

14) The rally; Politician

15) The struggle for justice; Politician

16) Brochure News 1-2-3-4-5 volume; Actuality

17) Mastro Pippa Vol. 1-2-3-; Politicians

18) The Women's Day Romance

19) The elected: Essay

20) Tales; Novel

21) The stars smile from heaven; story

22) The chorus of cicadas. Novel

23) The way of Wise Faith

24) Metaphors: Romance
25)   U Picciliddru Montelusa. Novel
26)

16-12-2016

youcanprint

Finito di stampare nel mese di Gennaio 2017
per conto di Youcanprint *Self - Publishing*

www.ingramcontent.com/pod-product-compliance
Lightning Source LLC
Chambersburg PA
CBHW021045090426
42738CB00006B/200